Faroe Islands

the Bradt Travel Guide

James Proctor

edition
4

www.bradtguides.com

Bradt Travel Guides Ltd, UK
The Globe Pequot Press Inc, USA

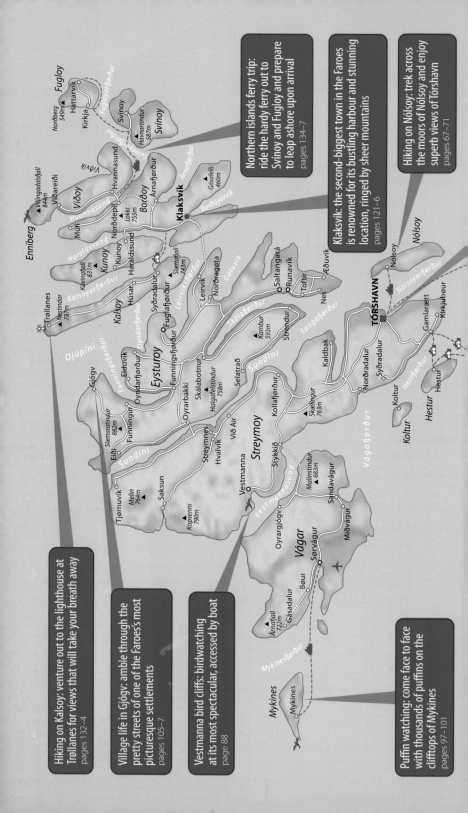

Northern islands ferry trip: ride the hardy ferry out to Svínoy and Fugloy and prepare to leap ashore upon arrival
pages 134–7

Klaksvík: the second-biggest town in the Faroes is renowned for its bustling harbour and stunning location, ringed by sheer mountains
pages 121–6

Hiking on Nólsoy: trek across the moors of Nólsoy and enjoy superb views of Tórshavn
pages 67–71

Hiking on Kalsoy: venture out to the lighthouse at Trøllanes for views that will take your breath away
pages 132–4

Village life in Gjógv: amble through the pretty streets of one of the Faroes's most picturesque settlements
pages 105–7

Vestmanna bird cliffs: birdwatching at its most spectacular, accessed by boat
page 88

Puffin watching: come face to face with thousands of puffins on the clifftops of Mykines
pages 97–101

Enniberg

Fugloy

Norðberg 549m ▲ · Hattarvík
Kirkja
Svínoy
Hvannartindur 587m ▲
Svínoy

Villingadalsfjall 844m ▲ · Viðareiði
Viðoy
Múli
Hvannasund
Norðdepil · Lokki
Borðoy · Klaksvík
Gøtueiði 460m ▲
Borðoyarvík

Kívingfjall 831m ▲
Kunoy
Kunoy
Haraldssund
Slættaratindur 755m ▲

Trøllanes · Nestindar 787m ▲
Kalsoy
Húsar · Syðradalur
Mikladalur
Fuglafjørður
Slættaðfjall 743m ▲
Leirvík
Norðragøta
Runavík
Saltangará
Toftir
Nes
Æðuvík

Djúpini
Eldvík · Funningsfjørður
Oyndarfjørður
Funningur
Skálabotnur · Halgafelstindur 758m ▲
Selatrað
Kambur 593m ▲
Strendur
Kaldbak
Norðradalur
Syðradalur

Gjógv
Slættaratindar 882m ▲
Eiði
Funningur
Oyrarbakki
Streymnes
Við Áir
Hvalvík
Saksun
Melin 764m ▲
Tjørnuvík
Kópsenni 790m ▲

Vestmanna
Kollafjørður
Skælingur 763m ▲
Kvívík
Streymoy
Stykkið

TÓRSHAVN
Nólsoy
Gamlarætt
Kirkjubøur
Hestur
Koltur

Oyrargjógv
Vágar
Sandavágur
Miðvágur
Málinstindur 683m ▲

Sørvágur
Bøur
Gásadalur
Árnafjall 722m ▲

Mykines
Mykines

Tórshavn: for great bars, harbourside restaurants and engaging museums, the Faroese capital is unbeatable
pages 39–61

End of the road: visit windswept Akraberg and take in the dramatic seascapes at the Faroese Land's End
pages 158–9

Suðuroy sea cliffs: stand atop the majestic Beinisvørð cliffs to understand why they've inspired dozens of poets and artists
pages 148–59

NORTH

ATLANTIC

OCEAN

Sandoy
Tindur 479m
Skálavík
Skarvanes
Dalur
Skúvoyarfjørður
Sandur
Skúgvoy
Skúgvoy

Dímunarfjørður

Stóra Dímun

Lítla Dímun

Suðuroyarfjørður

Sandvík
Hvalba
Hvalbiarfjørður
Trongisvágur
Gluggarnir 610m
Tvøroyri
Froðba
Krambatangi
Trongisvágsfjørður
Borgarknappur 574m
Fámjin
Suðuroy
Vágur
Vágsfjørður
Akrar
Lopra
Lopransfjørður
Sumba
Beinisvørð
Akraberg

N

Bradt

0   8km
0   5 miles

KEY
■ Capital
● Major town
● Other town
○ Village
— Road
⋯ Road tunnel
✈ Airport
⛴ Vehicle ferry
⛴ Passenger ferry
🐦 Birdwatching
🗼 Lighthouse

Faroe Islands
Don't miss...

Picturesque villages
Dozens of tiny hamlets dot the Faroe Islands, providing a glimpse of life in a land of extremes – a visit to the turf-roofed church of Funningur is a highlight of any trip (KC/VFI) page 107

Vertiginous sea cliffs
Justifiably famous for their record-setting heights, sea cliffs such as Enniberg in northern Viðoy and Beinisvørð (shown here) in southern Suðuroy play host to dozens of species of seabirds
(EC) page 157

Tórshavn

Named after the Norse god of war, the beguiling Faroese capital of Tórshavn ('Thor's Harbour') is dotted with brightly coloured wooden houses and bursting with Faroese charm

(ÓF/VFI) pages 39–61

Island-hopping by helicopter

One of the best (and fastest) ways to see many of the more isolated corners of the Faroes — soar above the jagged coastlines for a bird's-eye view of the stunning landscape

(EC) pages 27–8

Mykines

The most remote and enigmatic of the Faroe Islands, Mykines can be cut off by bad weather for days, but the tussocky valleys and rich birdlife are worth the challenge

(JP) pages 97–101

Faroe Islands in colour

left Hans Pauli Olsen's sculpture of the seal woman stands 2.5m tall on the rocky coast of Kalsoy (NF/S) page 132

below The second biggest town in the Faroes, Klaksvík on Borðay is encircled by mountains (EC) pages 121–6

bottom The international music festival G! is held in Gøta in July (ÓF/VFI) page 113

above   Sitting snugly around the head of the tooth-shaped Vágafjørður, Míðvágur is a typically vibrant Faroese village (SS) pages 89–92

right   Turf-roofed houses at Saksun, Streymoy (VFI) pages 79–82

below   During the summer months, the population of Fámjin increases significantly as people return for the sheep herding and hay season between July and the end of August (EC) pages 154–5

above left   Sailing is one of the best ways to see the islands in their natural splendour – catch a ride on the *Norðlýsið* schooner from Tórshavn (OF/VFI) pages 60–1

above right   Take a boat trip to the Vestmanna bird cliffs, one of the best excursions in the islands (DC/VFI) page 88

below   The final of the summer boat races takes place on Ólavsøka, the Faroese national day (ÓF/VFI) pages 30–1

AUTHOR

James Proctor first visited the Faroe Islands in 1992 on board the *Smyril* ferry sailing from Aberdeen and has been back and forth ever since. Accompanied half of the way by a pod of dolphins and buffeted by gale-force winds and stormy seas during the rest of the journey, James's love affair with the North Atlantic got off to a flying start. Whilst working as the BBC's Scandinavia correspondent, he produced a series of television and radio reports about the islands, concentrating on the issues of independence and whaling. James now divides his time as a freelance travel writer between the south of France and his  forest retreat in Sweden. He has also written Bradt's *Lapland* and *West Sweden* guides and co-written other guides to Iceland, Reykjavík, Sweden and Finland.

AUTHOR'S STORY

Ever since mistakenly studying Swedish at university (I actually signed up to do Spanish but went to the wrong lecture room), I have been fascinated by the Nordic countries. Although they share a common history and culture, they are remarkably different from each other and a visit to one Nordic nation only whets the appetite to learn more about the others. Despite the Faroes being the least well known of the Nordic family, like many people, I felt I somehow knew them before I even went there. Their name was buried somewhere in my subconscious after all those mentions of the shipping forecast on the radio. However, it was with a certain degree of trepidation that I approached the docks in Aberdeen one stormy afternoon in 1992 and set eyes on the alarmingly small boat that was to take me across the North Atlantic to the Faroes: all that talk of northerly gale force 8, increasing to storm force 10 later, certainly gave me second thoughts. Indeed, *Smyril* bobbed like a cork on the truly enormous waves all the way up to Tórshavn. After my arrival, I ate dinner with friends and watched as dense banks of fog rolled their way up the street outside our window, engulfing cars and entire houses. Later, the fog was to vanish as quickly as it had appeared, giving way to brilliant sunshine which bathed Tórshavn and the surrounding hillsides in the golden light that is so typical of the northern sky in late spring. I soon realised that I was somewhere quite extraordinary; the combination of wild weather and unforgiving landscape in the Faroe Islands is like nowhere else. After that first trip to the Faroes, I soon became a devoted fan of these 18 remote, windswept islands lost in the North Atlantic and quickly added them to my list of special places. I hope you will, too.

PUBLISHER'S FOREWORD · Hilary Bradt

There is something appealing about a place where visitors are advised to pack woolly hats and gloves for an August holiday! The Faroes are not for conventional holiday-makers, but then nor are Bradt guides. This group of islands offers a blend of the exotic and the familiar (at least to fans of BBC weather forecasts), but where nature is the main attraction and there are more puffins than people. Sounds like my kind of place.

Reprinted April 2018   Fourth edition published May 2016   First published 2004

Bradt Travel Guides Ltd
IDC House, The Vale, Chalfont St Peter, Bucks SL9 9RZ, England
www.bradtguides.com
Print edition published in the USA by The Globe Pequot Press Inc,
PO Box 480, Guilford, Connecticut 06437-0480

Text copyright © 2016 James Proctor
Maps copyright © 2016 Bradt Travel Guides Ltd
Photographs copyright © 2016 Individual photographers (see below)
Project Managers: Maisie Fitzpatrick and Katie Wilding
Cover image research: Pepi Bluck

ISBN: 978 1 78477 013 6 (print)
e-ISBN: 978 1 78477 158 4 (e-pub)
e-ISBN: 978 1 78477 258 1 (mobi)

British Library Cataloguing in Publication Data
A catalogue record for this book is available from the British Library

Photographs Arne List (AL); Corbis: Adam Woolfitt (AW/C); Erik Christensen (EC); James Proctor (JP); Markus Varesvuo (MV); Nature Picture Library: Robert Thompson Photography Limited (RT/NPL); Shutterstock: Andrea Ricordi (AR/S), Attila JANDI (AJ/S), Galyna Andrushko (GA/S), Nick Fox (NF/S); SuperStock (SS); Visit Faroe Islands: Absalon Hansen (AH/VFI), Adam Burton (AB/VFI), Atlantic Airways (AA/VFI), Daniele Casanova (DC/VFI), Kimberley Coole (KC/VFI), Ólavur Frederiksen (ÓF/VFI)

Front cover Gannets (*Morus bassanus*) (RT/NPL)
Back cover Aerial view of Tindhólmur (AA/VFI)
Title page Atlantic puffins (*Fratercula arctica*) (AH/VFI); view towards the mountain of Slættaratindur on the island of Eysturoy (AB/VFI); there are approximately 80,000 sheep in the Faroe Islands (ÓF/VFI)

Maps David McCutcheon FBCart.S; includes map data © OpenStreetMap contributors.

Typeset by Wakewing, Chesham
Production managed by Jellyfish Print Solutions; printed in India
Digital conversion by www.dataworks.co.in

Acknowledgements

If there is one person in the Faroe Islands who embodies the spirit of the islands, it is Súsanna at Visit Faroe Islands; creative, energetic and always willing to help. I am indebted to Súsanna for her tireless pursuit of off-beat facts, re-worked travel schedules and even international couriers. Thanks are due, too, to Guri and Levi at HQ for allowing me to take over their office space and supplying endless coffee and good humour. That sofa on the top floor really does belong to me now, you know!

Thanks, too, to Súsanna Sondum and colleagues at the city tourist office for help with last-minute queries – and, on previous visits, with those Barbary pirates of Hvalba. Hildur of 62 North fame remains, as ever, a friend in need – especially with all those last-minute documents. Thanks H! Friðbjörg in Klaksvík is always full of advice and tips and is a fount of knowledge on those curious, handknitted hold-up-your-socks-thingies.

Elsewhere in the islands, a big thanks go out to Eirik Suni in Gjógv and Maria at Atlantic as well as the countless people I encountered on my travels across the islands who offered advice and a guiding hand.

FEEDBACK REQUEST AND UPDATES WEBSITE

Although I am a regular visitor to the Faroe Islands, prices and places change frequently and I would be delighted to hear your experiences of travel in the Faroes. Did you discover a new spot for dinner, a thrilling adventure tour or a cosy new guesthouse or hotel? Has this guide been useful? What would you like to see changed? Your information will make future editions of this guide even better, so why not write to us and tell us about your experiences? Contact us on 01753 893444 or e info@bradtguides.com. We may post 'one-off updates' on the Bradt website at www.bradtupdates.com/faroes. You can also visit this website for updates to information in this guide. Alternatively you can add a review of the book to www.bradtguides.com or Amazon.

Contents

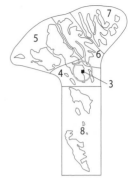

Introduction   VI

PART ONE   GENERAL INFORMATION   1

Chapter 1   Background Information   3
Geography and climate 3, Natural history 4, History 9,
Government and politics 15, Economy 15, People and
culture 16

Chapter 2   Practical Information   20
When to visit 20, Faroese highlights 20, The weather 22,
Information and maps 22, Tour operators 22, Embassies
and consulates 23, Getting there and away 23, Health and
safety 25, What to take 26, Money and costs 26, Getting
around the islands 27, Accommodation 28, Eating and
drinking 29, Public holidays 30, Shopping 31, Arts and
entertainment 32, Customs and tax-free goods 33, Media,
communications and time 33, Interacting with local
people 35, Giving something back 35

PART TWO   THE GUIDE   37

Chapter 3   Tórshavn   39
Getting there and away 42, Getting around 43, Tourist and
weather information 43, Where to stay 43, Where to
eat and drink 47, Entertainment and nightlife 49, Other
practicalities 51, What to see and do 51

Chapter 4   Around Tórshavn   63
Kirkjubøur 64, Nólsoy 67, Hestur 71, Koltur 71, North to
Kaldbak 73

Chapter 5   Streymoy and the Western Islands   75
Where to go 76, Getting around 77, Kollafjørður and
around 77, Tjørnuvík 83, West to Kvivik and
Vestmanna 84, The western islands: Vágar and Mykines 88

Chapter 6   Eysturoy   103
Where to go 103, Getting around 104, Northern
Eysturoy 104, Southern Eysturoy 113

| Chapter 7 | **The Northern Islands** | **119** |

Where to go 119, Getting around 121, Borðoy 121,
Viðoy 128, Kunoy 130, Kalsoy 132, Northern outposts:
Svínoy and Fugloy 134

| Chapter 8 | **The Southern Islands** | **139** |

Where to go 140, Getting around 140, Sandoy 141,
Skúgvoy 145, Stóra Dímun 147, Lítla Dímun 147,
Suðuroy 148

Appendix 1	**Language**	**160**
Appendix 2	**Glossary of Faroese geographical terms**	**166**
Appendix 3	**Further Information**	**168**
Index		**170**
Index of advertisers		**172**

LIST OF MAPS

Eysturoy	102	Southern islands	138
Faroe Islands	1st colour section	Streymoy and the western	
Fuglafjørður	110	islands	74
Glyvrar, Saltangará and		Tórshavn, overview	40–1
Runavík	116	Tórshavn, around	62
Klaksvík	122	Tórshavn, centre	44–5
Northern islands	120	Tvøroyri	150
Sørvágur	95	Vestmanna	86

KEY TO SYMBOLS

⁞⁞⁞⁞⁞ Pedestrianised street	🚲 Cycle hire	🎭 Theatre/cinema
---------- Footpath	🚩 Tourist information	🔱 Statue/monument
≡≡≡≡≡≡ Tunnel	$ Bank	🚹🚺 Male/female toilets
--⛴-- Car ferry	✉ Post office	🏟 Stadium
--🚢-- Passenger ferry	🏛 Important/historic building	🕍 Lighthouse
✈ Airport (international)	🏰 Castle/fortress	➤ Bird nesting site
🚁 Helicopter service	✝ Church/cathedral	• Other place of interest
⛽ Petrol station/garage	☆ Nightclub	▲ Summit (height in metres)
🚌 Bus station etc	✚ Hospital/clinic	▨ Urban park
🚗 Car rental	🏛 Museum/gallery	

Introduction

Attention all shipping. The Met Office issued the following gale warning to shipping at 17.25 GMT on Monday 23 January. Fair Isle, Faroes, southeast Iceland: northerly gale force 8 expected soon, veering northeasterly, increasing to storm force 10 later.

Shipping forecast, BBC Radio

Arguably best known for their dramatic appearance in the BBC shipping forecast, the Faroe Islands are one of Europe's best-kept secrets. Wild, wet and windy, these 18 volcanic islands, far out in the North Atlantic, are mercifully still off the main tourist trail. Travel here and you'll discover a different world – a realm of austere beauty where crystal-clear mountain streams cascade down verdant hillsides dotted with turf-roofed homes, their timber walls painted a mêlée of reds, yellows and blues; a world where sea cliffs, teeming with birdlife, plummet precipitously into the churning Atlantic below; a world where the sea is all-powerful, giving and taking away.

This geographically isolated land of towering layer-cake mountains and deep rounded valleys, sparkling fell-top tarns and shorelines gnawed into countless craggy inlets is of such elemental wonder that first-time visitors soon become ardent devotees, returning time and again to the Faroes, one of Europe's last places. True, the weather can be unreliable, even downright inclement at times – but the good news is that conditions in the middle of the Atlantic change fast, so you'll never have long to wait for a glimpse of the sun. There's sound logic behind the Faroese saying: 'If you don't like the weather, wait five minutes!' The quality of the light in the northern sky, which attracts countless artists to the islands, and the purity of the air are perhaps two of the most difficult things about the Faroes to qualify on paper – visit, though, and you'll soon appreciate this most alluring side of island life.

Thanks to regular air links to no fewer than five European countries and a well-appointed ferry plying the waters of the North Atlantic, it has never been easier to reach the Faroe Islands. Whether you're looking to hike across tussocky moorland landscapes to imposing lighthouses perched on rocky promontories, watch seabirds in their natural habitat atop vertical cliff faces or simply island-hop around the Faroes exploring traditional villages and hamlets as you go, you're sure to find an itinerary to please. This is a country where gliding across narrow sounds and fjords by mail boat or skimming scree-topped pyramidal peaks by helicopter are just two of the options for getting around. Travel in the Faroes is not only well integrated, but also incredibly good value. Given the rigours of the climate, quality of life is important to the Faroese; consequently, the islands' infrastructure is well developed, accommodation is warm and snug and eating out throws up an array of options – everything from pan-fried puffin breast to whale meat could be on the menu alongside more conventional dishes.

As a Scandinavian specialist, I have not only travelled widely across the Nordic countries but have also lived and worked in the region. I speak several Scandinavian languages and have, over the years, developed an extensive network of friends and colleagues throughout the Nordic area. Based on this experience, it is with great pride that I recommend a trip to the Faroe Islands; this is still one of the few places in Europe where life moves at an enviably sedate pace and where the forces of nature and vagaries of the climate mean everything to the people who live here. A visit to the Faroes is a marvellously rewarding experience. All 18 islands are waiting to welcome you. Open your eyes and enjoy.

HOW TO USE THE MAPS IN THIS GUIDE

KEYS AND SYMBOLS Maps include alphabetical keys covering the locations of those places to stay, eat or drink that are featured in the book. Note that regional maps may not show all hotels and restaurants in the area: other establishments may be located in towns shown on the map.

GRIDS AND GRID REFERENCES Several maps use gridlines to allow easy location of sites. Map grid references are listed in square brackets after the name of the place or sight of interest in the text, with page number followed by grid number, eg: [40 B2].

FOLLOW BRADT

For the latest news, special offers and competitions, subscribe to the Bradt newsletter via the website www.bradtguides.com and follow Bradt on:

- ⓕ www.facebook.com/BradtTravelGuides
- 🐦 @BradtGuides
- 📷 @bradtguides
- ⓟ www.pinterest.com/bradtguides

ATTENTION WILDLIFE ENTHUSIASTS

For more on wildlife in the Faroe Islands, why not check out Bradt's *Wildlife of the North Atlantic*? Go to www.bradtguides.com and key in FAROEWILD20 at the checkout for your 20% discount (while stocks last).

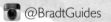 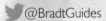

Part One

GENERAL INFORMATION

FAROE ISLANDS AT A GLANCE

Location In the middle of the Gulf Stream in the North Atlantic at 62°N, halfway between Scotland and Iceland

Neighbouring countries Closest land is North Rona, part of Scotland's Outer Hebrides, 257km (139 nautical miles) to the south

Size 1,399km² (545 square miles)

Area Faroese archipelago, 113km (70 miles) long and 75km (47 miles) wide. Total coastline of 1,100km (687 miles). No point in the Faroes is further than 5km (3 miles) from the sea.

Islands 18 volcanic islands separated by narrow sounds and fjords arranged roughly in the form of an arrowhead. All but one are inhabited.

Heights Highest mountain 882m (2,883ft); average height above sea level 300m (980ft)

Climate Average 3°–11°C, winter–summer

Population 48,704 (and roughly twice as many sheep)

Capital Tórshavn (population 19,800)

Status Self-governing region within the Kingdom of Denmark

Language Faroese. Danish has equal status in all official affairs.

Religion Evangelical Lutheran

Currency Faroese króna/Danish krone (kr)

Exchange rate £1 = 9.54kr, US$1 = 6.60kr, €1 = 7.46kr (February 2016)

International telephone code +298

Time GMT (winter); GMT+1 (summer)

Electrical voltage 220V; European two-pin plugs

Weights and measures Metric

Flag Red cross fringed with blue on a white background

Public holidays 1 January, Maundy Thursday, Good Friday, Easter Sunday, Easter Monday, 25 April, Common Prayers' Day (May), Ascension Day, Whit Sunday, Whit Monday, 5 June, 28–29 July (Ólavsøka), 24–26 December, 31 December

1

Background Information

GEOGRAPHY AND CLIMATE

The geography – and geology – of the Faroe Islands is remarkably consistent and straightforward to get to grips with. The islands are what remain of an eroded plateau of volcanic basalt which was composed during four periods of rock formation; these different layers of rock help to give the mountains on several of the islands their terraced appearance. During the ice age, the Faroes were covered by a vast layer of ice. Gradually, over time, the ice sheet melted and broke up into smaller glaciers which in turn created the glacial features that dominate the Faroese landscape today. The Faroese mountains provide textbook examples of glacial activity: a series of mountain slopes rising steeply from a valley floor to culminate in the sharp ridges (*arêtes*), cirques and pyramidal peaks typical of the head of a glacier; in parts of the islands, where the sea now covers what would have been a valley floor, deep rounded valleys (originally cirques at the head of a glacier, known as *botnur* in Faroese) are all that remain of the land that once bore the tremendous bulk of a glacier. The tallest and most sheer sea cliffs, often perpendicular in character, are found in the north and west of the country where the land is at its highest and most rugged. The rock strata slopes slightly towards the south and east with the result that the coastline here is much gentler and more eroded. It's a harsh yet austere beauty, repeated throughout the country, though at its most breathtaking in the northern islands where the houses are seemingly stuck on the steep mountainsides, their brightly painted colours contrasting with the grey-brown basalt behind and the deep blue of the sea in front. On the islands further south, the landscape is softer, with lower, gentler hills and larger expanses of farmland. For a detailed glossary of Faroese geographical terms, see *Appendix 2*, pages 166–7.

CLIMATE The weather is maritime, quite changeable and totally dominated by the Gulf Stream which encircles the islands and moderates the climate, giving an annual average range between 3°C in winter and 11°C in summer. In sheltered valleys the temperature can often reach into the high teens; however, the highest temperature ever recorded in the islands is a balmy 22°C. The Faroes also lie in the stormiest part of the North Atlantic, directly in the path of the majority of Atlantic depressions, and as a result are cloudy, wet and windy throughout the year. In winter, temperatures are relatively mild for the high latitude (the Faroes are warmer in winter, for example, than Denmark, 6° of latitude further south), harbours never freeze and although snowfall does occur it is generally short-lived. Winter storms though can rage for days, cutting off some of the smaller islands. Conversely, in summer, days are cool and rather cloudy. Throughout the year, mist (Tórshavn is

Month	Average rainfall (mm)	Wet days	Month	Average rainfall (mm)	Wet days
January	149	25	July	79	18
February	136	22	August	96	20
March	114	23	September	132	12
April	106	22	October	157	24
May	67	16	November	156	24
June	74	16	December	167	26

particularly prone to fog in the summer months) and rain are common, but weather changes are rapid and there are nearly always variable conditions prevailing on different islands. The two main southern islands, Sandoy and Suðuroy, for example, have more sunny days than the northern islands and are generally a shade warmer.

NATURAL HISTORY

FAUNA Other than the vast numbers of seabirds that are attracted to the Faroe Islands, visitors will notice a distinct lack of fauna. The islands have no indigenous mammals due to their isolated location in the middle of the North Atlantic and all animals currently found in the Faroes have been introduced here.

Seabirds Although there has been a steady decline in the seabird population in the Faroes since the 1950s, with a severe drop in numbers recorded during recent years due to falling fish stocks, it's nevertheless estimated that there are two million pairs of seabirds in the Faroe Islands during the breeding season. This is unmistakably the best time to watch birds in the islands – simply find yourself a suitable cliff, sit down, remain quiet and watch and smell the spectacle: a cliff face populated by hundreds of thousands of seabirds is not only an audio-visual delight, but also one that won't fail to leave your nose unstimulated either. Each species of bird has its own favourite spot on the cliff – **puffins** (*Fratercula arctica*), for example, will be found on the steep grassy slopes at the top of the cliff and a colony is easily recognised by the luxuriant green colour of the surrounding vegetation which thrives on the birds' nutrient-rich droppings. They also appreciate grassy tufts on the top of sea stacks. The birds burrow about 1m into the slope where the female lays a single egg. Moving down the cliff face, **guillemots** (*Uria aalge*) and **kittiwakes** (*Rissa tridactyla*) come next, closely packed together on the narrow shelves towards the top of the cliff. Although there are some cliffs preferred only by kittiwakes, these two species, the former a black-and-white member of the auk family (members of which, incidentally, lay their eggs straight onto the cliff face or into holes in the rock), the latter a small white gull with grey wings and black wing tips, are often found nesting together; kittiwakes are among the noisiest of all the seabirds and their nests become a stinking pile of guano by the end of the breeding season. **Razorbills** (*Alca torda*) are similar in appearance to guillemots but have a blacker back and a thicker bill with a white line – they can sometimes be found on small ledges and crevices amongst the guillemots but they are much fewer in number and in smaller colonies. Four hundred years ago, the **fulmar** (*Fulmarus glacialis*) was so rare it was thought to be a bad omen heralding the arrival of terrible weather – today it is the most common seabird in the islands and can be found scattered across the cliff face. This is one of the most elegant fliers of all seabirds, gliding effortlessly on outstretched grey wings along the top of the cliff. This large seabird is similar to a gull, stout with a thick neck, whitish head, neck and breast. At the bottom of the cliff, you'll find the **shags** (*Phalacrocorax aristotelis*), large black birds with an unusual green eye, whose plumage often looks scaly. In a few locations around the islands, you might be lucky (or unlucky) enough to come across the **great skua** (*Catharacta skua*), a massive, heavily built bird with dark-brown feathers throughout, except light patches on its outstretched wings. Known for attacking other seabirds and forcing them to vomit up their food, this powerful flier will also swoop from the air on anything – or anyone – who comes too close to its nest. Its sturdy bill with a hooked tip is best kept away from your head by holding your arm in the air to distract the birds away from your scalp. Another bird renowned for direct hits on human heads is the **arctic tern** (*Sterna paradisaea*), a slender, elegant creature with grey and white plumage. Its forked tail, long, pointed wings, black head and blood-red beak are a scene straight out of Alfred Hitchcock when coming in for the attack. The largest seabird in the North Atlantic can also

WHERE TO WATCH SEABIRDS IN THE FAROES

PUFFINS Northern islands; Eysturoy; Vestmanna bird cliffs; Saksun cliffs; Viðvík bay, Vágar; Mykines

GUILLEMOTS Largest colony on Skúgvoy; northern islands; Eysturoy; Vestmanna bird cliffs; Saksun cliffs; Mykines; Sandoy

ARCTIC TERN Kirkjubøurhólmur at southern end of Streymoy; Skúgvoy; Sumbiarhólmur at southern end of Suðuroy

RAZORBILLS Look for them where you see kittiwakes

FULMARS Throughout the islands

KITTIWAKES Northern islands; Eysturoy; Vestmanna bird cliffs; Saksun cliffs; Mykines; Sandoy

GANNETS Mykineshólmur

MANX SHEARWATERS/STORM PETRELS Largest colony on Nólsoy; Mykines

SHAGS Northern islands; Eysturoy

GREAT SKUAS Svínoy; Skúgvoy

be seen in the Faroes; with a wingspan of 2m, the **gannet** (*Morus bassanus*) breeds predominantly on Mykineshólmur in the far west of the country. These white birds with yellow heads and black wing tips are tremendous divers, sweeping down on their prey from a height of up to 40m.

The largest colony of **storm petrels** (*Hydrobates pelagicus*) anywhere in the world is in the Faroes. As a precaution against predators (they are particularly wary of rats and will not nest anywhere the rodents are found), Europe's smallest seabird can only be seen on land at night; during the day these small black birds, similar in size to a chaffinch but with longer wings, can be seen flitting around bat-like in the half-light.

Other birds As far as other species of birds are concerned, the small size and isolated location of the Faroe Islands mean that the overall number of non-seabirds is low. There is, however, a good collection of waders and divers including the **oystercatcher** (*Haematopus ostralegus*), **whimbrel** (*Numenius phaeopus*), **curlew** (*Numenius arquata*), **redshank** (*Tringa totanus*), **red-necked phalarope** (*Phalaropus lobatus*) and **red-throated diver** (*Gavia stellata*), as well as passerines such as the **meadow pipit** (*Anthus pratensis*), **chiffchaff** (*Phylloscopus collybita*) and **redwing** (*Turdus iliacus*). The most common duck is the **eider** (*Somateria mollissima*) and the only bird of prey is the **merlin** (*Falco columbarius*), or *smyril* in Faroese – a name which launched an entire international shipping line.

Birdwatching Summer is the best time to watch birds in the Faroes. Although the various species return to the islands at different times of the year, most of them are back in residence for the breeding season between late May and mid-August, which reaches its peak between the end of June and the beginning of July. Not only is the unpredictable Faroese weather at its best at this time of year but you'll also benefit from the long, light northern nights. Make sure you bring a decent pair of binoculars with you as they will greatly enhance your viewing pleasure and the number of species you can see. As for seeing the nocturnal storm petrel, the best bet is to take the tours run by Jens-Kjeld Jensen on Nólsoy since the colonies are difficult, if not dangerous, to find in the dark; see page 69 for details. Remember, too, not to disturb nesting birds as you may cause them to abandon their nests and lose their chicks, and do not collect eggs.

Marine life Agricultural land has always been scarce in the islands and over the centuries the Faroese have come to regard the seas around their islands as their garden, harvesting the fish and whales found here. Although fish numbers have been falling in recent years due to overfishing, the North Atlantic is still rich in fish. The main species are blue whiting, saithe, cod, capelin, herring, mackerel, haddock and redfish as well as lobster and scallops.

Whales Several species of whale also inhabit Faroese waters: longfin pilot whales (*Globicephala melas*), killer whales (*Orcinus orca*) and fin whales (*Balaenoptera physalus*) can all be found here, as well as harbour porpoises (*Phocoena phocoena*), bottlenose (*Tursiops truncatus*) and white-sided dolphins (*Lagenorhynchus acutus*). Sadly, though, it is unlikely that you will see large numbers of whales or dolphins whilst in the islands – you will probably have to make do with the odd distant glimpse offshore – since the islands have yet to offer whale-watching tours.

The only whale still hunted by the Faroese, the **longfin pilot whale** generally lives in pods of between ten and 50, preferring deep water where squid, its main source of food, is abundant. Jet black or dark grey in colour and weighing around two to three tonnes when fully grown, the pilot whale can be recognised by its strong blow (often more than 1m high), bulbous forehead, its prominent dorsal, fin which is set quite far forward, and unusually long flippers. Young whales may breach, an activity which becomes rarer as they grow older, although spyhopping (the technical term for poking their heads out of the water and having a look around) and lobtailing or tail-slapping are regularly observed. Pods of pilot whales are sometimes driven ashore by small fishing boats where they are then forced to beach and are killed for their meat. This traditional hunt has taken place in the Faroes for centuries and is considered by the Faroese an ancient right; over the years the meat produced from the kill has helped to keep many isolated communities alive.

The **killer whale**, also known as the orca, is the largest member of the dolphin family and is easily recognised by its black, white and grey markings (there's a white patch behind each eye) and massive triangular dorsal fin (male) set slightly forward of the centre of the body; this is the whale popularly featured in the film, *Free Willy*. The term killer whale is confusing since they do not eat people, or indeed act violently within their pod. Their main sources of food are fish and seals, although they do also eat squid, and they are generally found in deep water but will enter shallow bays and estuaries, particularly in summer and autumn when herring move closer to the coast. The killer whale is inquisitive and highly acrobatic when on the surface, often leaping out of the water, lobtailing, flipper-slapping and spyhopping. Although individual animals may separate themselves from a pod, they are generally found in groups of up to 25; when fully grown they can weigh up to nine tonnes.

Weighing up to 80 tonnes (the equivalent of around 2,000 people standing on one spot), and measuring up to a whopping 26m, the **fin whale** is the second-largest animal on earth. This animal was extensively hunted and its numbers plummeted accordingly; it's thought the fin whale population today stands at around 120,000. It can be recognised by its exceptionally large size, grey body, small fin sloping backwards about three-quarters of the way down its body, and its tall narrow blow, typically occurring between two and five times at intervals of ten–20 seconds. The fin whale also has around 100 throat grooves, which generally reach down to its navel. Occasionally the animal will breach clear of the water. The fin whale is a fast swimmer (around 30km/h) and generally lives in small groups numbering around five. This whale first appears off the Faroes around March, though it's not until late May or early June that it's present in large numbers.

Porpoises and dolphins

Smaller than a human being at roughly 1.5m in length, the **harbour porpoise** is not easy to spot. It's quite shy and is very wary of boats. The best thing to listen out for is its blow which, although not often seen, sounds rather like someone sneezing. This dolphin has black lips (rather than a beak), a chin and a nondescript grey-black body (white underside) with a low fin in the shape of a triangle but with a blunt tip. It is generally found within 10km of the shore and particularly appreciates shallow bays and estuaries where it feeds on shrimp and fish; look out for it rising to the surface about four or five times in a row at 15-second intervals.

Although the **bottlenose dolphin** is relatively rare around the Faroes, it does appear from time to time and usually congregates in groups of ten or so. A classic dolphin in appearance, with bluish-grey flesh, a protracted beak and pointed flippers, it is very active on the surface, sometimes breaching and riding on the wake of boats. Its dorsal fin is slightly hooked and is positioned in the centre of the body. Weighing up to 600kg, the bottlenose feeds mostly on fish and squid, though it will also consume shrimp.

The **white-sided dolphin** is so named because of its distinctive white and yellow streaks, which stretch from its dorsal fin (slightly forward of the centre of its body) to its tail. This large animal, weighing around 200kg and measuring about 2m in length, can often be seen alongside longfin pilot whales in groups of anything up to 50, though it prefers smaller pods closer to the shore. It has a gently sloping forehead and a black ring around its eye. The white-sided dolphin is very agile and often breaches and lobtails, surfacing to breathe about every 15 seconds. Its diet consists of squid and fish, occasionally shrimp.

Unfortunately, the exact populations of the above mammals are not known exactly, although it is believed that longfin pilot whales are very common throughout the North Atlantic. It's for this reason that the International Whaling Commission has excluded the pilot whale from its endangered species list, making it legally possible for the Faroese to continue their traditional hunt for the whale whilst still conserving numbers. As far as the conservation of fish stocks is concerned, the Faroese fishing industry has for several years employed a system of 'fishing days' rather than quotas which, it's argued, better conserves fish numbers rather than simply hoovering up large numbers of fish to fill quotas.

FLORA One of the first things that visitors to the Faroe Islands notice is the distinct lack of trees. Although there are a handful of small plantations – mostly of spruce, ash, maple and willow – dotted around the islands, there are no indigenous trees; the islands' 80,000 or so sheep nibble anything they come across, putting paid to any chance a tree may have of re-establishing itself elsewhere. In fact, anything that does grow in the Faroes has been brought to the islands by birds, the wind, the sea currents or, since the time of the Settlement, by people. Today there are around 400 species of flowering plant (a quarter were introduced by man) and around 30 or so mosses and fungi. The islands are characterised by large areas of hilly grassland divided into the homefield (the area immediately enclosing a village) and the outfield (everything on the other side of this division, ie: valley sides, mountaintops, etc). During the summer months, the sheep are not allowed in the homefield, where vegetables are cultivated, and it's here that you'll find the islands' various buttercups, violets, wild orchids and cranesbill. In the outfield the terrain can often be boggy and peaty, and it's here that you'll come across plants that can tolerate high amounts of water such as cottongrass and rushes. Buttercups are one of the few wild flowers you'll see in the outfield among the sheep because they have a bitter taste and are poisonous. Often in the proximity of bird cliffs you'll find angelica which, during previous centuries, was cultivated as a vegetable; it particularly likes soil that is rich in phosphates and nitrates, caused by bird droppings. Faroese mountaintops are renowned for their extensive areas of camomile, knotgrass, lady's mantle and sorrel. Ravines and gorges are the places to look for the several varieties of saxifrage that grow in the islands because here they can grow out of the reach of sheep; five of the most beautiful are the mossy saxifrage (*Saxifraga hypnoides*), alpine saxifrage (*Saxifraga nivalis*), purple saxifrage (*Saxifraga oppositifolia*), Irish saxifrage (*Saxifraga rosacea*) and starry saxifrage (*Saxifraga stellaris*).

During the summer months you should keep to established paths when walking through the homefield and take special care not to walk through hayfields, which will provide much-needed fodder for sheep and cattle through the long winter months. Although Faroese nature is fragile, there are no special conservation issues as such – nevertheless, you should not import large numbers of cans and plastic bottles which, when discarded, can destroy the delicate environmental balance and endanger birds.

HISTORY

Although the Faroe Islands have never been linked politically with Iceland, 400km to the northwest, their histories frequently overlap. In both cases some of our best glimpses of early life come from the stories or *sagas* written down around the 13th century. Neither Iceland nor the Faroes had an indigenous population to be conquered or subjugated when the first brave travellers arrived from the south and east. Both were visited first, in all probability, by Irish monks but owe their early development to the Vikings. Both had to come to terms with centuries of rule from Norway and Denmark, and both have struggled to establish their independence – the Icelanders succeeded eventually, although the Faroes remain to this day a Danish dependency.

EARLY SETTLERS There is still much academic debate about the voyages of the Irish abbot St Brendan in AD560–67. According to the stories passed down to future generations, he went in search of 'The Promised Land of the Saints' and had many adventures along the way, but historical evidence of his travels is scant to say the least. His story was long considered a legend, but it spoke of his visit to the 'Island of Sheep and the Paradise of Birds', several days' sailing distance from Scotland. The literal translation of the Faroese word for the islands, *Føroyar*, is indeed 'The sheep islands', and Mykines in particular has a massive bird population, but this wasn't enough to convince the sceptics. Recently, researchers have unearthed archaeological signs of cultivated fields from the same period, and gravestones with what appear to be Celtic crosses have been discovered in an ancient churchyard in Skúgvoy, all of which gives credibility to the theory that even if St Brendan himself never visited, Irish monks were indeed the first humans to set foot here.

The arrival of the Norsemen in the 9th century is not in dispute, on the other hand. These visitors were not Vikings in the sense that most people imagine them. Rather, they were farmers and peasants who were either in search of new lands or forced to flee Scandinavia for religious or other reasons.

If the *Færeyinga Saga* or *Saga of the Faroe Islanders* is to be believed, the first Norse settler was a man named **Grímur Kamban** who probably made his way north from Viking-settled Ireland. A Norse system of administration was quickly established, remarkably democratic for the time. There would have been local meeting places for discussion of the islands' development and the settlement of disputes, and the main parliament or *ting* (people's assembly) sat at Tinganes in Tórshavn. This would have been the final arbiter of the law and the place where any unresolved disagreements were sorted out. It was also the main place of worship to the Norse gods.

The *Saga* tells us of the Faroes' conversion to Christianity around AD1000, around the same time as in Iceland. By all accounts it was a far from peaceful transition. The new religion was brought to the islands by **Sigmundur Brestisson**, a member of the dominant Gøtuskeggjar family, who went to Norway and promised the Norwegian King Olav that he would convert his home people on his return. The Faroese farmers refused, and an increasingly bloody period followed in which the battle for religion became entwined with resistance to Norwegian influence more generally.

THE INFLUENCE OF SCANDINAVIA The victory of the Christians brought many social changes in its wake. Family allegiance was replaced by loyalty to the Church and, in effect, to Norse rule. But, as might be expected, there was a lot of passive resistance and it took centuries before the traditional customs and beliefs had all but disappeared. According to the *Saga,* the *ting* agreed in 1035 to accept Norwegian control and to become a part of the Kingdom of Norway.

It was a dark period for the Faroes because, despite a healthy economic outlook, the islands became more and more dependent on Norway, both politically and financially. By 1035, the *ting* had lost its ultimate power and the traditional, locally administered fishing industry fell prey to foreign intervention, first from Norway and then from the Hanseatic League. The Church demanded not just the people's faith but more and more of their money too. When the construction of the Magnus Cathedral began around 1300 at Kirkjubøur, the financial demands on the local population to pay for it were so great that there was apparently a revolt against the bishop. By all accounts the fact that the cathedral remains unfinished to this day – it still has no roof – is a testament to the ferocity of the opposition. But that a cathedral should have been contemplated at all is evidence of the growth of the islands both in importance and in numbers of inhabitants. By the end of the 13th century, it's thought that around 4,000 people lived here.

The so-called 'Sheep Letter' of 1298 gives a rare insight into the social structures of the time. It was drawn up to regulate the division of land and, as the name implies, to lay down some rules for the rearing of sheep. Remarkably, it remained in force until the middle of the 19th century. The Letter suggests that by the time of its drafting, the first settlements, owned by a small number of families, had been broken up into smaller landholdings and farms and that the population was now more spread out across the islands, although by now the Church controlled around 40% of the land. The Faroes were now sufficiently well established to provide opportunities for trade that its absentee rulers couldn't resist exploiting.

Norway's king, **Magnus the Lawmaker**, wasn't content with having a cathedral that bore his name. He now tried to establish a trade monopoly too, insisting that all commerce take place through the Norwegian port of Bergen. Here, of course, customs taxes would be levied. But his ships couldn't compete with the much more efficient vessels of the newly formed Hanseatic League in northern Germany. This, coupled with the plague that struck Norway to devastating effect, drastically reduced the king's power in the Faroes and led to a more competitive economic environment.

In 1380 the crowns of Denmark and Norway were formally united, although with the Danes as the dominant partner. Danish law took effect in the Faroes and the *ting* became little more than a talking shop. One of the world's oldest parliaments had effectively been dissolved. At the same time the Catholic Church increased its land-grab; the islands entered a period of economic and cultural decline that amounted to something of a Dark Age with local customs and the local economy being increasingly smothered by the power of Denmark.

AFTER THE MIDDLE AGES The next major landmark in Faroese history didn't come until 1535 when King Christian III of Denmark granted exclusive trading rights to a Hamburg merchant, **Thomas Köppen**, and with it the right to collect taxes. After a bitter civil war at home, the Danish crown was desperately short of money. The Faroe Islands had already been offered to England's King Henry VIII in return for cash, but he turned them down. If he'd accepted, the Faroes might well be today what many ill-informed people believe them to be anyway – some far-flung extension of the British Isles.

The year 1535 had an even more profound effect on the islands with the advent of the Reformation. Denmark had now adopted the Lutheran Protestant religion and decided to impose it on its foreign territories too. It was hailed as an exercise in enlightenment, but the impact on the islands was generally a negative one. Danish replaced Latin as the language of the Church, and priests, who had been educated until now at Kirkjubøur on Streymoy, had to go to Copenhagen for their training. Before long there were more Danish clergymen than Faroese. By 1557 the local bishopric was abolished altogether and for religious purposes the islands came under the tutelage of Bergen. King Christian III had already confiscated two-thirds of Church lands, leasing much of it to Köppen, and now he grabbed the remainder. This he rented out to tenants known as *kongsbøndur* or king's farmers. Uniquely these lands couldn't be split up among family members, so the tenants who held them went on to become relatively wealthy and powerful. The reform was a major force for stability in Faroese society.

TRADE Over the following century the trade monopoly passed through different hands, almost all of them foreign. The most notable exception was a Faroese adventurer, **Magnus Heinason** (1548–89), who promised to tackle the problem of pirates in the waters off the islands and, in return, was allowed to build a fighting ship and the fort at Skansin in Tórshavn. He is still regarded as something of a national hero, although he wasn't beyond bullying and cheating his fellow countrymen in pursuit of a good profit for himself. The problem of piracy didn't go away, and the growth of smuggling undermined the monopoly more and more as time went on.

In the mid 17th century the Faroes were all but handed over to one man, **Christopher Gabel**, who had almost total political and economic control. He passed all of it on to his son, Frederik, on his death. Both men assumed the title of Governor and are remembered for the harshness of their rule and, as ever, their readiness to profit from the islanders' efforts. They tried to fortify Skansin still further, using unpaid workers from Tórshavn. What followed was a mini revolution. A formal complaint was made to Denmark, but the locals took matters into their own hands and mysterious fires and an explosion in a gunpowder store destroyed many of the buildings owned by the Gabels' company. In 1677 the town was subjected to a violent raid by French pirates and, once again, the Danes were forced to think about how best to restore some kind of peace and economic prosperity to the Faroes. A Royal Commission was dispatched to come up with suggestions, but the king's preferred solution was simply to take back power himself.

Faroese historians regard the subsequent period as a distinct change for the better. Corruption all but disappeared and some semblance of fair trade was restored. Unfortunately little was done to improve communications between the islands themselves and people still had to travel to Tórshavn in all weathers to collect supplies. Famine and death on the more outlying islands were not uncommon.

The wealthy *kongsbøndur* were able to consolidate their power still further and in 1777 passed the so-called 'slave law' which forbade marriage to anyone who didn't own enough land to support a family. Despite its obvious unfairness, the law was designed to control the population so the Faroes could remain self-sufficient. It didn't work, and before long new settlements had to be established to house the growing number of islanders and the importation of food, especially corn, became a necessity.

Meanwhile the political upheavals in Europe continued to have an impact on the islands. The outbreak of the Napoleonic Wars disrupted trade and in 1808 an English brig, the *Clio,* entered Tórshavn and briefly captured the fort at Skansin. Economically, fishing was growing in importance so that by 1840, fish and fish products made up almost 40% of exports from the islands. The growth of fishing had a powerful social impact too, with men away from home for long periods of time and women taking on greater responsibilities as a result. Faroese society was entering a period of flux that would help generate a political demand for greater independence. As a first step, the trade monopoly was finally abolished on 1 January 1856. This had been demanded by the islanders themselves, although the reasons for abolition had far more to do with the fact that the monopoly was losing the Danish crown money. With its passing, the idea that Denmark was not, after all, all-powerful began to grow.

POLITICAL CHANGE These stirrings of nationalist sentiment had been encouraged earlier in the century when the Faroese parliament, already renamed the *Løgting* to fit in with the Scandinavian system of local government, was finally abolished altogether. Danish law was now supreme. The practical effect was minimal but the psychological impact was far more profound. Add to that the use of Danish rather than Faroese in all official dealings and then, in 1849, the legal assumption of the islands into Denmark itself, and it was inevitable that local noses would be put severely out of joint. The concept of Home Rule was discussed openly for the first time. In 1852 the Løgting was re-established as a kind of regional council with only advisory powers. It had 20 members, 18 of them elected by the various districts. The language question generated the greatest resentment but this led some to start questioning the threat to Faroese culture as well.

Just how much anger lay below the surface was revealed when, in 1888, a small group of young men advertised a meeting with the words: 'Everybody is invited to come to the house of the Løgting on Boxing Day at 3 p.m. where we will discuss how to protect the Faroese language and the Faroese culture.' It was standing room only. There were bold speeches about the time having come for the Faroese people to stand up and protect their heritage. An organisation called the *Føringafelag* was formed as a direct result of the meeting to fight for both the language and the self-sufficiency of the islands.

The young radicals were opposed by many of the wealthier landowners, who feared higher taxes to pay for local self-government. Indeed it was the opponents of Home Rule that formed the Faroes' first political party, the Union Party, to campaign for even closer links with Denmark. In response, **Jóhannes Patursson**, one of the young men behind the Boxing Day meeting, formed the Self-Rule Party to fight for gradual moves towards independence. The battle lines were drawn, but the conservatives still held the upper hand and after a centrist Social Democratic Party was formed in 1927, the radicals were kept out of power until World War II.

The conflagration that hit Europe had a sudden and dramatic effect on the Faroe Islands. Denmark quickly fell to Germany and Britain sent troops to the islands to prevent them also falling under Nazi control. Needless to say the British were more concerned about the strategically important North Atlantic shipping lanes than the welfare of the islanders, but the effect was the same: the changes came with remarkable speed.

A Faroese ship on its way to Aberdeen was intercepted by a British warship and ordered to lower the Danish flag and to fly the Faroese flag instead. The Danish governor of the islands protested but was overruled, and the BBC announced that all Faroese shipping would fly the islands' own flag from then on. The day of the announcement, 25 April, has been the national flag day ever since. In practice, the Faroese enjoyed Home Rule in all but name during the war years and in return they braved the dangerous seas to the south to deliver much-needed fish to the British Isles. There was a high cost to pay in human lives but the economy prospered and the islands built up their own financial reserves for the first time.

By the end of the war the political plates had shifted. Despite a rearguard action by the conservative parties, the people voted narrowly in a referendum for independence from Denmark. The Danish Prime Minister agreed – at first – and it seemed that self-government was indeed on the way. A change of heart by the Danish government swiftly followed when it was felt in Copenhagen that Danish national honour was being challenged. So, far from greater independence, the Faroes suffered the indignity of having the Løgting dissolved by the King of Denmark and new elections ordered. The new Løgting agreed instead to a middle way of greater self-rule within the union with Denmark and the Faroese Home Rule Act was duly passed and came into effect on 1 April 1948.

The Faroes has shifted from being a mere county of Denmark to a 'self-governing community within the Kingdom of Denmark', a status it holds to this day. But the battle goes on, though with none of the fervour of the 1940s. In 1948, a new political party was formed to insist that the referendum result be honoured and the islands be given full independence. In recent years that came tantalisingly close, but never close enough. The post-war settlement has survived – just – not least because it gives a substantial measure of self-rule to the islanders themselves. Having said that, the current compromise has some confusing inconsistencies.

The Løgting is now wholly democratic and the representative of Denmark in the islands has no vote in its proceedings. There is a Faroese prime minister, the *Løgmaður*, and a cabinet. Its powers cover taxation, customs, communications, education, sanitation and the post office. Faroese stamps are a great money-spinner for the islands. But while Faroese is the official language of domestic politics and national life, Danish must still be taught in all schools as a link to the motherland. Denmark controls the police, defence and foreign policy, and the currency. There is a Faroese currency, the Faroese króna, but it is tied to the Danish currency and Faroese banknotes are printed and issued by the National Bank of Denmark. But trade, that historically contentious issue, has been left in the hands of the Faroese.

So, when Denmark joined the European Union, it happened that the Faroes refused to go in with them, choosing to stay outside and preserve their fishing rights. If the Danes were ever to vote to join the Eurozone, the position of the Faroes would prove an interesting side issue.

THE 90S FINANCIAL CRISIS The islands have benefited financially from the link with Denmark. They pay no direct taxes to Copenhagen but receive subsidies that amount to some 14% of their gross domestic product.

The continued existence of the 200-mile exclusion zone for fishing helped the Faroese economy prosper in the post-war years. For a while the population was enjoying the world's highest standard of living and the Faroese were spending up to ten times as much as their Danish counterparts. Road and tunnel building brought the islands' communities closer together but for the population the cost per head was high. The Faroese were living on borrowed time, and for that matter on borrowed money. It couldn't last.

The fishing industry had been cushioned by over-generous government subsidies during the good years. So when drastic falls in fish stocks in the North Atlantic, due to overfishing, hit the fishermen hard, the knock-on effects for the entire community were catastrophic. The Faroes had become a centre of expertise for high-tech, high-yield fishing equipment but now they had to pay the price of their success. The annual catch fell dramatically at the same time as fish prices were taking a tumble and, as a result, the whole economy was suddenly plunged into crisis.

The national bank was supporting massive debt and as people increasingly defaulted on their loans, the bank itself went under. In October 1992, the receivers were called in and the Faroese had no choice but to go cap in hand to Denmark to ask the government there to bail them out. It was a terrible humiliation that affected everyone in the islands. In return for financial support that eventually reached almost two billion Danish kroner, the Danish National Bank effectively took control of its Faroese equivalent. Not surprisingly the Danes demanded major reforms in return for their support. There was an emergency budget that produced lower public spending, higher taxes and cuts in wages for public employees. Unemployment rose to over 20% and the fishing industry was crippled, with half its boats and processing plants in receivership. Then, to make matters worse, the Faroese government discovered that an apparently generous offer to allow a Faroese takeover of the islands' second-biggest bank from the Danish National Bank had a painful sting in the tail. Contrary to what they had been told, the bank was itself in serious debt, something the new owners only discovered 48 hours after taking it over. By October 1993 the islanders were back asking Copenhagen for more cash. The Danish media attacked them ferociously as if they were spoiled and irresponsible children. Demands for an official enquiry into the bank issue were refused and things looked bleaker than ever until a Danish journalist revealed the extent of the scandal, with evidence of a high-level conspiracy effectively to bankrupt the Faroes completely. The revelations led to a compromise with a big reduction in the islands' debt and an interest-free loan from the shamed Danes.

The last few years of the 20th century were a period of recovery. Fish stocks stabilised and the catch increased once more. Some of the 5,000 or so people who had left the islands during the slump started to return as the economy picked up considerably. But the political impact of the crisis was more long-lasting. For only the second time ever pro-independence parties won a majority in the Løgting with a programme designed to achieve full independence by the year 2000. Denmark agreed to negotiate and experts were asked to investigate how the Faroes might manage if they decided to go it alone. The experts predicted that a Faroese state would be viable and plans were laid for independence subject to a vote in favour in a referendum.

Then suddenly it all went wrong. The Faroese accused the Danes of bad faith in the negotiations. The Danish government insists the Faroese plans were unworkable, although there are suspicions that Copenhagen was afraid Greenland would follow the Faroes down the path to independence and decided instead to stop the process in its tracks. By the spring of 2001 Prime Minister Anfinn Kallsberg was forced to tell the Faroese people that he was now convinced Denmark had never intended to grant the islands their freedom. Could the Faroes achieve full nationhood by themselves? They concluded that they couldn't. The plans had relied on gradually reducing Danish subsidies over 12 years but that was not on offer any more, if indeed it ever had been. So the planned referendum for May 2001 was cancelled.

Since then, the islands have adopted a policy of gradually taking greater control of the school and health systems, with less dependence on Danish grants, along with attempts at economic diversification to protect the islands from future upheavals in the fishing industry.

THE FAROE ISLANDS TODAY The discovery of oil deposits has excited a lot of optimism for the future, not least because Denmark signed away any rights to oil and mineral finds before the discovery was made. So far it seems the oil may be hard to extract and, while the first drilling started in 2001, exploration is still underway on the southern edge of Faroese territorial waters in the hope of finding oil in commercially exploitable quantities. Optimists point out that it took Norway over 30 attempts to strike gold, and exploration off the Faroes is still in the very early stages. On land, tunnel fever remains high following the success of the subsea link to Klaksvík. Initial work has now begun on a new tunnel to link southern Streymoy with Eysturoy; a second tunnel from Streymoy to Sandur is set to follow.

GOVERNMENT AND POLITICS

Since the Home Rule Act, passed on 23 March 1948, the Faroe Islands have been a self-governing region of the Kingdom of Denmark. They have their own prime minister and government, parliament, flag, currency (albeit tied to that of Denmark), national airline – even football team. Unlike Denmark, the Faroes are not part of the European Union and all trade with EU countries is governed by specially negotiated treaties drawn up in consultation and co-operation with the Danish foreign ministry. The islands are represented in the Danish parliament, the *Folketing*, by two MPs. Although for all intents and purposes the islands are self-governing, Denmark is still responsible for policing, defence and justice. However, it is the intention of the Faroese administration to gradually take control of all the islands' affairs in preparation for the possibility of full independence some time in the future. Public opinion, however, remains divided on the issue of independence – not least because the generous subsidies which the Danes pour into the islands, funding everything from childcare to healthcare, would cease, leaving the Faroese totally dependent on their own resources for continued prosperity.

ECONOMY

FISHING The Faroese economy is totally dependent on fishing and fish rearing and the islands operate a 200-mile exclusive fisheries zone offshore. Fisheries products, including farmed salmon, account for more than 95% of total exports and nearly half of the Faroese gross domestic product. Few other countries have such a degree of dependency on living marine resources, hence safeguarding the marine environment and ensuring its sustainable use are top priorities for the Faroese government. With around 190 fishing vessels working the waters of the North Atlantic, the fishing fleet is among the most modern afloat, comprising mainly coastal vessels and long-liners as well as a number of ocean-going trawlers. The islands operate a fisheries management system of fishing days rather than quotas, which entitles vessels to fish for a set number of days per year irrespective of how much fish they catch. In recent years the Faroese fish-farming industry has undergone tremendous growth and today represents a significant component of the country's economic activity. The clean temperate waters around the islands are ideal for fish farming, particularly of Atlantic salmon, and most islands in the archipelago now have one or two fish farms in operation.

WHALING Although many different species of whales can be found in the waters around the Faroe Islands, the only whales the Faroese catch today are small pilot whales which are driven ashore into shallow bays during whale drives (Faroese *grindadráp*) and killed by a deep cut through the spinal cord: death is almost immediate. Pilot whales, so called in English because of their habit of following a leader or pilot and known as *grindhvalur* in Faroese, are actually a species of large dolphin and can be found across the North Atlantic from Canada to Norway. The whales are not on the endangered species list drawn up by the International Whaling Commission and experts estimate there are around 700,000 pilot whales in the North Atlantic. The Faroese catch around 900 whales each year in several drives. The meat and blubber have long been a staple part of the national diet. Whales are shared among the participants in a whale drive and residents of the local district where they are landed.

Whaling began with the settlement of the Faroes in the 800s, though it wasn't until 1584 that records began to be kept showing the numbers killed and documenting strandings of pilot whale schools. When commercial whaling began in the second half of the 20th century it was blubber rather than meat that was the most sought-after product. The blubber was boiled down on site into oil which was then used for heating and the production of soaps and cosmetics. Then, in the 1970s and 80s, a market developed in Japan for whale meat. Whales were caught in the Faroes until 1984 (the last big whale caught in the islands was a fin whale winched ashore at the former whaling station, við Áir, on Streymoy) when protests were reaching a peak and environmental groups such as Greenpeace began flexing their muscles, calling for boycotts of seafood from whale-hunting nations. Public opinion in the Faroes is strongly in favour of whaling and most people would like to see its resumption. The government in Tórshavn has closely followed the situation in neighbouring Iceland where commercial whaling was recommenced in late 2006. In recent years, Greenpeace has attempted to draw international attention to the Faroese whale drive, though with little success as the number of hunts has not diminished.

PEOPLE AND CULTURE

According to the latest demographic figures available for the Faroes, 48,704 people live in the islands, 20,235 (about 42%) of them in the capital, Tórshavn, and 4,893 in Klaksvík, the country's second town on the island of Borðoy. Population density in the Faroes is 35 people per km², considerably more than Iceland's 3 per km² though much less than Denmark's 124 per km². The Faroese are of Scandinavian origin, descendants of Vikings who came originally from southwestern Norway. It's estimated that around 25,000 Faroese now live in Denmark, bringing the total number of speakers of Faroese to around 70,000. Although there are a number of Danes living in the islands, and small numbers of other nationalities, immigration to the Faroes is still relatively small. It is not common to see any other skin colour than white in the islands.

LANGUAGE Today, **Faroese** is the official language of the Faroe Islands, used in schools, administration, the Church and the media. A Viking tongue, brought to the islands with the first settlers around AD800, it's a grammatically complicated language, composed of many case endings, genders and dialects, which not surprisingly few visitors take the trouble to learn. However, its history is a fascinating, and ultimately successful, struggle for survival against much more prestigious Danish, the national tongue of a kingdom and empire. Indeed, Faroese is one of only two languages (both variants of Old Norse, the language spoken in Scandinavia during the Viking period) exported by the Vikings which still exists today. Between the 13th and 18th centuries, Norn, the Norse spoken in the Scottish Hebrides, the Isle of Man, Orkney and Shetland died out, with the result that Faroese and Icelandic are today the closest relatives to the original language of the Vikings.

Delve into the history of Faroese and you'll quickly come up with some quite remarkable facts: the first monolingual Faroese–Faroese dictionary was only published in 1998, the first Bible in Faroese didn't appear until 1961 and the language only won official status in the islands in 1948 with the introduction of the Home Rule Act. The reason for this rather late coming-of-age is quite simple: over the centuries Faroese, little more than a ragtag of dialects spoken by farmers and fishermen with no written form, always played second fiddle to Danish, the respected language of merchants and officials. In 1380, when Norway and its dependencies, which then included the Faroe Islands, became part of the Dano-Norwegian kingdom, the status of Danish as the official language of the crown was confirmed right across the new kingdom, including the far-flung Faroes, which few people in Denmark at the time had even heard of. It was a status that the Reformation only served to reinforce – Luther's aim was that the word of God be translated from Latin into the language of the people, which, in the view of the Danish Church, was most definitely Danish. For over 400 years during the period of Danish administration, Faroese stagnated; it remained little more than a collection of peasant dialects spoken by countryfolk amongst each other. Any communication with the authorities had to be carried out in Danish since no official could speak, or indeed had any intention of learning, Faroese. In fact, it wasn't until 1823 that the first Faroese text, the Gospel of St Matthew, was published in the vernacular. Ironically, it was met with much derision by the islanders themselves and the experiment wasn't repeated for another 20 years. A similar problem was encountered in 1856 when the theologian **V U Hammershaimb** chose to preach in Faroese rather than Danish, the official language of the Church; there was great indignation amongst the congregation who didn't deem their lowly tongue worthy of the great words of God.

The abolition of the Danish trade monopoly the same year marked a turning point in the islands and in the fortunes of the Faroese language. People became more mobile, trade (and ultimately contact with the outside world) increased and in the 1870s the Faroese began sloop fishing, laying the first tentative steps towards economic growth and independence – national confidence and linguistic credibility naturally increased. Although compulsory schooling was introduced by the Copenhagen authorities in 1840, the language of instruction remained Danish and the range of subjects heavily Denmark-orientated. It was a common complaint

THE MAN BEHIND THE SPELLING: HAMMERSHAIMB

Faroe Islanders often complain that the spelling of Faroese bears little resemblance to its pronunciation. Today, words are spelt in line with their Old Norse origins, despite the fact that they are no longer pronounced this way. The man who drew up today's archaic spelling rules was **Venceslaus Ulricus Hammershaimb** (1819–1909), whose name alone is a spelling nightmare. A Lutheran minister and folklorist, Hammershaimb launched his complex spelling system in 1846 to create a single standard form for every word, irrespective of its different regional pronunciations. In 1889, Faroese linguist **Jakob Jakobsen** (see box, page 18), proposed reforms to Hammershaimb's spelling rules but they were thrown out by a special committee a few years later after a heated national debate. Accordingly, Faroese spelling causes great problems for today's schoolchildren who struggle to understand why the letter 'ð' is written but never pronounced and why the letter 'g' can seemingly have any number of pronunciations.

among Faroese students that they learnt everything about the history of Denmark from the Stone Age to the present day yet nothing about their own country or traditions. In fact, oral Faroese only became an official subject in the curriculum in 1912, the written version of the language being introduced in 1920. As late as 1938 Danish remained the official language of education in the Faroe Islands. However, following World War II, the Home Rule Act of 1948, which made the islands a self-governing region of the Kingdom of Denmark, finally brought official recognition of the Faroese language, which, today, is the national language of the Faroe Islands. Danish, however, still has official status with Faroese in public affairs and all laws passed by the Faroese parliament are painstakingly translated into Danish. Yet, the battle is still not won. Faroese, a language spoken by around 48,000 people in the islands themselves, is under constant pressure from Danish (many television programmes are broadcast in Danish without subtitles) and English with the result that many foreign words are seeping into the language and diluting what the Faroese claim is one of the purest languages in Europe thanks to centuries of (Danish-imposed) isolation. In fact, until the early 2000s, dictionaries between Faroese and any language other than Danish simply didn't exist. For words, phrases and grammar, see *Appendices 1* and *2*, pages 160–5 and 166–7. Jonathan Adams and Hjalmar P Petersen have an excellent language course, *Faroese: A Language Course for Beginners* (see *Appendix 3*, page 169, for details).

A LESSON LEARNT: THE DEATH OF NORN

Jakob Jakobsen (1864–1918) was a Faroese linguist who, at the age of 29, began studying the remnants of **Norn**, the Old Norse language once spoken in the Shetland Islands and a sister language to his mother tongue, Faroese (both languages were mutually intelligible). The Scandinavian language that evolved into Norn was brought to Shetland by Norwegian Vikings in the 800s and, indeed, Shetland remained part of Norway until 1472 when the islands were officially annexed by an Act of Parliament to the Scottish crown.

From 1893, Jakobsen spent three years in Shetland, travelling across the islands interviewing local people and jotting down dialect words and place names which he considered to be of Norn origin; the result was his *Etymological Dictionary of the Norn Language in Shetland*, published in 1928, which included an impressive 10,000 entries. In 1894 Jakobsen reported that there were still people on the island of Foula who could repeat sentences in Norn and possibly men who had lived into the second half of the 19th century who could speak the language.

Today, the last native speaker of Norn is considered to have died around 1850, though the language had effectively died out between 1775 and 1800 due to increasing immigration from mainland Scotland and the use of English as the official language of administration, law and religion. In the early 1900s, the death of Norn was cited by Jakobsen and other promoters of Faroese as a cautionary example of what could happen to their own language in the face of Danish linguistic supremacy: Faroese, like Norn, was an unwritten language used on the periphery of a larger empire which spoke a different language. Significantly, what saved Faroese from extinction was the lack of large-scale immigration into the Faroe Islands (the exact opposite of what happened in Shetland), which meant the islanders could still get by speaking Faroese in their daily lives.

RELIGION   Religion is important to the Faroese and 84% of the population belongs to the established national church in the islands, the Evangelical–Lutheran Føroya Kirkja, which has 61 churches in the Faroes; three out of every four weddings are held in one. In addition to the national church there are several other religious communities in the islands, including the Plymouth Brethren (13% of the population are members), the Catholic Church, the Salvation Army, the Pentecostal movement, Seventh Day Adventists, Jehovah's Witnesses, the Philadelphia Congregation and the Baháʼí faith.

ARTS AND CULTURE   The arts scene in the Faroes is in its infancy. The lack of a written language for centuries combined with a subsistence lifestyle meant there was little time left for the finer things in life. Culture as we know it was essentially limited to the chain dance, which is still going strong today. The dancers hold hands to form a chain or ring which moves slowly to the left in a heavy rhythm marked by two double steps to the left and one to the right. This form of dancing began in France, where it was known as the *branle simple*, from where it spread across Europe, eventually reaching the Faroes, now the only place it still exists. The singing of the dancers is the only music and the texts used are mainly those of the *kvæði* – lengthy medieval ballads written in 6/4 time which tell of heroic deeds of the period. Although the ballads were never written down, they were passed orally from generation to generation.

It was in this manner, too, that the first Faroese stories were passed on, though once again they were not written down. Over the years a number of minor authors and poets came and went, but it was not until the early 20th century, with the acceptance of a standardised written language, that writing began to progress. However, it's the work of **William Heinesen**, born in Tórshavn in 1900, that really marks the beginning of the Faroese novel. Although regarded as one of the Faroes' greatest writers, Heinesen wrote in Danish rather than Faroese, Danish being considered the language of culture in his day.

A similarly delayed start was also the case for the visual arts in the islands. Although several new artists are now coming to the fore, there is little tradition of painting or sculpture in the islands. The most renowned artist in the Faroes is undoubtedly **Sámal Joensen-Mikines**, whose work is displayed in the National Art Gallery in Tórshavn. Drawing heavily on the unforgiving character of the Faroese landscape, his and his successors' work has produced some inspired interpretations of land, sea and sky. One of the latest stars to emerge is **Tróndur Patursson**, whose work with stained glass in particular has won him justifiable praise, while a group of new artists, such as **Øssur Johannesen** and **Edvard Fuglø**, are moving away from the use of traditional motifs and taking Faroese art in a new contemporary direction.

1

2

Practical Information

WHEN TO VISIT

Undoubtedly the best time to be in the Faroes is during the long days of **summer**. From May to the end of July, when the evenings are light and the weather is at its most stable, the islands show their best side: wild flowers grow amid the deep-green tussocky grass of the valley slopes, the waterfalls glisten against the patchwork of whites and blues of the northern sky and everywhere the air is heavy with the scent of freshly mown hay and full of the calls of thousands of birds. August and September, too, are delightful months to be in the islands; the days are still long and can be pleasantly warm. September, in particular, can be a great time to have the islands to yourself; most other tourists have left and you can hike without seeing a soul and experience the unsullied Faroese nature totally undisturbed. However, the weather now is on the change and the first of the winter storms is never far away. Although **autumn**, and especially **winter**, are not ideally suited to tourism in the Faroes, there is nevertheless a certain masochistic pleasure to be gained from being buffeted by winds and rain, the intensity of which you will probably never have experienced before. The downside, of course, is that daylight is scarce at this time of year, and in December and January, it's already starting to get dark around 14.00–14.30 – it's black by 14.30–15.00. Under a fresh fall of snow, the elemental beauty of the Faroese landscapes of mountain peaks and deep valleys is certainly breathtaking, but it's worth remembering that many attractions are closed or inaccessible during the long winter months. **Spring** brings a new lease of life to the islands, and daffodils and snowdrops are in full bloom in the Faroes way before they even start to peek out of the ground in Iceland, for example, barely an hour's flight to the north. March and April are incredibly satisfying months to visit the country – not only can you appreciate the fresh leaves on the trees and the newly opened flowers, but the birds are starting to return, a sure sign that spring has arrived.

FAROESE HIGHLIGHTS

The Faroe Islands have three things in plenty: vast areas of unspoilt mountainous terrain perfect for hiking; vertical sea cliffs teeming with birdlife ideal for ornithologists; and picturesque villages of wooden houses topped with turf roofs waiting to be discovered. If you have only a couple of days in the Faroes, it makes sense to concentrate on the capital, **Tórshavn**, and the immediate vicinity, perhaps adding in a visit to the medieval cathedral at **Kirkjubøur** or a boat trip across to **Nólsoy**. With a little more time, it's definitely worth seeing the spectacular bird cliffs at **Vestmanna**, a boat tour every visitor to the islands should try to make, and taking a trip anywhere by helicopter – most dramatically past the remote outpost of **Stóra Dímun**. An ideal week's holiday in the islands could include all the above plus a trip to **Mykines** to see the puffins and gannets or a visit to **Klaksvík** and a tour of the northern islands – a hike out to one of the world's tallest vertical sea cliffs, **Enniberg** on Viðoy, or an unforgettable boat trip across stormy seas to the island of **Fugloy** where there are some wonderful coastlines to discover (returning by helicopter if you can), or a hike out to the lighthouse on northern **Kalsoy** for the best views anywhere in the country. With two weeks at your disposal it's well

WEATHER CONDITIONS

Faroese	Danish	English
skýfrítt	skyfrit	bright
smáskýggjað	let skyet	fair
skýggjað	skyet	cloudy
samdrigið	overskyet	overcast
skýggjað loft	vekslende skydække	variable clouds
tjúkt	lavt skydække	low clouds/hill fog
grátt	gråvejr	dull
támut	diset	misty/hazy
mjørki	tåget	fog/foggy
pollamjørki/mjørkaflókar	tågebanker	fogbanks
sól	sol/solskin	sun/sunny
sólglottar	solstrejf	sunny spells
turt	tørt	dry
sirm	finregn/støvregn	drizzle
regn	regn	rain
ælingur	byger	showers
hækkar	drejer	veering/backing
lækkar	drejer	veering/backing
hvirlur	vindstød	gusts
vátaslettingur	slud	sleet
heglingur	hagl	hail

WIND

Faroese	Danish	English	Beaufort wind scale	Wind (m/sec)
stilli/logn	stille	calm	0	0.0–0.2
fleyr	svag luftning	light air	1	0.3–1.5
lot	svag brise	light breeze	2	1.6–3.3
lítíð lot/gul	let brise	gentle breeze	3	3.4–5.4
andøvsgul	jævn brise	moderate breeze	4	5.5–7.9
frískur vindur/ stívt andøvsgul	frisk brise/ frisk vind	fresh breeze/ fresh wind	5	8.0–10.7
strúkur í vindi	kuling/hård vind	strong wind	6	10.8–13.8
hvassur vindur	stiv kuling	near gale	7	13.9–17.1
skrið	hård kuling	gale	8	17.2–20.7
stormur	storm	strong gale	9	20.8–24.4
hvassur stormur	stærk storm	storm	10	24.5–28.4
kolandi stormur	orkanagtig storm	violent storm	11	28.5–32.6
óðn	orkan	hurricane	12	32.7–36.9

worth considering hiking, perhaps on **Vágar** or **Suðuroy** and touring the villages of **Streymoy** and **Eysturoy**, in particular **Saksun**, **Tjørnuvík** and **Gjógv**.

THE WEATHER

The statement that the Faroes can experience all four seasons in just one day may well have become a cliché over the years, yet it remains a fact with which any visitor to the islands will become all too familiar. A morning may start out beautifully sunny and warm, only for dark menacing clouds to roll in off the Atlantic within an hour or so, and by lunchtime it's pouring with rain. Then, slowly, the clouds disperse, there's a brilliant rainbow, and the sun comes out again by mid afternoon – only for the wind to pick up by evening and almost knock you flat. Faroese weather is certainly very changeable and it pays to be one step ahead and have raingear with you at all times. Don't forget that if the weather turns, it's alarmingly easy to become stranded on one island or another (it has happened to me on several occasions) with no choice but to batten down the hatches and sit it out.

INFORMATION AND MAPS

The best source of information on the Faroes is the internet. The website of the Faroese tourist board, VisitFaroeIslands (see ad, inside back cover), should be your first port of call when trying to assemble information; check out www.visitfaroeislands.com. Alternatively, should you wish for specific information relevant to Tórshavn or any of the other towns or islands, it's better to contact the individual tourist office or *kunningastova* concerned; see the individual entries in the text for details.

MAPS The best map of the Faroes is the *Føroyar 1:100,000* by Solberg. It is readily available in the bookshops in Tórshavn and costs around 150kr. For more detailed mapping, particularly for hiking purposes, you should get hold of the *Føroyar Topografiskt kort 1:20,000*, by the same publisher, which breaks the islands down into 37 individual sheets; they, once again, are readily available in Tórshavn.

TOUR OPERATORS

Although the Faroes are geared up for individual travel, with a full range of accommodation and transport options to ensure a trouble-free stay, there are a number of tour operators who also specialise in holidays to the islands. The main ones are listed below.

UNITED KINGDOM

Ramblers Holidays ✆01707 331133; e info@ramblersholidays.co.uk; www.ramblersholidays.co.uk

Regent Holidays See ad, inside front cover; ✆020 3588 2971; e regent@regentholidays.co.uk; www.regent-holidays.co.uk

Taber Holidays ✆01274 875199; e office@taberhols.co.uk; www.taberhols.co.uk

UNITED STATES

5 Stars of Scandinavia ✆+1 800 722 4126; e info@5stars-scandinavia.com; www.5stars-scandinavia.com

CANADA

Great Canadian Travel Company ✆+1 800 661 3830; e info@gctravel.ca; www.greatcanadiantravel.com

AUSTRALIA

Nordic Travel ✆+61 2 9968 1783; e info@nordictravel.com.au; www.nordictravel.com.au

FAROE ISLANDS

62° North Incoming See ad, 2nd colour section; ✆+298 34 00 60; e incoming@62n.fo; www.62n.fo

Green Gate Incoming ✆+298 35 05 20; e info@greengate.fo; www.greengate.fo

EMBASSIES AND CONSULATES

Abroad, the Faroe Islands are represented by Denmark, which has embassies and consulates around the world. European Union, US, Canadian, Australian and New Zealand nationals need only a valid passport to enter the Faroe Islands for up to three months. Some other nationalities require an entry visa for Denmark – consult your nearest Danish embassy or consulate for further information and note that a Danish visa does not give the right to enter the Faroes unless specifically stated.

United Kingdom Royal Danish Embassy, 55 Sloane St, London SW1X 9SR; ✆020 7333 0200; e lonamb@um.dk; www.storbritannien.um.dk

United States Royal Danish Embassy, 3200 Whitehaven St NW, Washington, DC 20008; ✆202 234 4300; e wasamb@um.dk; www.usa.um.dk

Australia Royal Danish Embassy, 15 Hunter St, Yarralumla, ACT 2600, ✆02 6270 5333; e cbramb@um.dk; www.australien.um.dk

Canada Royal Danish Embassy, 47 Clarence St, Suite 450, Ottawa, Ontario K1N 9K1; ✆613 562 1811; e ottamb@um.dk; www.canada.um.dk

Ireland Royal Danish Embassy, Iveagh Court, Harcourt Rd, Dublin 2; ✆01 475 6404; e dubamb@um.dk; www.irland.um.dk

New Zealand Royal Danish Consulate General in Auckland, 47A Normanby Road, Mt Eden, Auckland; ✆64 22 047 3500; e danish-in-auckland@mail.com; www.newzealand.um.dk

GETTING THERE AND AWAY

BY AIR The quickest and easiest way to reach the Faroe Islands is by the Faroese national airline, **Atlantic Airways** (✆ +298 34 10 00; e booking@atlantic.fo; www.atlantic.fo), which operates all routes to the islands exclusively. The international airline code for Atlantic Airways is RC and the airport code for the Faroes is FAE. It is important to note, though, that Atlantic only has through luggage transfer agreements with Scandinavian Airlines (SAS).

From the United Kingdom Atlantic Airways operate directly from Edinburgh (EDI) to the Faroes twice a week (on Fridays and Mondays) all year round, although services are reduced during the winter months. Flying time is in the region of

1 hour. When there is no flight from Edinburgh, connections can be made via Copenhagen (see below).

From mainland Europe An option that suits travellers coming from mainland Europe is to travel **via Denmark**. Most usefully, Atlantic flies between Copenhagen (CPH) and the Faroes twice daily. There are sometimes flights from Bergen in Norway, though schedules are prone to change. Flights to Copenhagen, in order to connect with Atlantic Airways, are available with most major European airlines. Atlantic's CPH–FAE return fares start at around 2,200 Danish kroner. Once again, book early for the cheapest fares.

From the United States The best way to reach the Faroes from the USA is to travel via Reykjavík with Icelandair (*www.icelandair.com; airline code FI*) or via Copenhagen with SAS (*www.scandinavian.net; airline code SK*). Flying with Icelandair, you'll sometimes need to change airports in Iceland; Icelandair flights arrive at the main international airport, Keflavík (KEF), and onward Atlantic Airways flights to the Faroes (1 hour) usually leave from Reykjavík city airport (RKV); both airports are linked by transfer bus.

From Canada Icelandair operates from several Canadian gateways (check the Icelandair website for the latest details) to Reykjavík, or pick up a flight to one of Icelandair's US gateways and transfer there for Iceland and then on to the Faroes.

From the rest of the world Getting to the Faroes from the rest of the world naturally involves first reaching either London or Copenhagen, from where connections are available as described above. It's worth remembering, though, that many online travel websites, such as Expedia, do not sell Atlantic Airways tickets. The best place to buy an Atlantic ticket is directly with the airline on their website, www.atlantic.fo.

BY SEA The Faroese-operated **Smyril Line** (*J Broncksgøta 37, PO Box 370, FO-110 Tórshavn;* ╲ *+298 34 59 00;* e *office@smyril-line.com; www.smyrilline.com*)connects the islands with **Hirtshals** in Denmark, and **Seyðisfjörður** in Iceland. Sailing patterns are complicated but essentially the *Norröna* (see below) sails twice weekly to Denmark and Iceland from mid-June to August; once weekly to both destinations at other times of the year. Although there can be no doubt that sailing the North Atlantic to the Faroes in the wake of the Vikings is a wonderfully romantic notion, it's really only sensible for those who want to take a vehicle with them on holiday – and for those with plenty of time. Smyril Line's ports are rather remote: Hirtshals is just 50km southwest of Skagen, the northernmost tip of Denmark, whilst Seyðisfjörður is located on the southeast coast of Iceland, a full 700km from Reykjavík.

The *Norröna* ferry In 2003, Smyril Line introduced a new ferry on their circuit of the North Atlantic. The new *Norröna* is the last word in luxury: shopping arcade, bars, nightclub, sauna and solarium, swimming pool and fitness centre are all on board. Weighing in at a whopping 36,000 tonnes and measuring 164m in length and 30m wide, it can carry nearly 1,500 passengers and 800 cars with a service speed of 21 knots; it underwent a partial refit in October 2007, further improving facilities. The current ship is a far cry from the previous *Norröna*, which was long overdue for retirement – however, the sheer size of the new vessel (complete with an enlarged terminal building in the tiny Tórshavn harbour) has created problems.

Manoeuvring it into the harbour when it's being buffeted by strong cross-winds is no mean feat and occasionally it is forced to divert to nearby **Kollafjørður**, where the approach is much easier. Although the *Norröna* is stabilised, being caught far out at sea with nothing to break the swells and towering waves sweeping in unopposed from the coast of North America is certainly not to everyone's liking. In the winter of 2007, for example, the *Norröna* lost power in heavy seas off Shetland and began to roll violently; 80 cars were damaged on the car deck.

Fares In peak season, a return foot passenger ticket from Hirtshals to the Faroes starts at 2,470kr in a couchette; cabin accommodation costs from another 200kr return; a car and passenger return costs 5,540kr, once again, before onboard accommodation is added. The full range of fares is available on the Smyril Line website which is the best – and cheapest – place to buy tickets.

HEALTH AND SAFETY with Dr Felicity Nicholson

The health risks while travelling in the Faroe Islands are minimal and healthcare is of an excellent standard. Language is rarely a problem and health workers are generally proficient in English. However, should you encounter any communication problems, the local tourist office should be able to point you in the direction of a doctor or dentist who does speak English. Under Faroese law, a national of any country is entitled to emergency healthcare in the case of an accident; it is the responsibility of the individual doctor treating you to decide just what 'emergency care' consists of. If, however, you suffer from a medical condition requiring regular treatment or medication, this is not free and you will have to pay for all treatment received. It is necessary to present your passport at the hospital to receive any form of emergency care. It goes without saying that you should have comprehensive travel insurance.

As far as safety is concerned, the main risks are the Faroese landscapes – vertical sea cliffs that drop into the sea from heights of up to 900m should obviously be approached with great care. It's also important to remember that when you're out in the countryside the weather can change at any moment and hiking conditions can very quickly become hazardous; however, with common sense, it's unlikely you'll encounter serious danger. In relation to crime, the Faroes are one of the safest parts of the world you will ever visit: police figures put the yearly number of break-ins and cases of theft at barely 500 for the entire country.

WOMEN TRAVELLERS Women travelling alone are unlikely to encounter any problems. Faroese males are generally well mannered and far too shy to create trouble. On Friday and Saturday nights in Tórshavn, when the beer starts to flow, it's obviously sensible to keep your wits about you but, once again, you're unlikely to become the target of abusive behaviour.

GAY FAROES Quite remarkably for a country where religion is still widely respected (and feared), there has been a sea-change in attitudes towards homosexuality in recent years. In 2006 it became illegal to discriminate on the grounds of sexual orientation following a change in the law. The new legislation was prompted by a well-publicised gay-bashing incident on a well-known musician in a pub in Tórshavn which appalled the public. More recently, in 2012, a staggering 5,000 people (over 10% of the population) marched through the streets of Tórshavn during Faroe Pride, calling for gay marriage to be legalised in the islands, in line with the law in Denmark. Taking their cue from other gay organisations, namely those in Iceland and Denmark, the newly formed Faroese LGBT group has won the support of the media in its campaign for equal rights and is a vocal opponent of any reactionary church leader or politician who argues against equality. For the first time ever, young gay Faroese now have role models to look up to and a public voice.

Faroe Pride is now an annual event and is undoubtedly the best time for any gay traveller to visit the islands; it's held on 27 July, the day before Olavsøka. Otherwise, there are occasional gay nights, organised by http://lgbt.fo, held at the Sirkus bar in Tórshavn. For more gay information about the Faroes, check out http://lgbt.fo or their Facebook page **f** lgbtforoyar. The islands' first out gay MP, Sonja Jógvansdóttir, was elected to parliament in September 2015 and is now pressing for the legalisation of gay marriage.

WHAT TO TAKE

The first thing to pack when planning a trip to the Faroes is a decent **waterproof jacket**. If you're considering hiking, **sturdy waterproof boots and trousers** are essential – you will doubtless find yourself on marshy ground at some point on your wanderings, even if it doesn't rain (unlikely) during your stay. Don't be tempted to bring an umbrella as they are no use whatsoever in the Faroes – it will only be blown inside out by the strong winds. A **waterproof cover for your rucksack** is also a wise thing to pack in your luggage. As crazy as it may sound for a summer holiday, it's also a good idea to take a pair of **gloves** and even a **woolly hat** with you because even in the middle of July up on the mountains it can be chilly when the wind starts blowing. A **tablet** or **smartphone** is useful for checking emails and getting the latest weather information; most accommodation offers free Wi-Fi. Your mobile phone is handy as an **alarm clock** for early-morning buses and ferries. As far as electricity is concerned, the Faroese supply is 220V and all plugs are the northern European two-pin standard (the same as throughout the rest of Scandinavia), for which **adaptors** are readily available at major airports.

MONEY AND COSTS

There are two **currencies** in the Faroe Islands, both of which have equal value: the **Faroese króna** and the **Danish krone**. Notes come in denominations of 1,000kr, 500kr, 200kr, 100kr and 50kr; coins in 20kr, 10kr, 5kr, 2kr and 1kr. Occasionally you may also come across 50 øre coins, ie: half of one krone. Since Denmark is not part of the Eurozone, the European Union's single-currency area, it is not possible to spend euros in the Faroes. If Denmark does join the Eurozone, it's unclear whether the European single currency will become legal tender in the islands since the Faroes, although part of the Kingdom of Denmark, are not part of the European Union. In February 2016, exchange rates for the Danish krone were roughly £1 = 9.54kr, US$1 = 6.60kr and €1 = 7.46kr.

The best way to get money in the Faroes is by using a debit card. This makes it possible to withdraw money from cashpoints much as you would do at home. The use of credit cards such as Visa and MasterCard is widespread and provides another way of paying for goods and also, of course, for withdrawing cash on credit. **Banks** are generally open 09.30–16.00 Monday–Friday and most have ATMs, even in remote villages.

COSTS AND BUDGETING Costs in the Faroe Islands are roughly in line with those you'll find in other countries in northern Europe. Accommodation, eating out and domestic travel, although not especially cheap, are on the whole good value. There are, though, two notable exceptions to the above statement. Alcohol is likely to be a third more expensive than you're used to paying at home (in a restaurant a bottle of wine costs around 250kr, whereas a half-litre of beer in a bar is about 50–60kr); and travel by helicopter is an absolute bargain – 215kr, for example, is all it costs to fly from Tórshavn out to Mykines.

Although tipping and bargaining are not expected in the Faroes, you may wish to round a restaurant bill up to the nearest large number, for example 126kr becomes 130–140kr, as a small sign of your appreciation.

When it comes to budgeting for a trip you should be able to get by on around 300–400kr per day if you're staying in a youth hostel, self-catering and not making too many trips around; 600–800kr if you want to stay in a guesthouse (sharing a room with one other person), eat out in a restaurant every so often and go for a couple of beers; and upwards of 800kr per day per person for (shared) hotel accommodation, sightseeing trips and eating out with alcohol.

GETTING AROUND THE ISLANDS

Travel around the Faroe Islands is a doddle. All 17 inhabited islands are connected by bus, ferry or helicopter – and in a couple of instances by all three. You'll often find that if your journey involves changing from bus to ferry or vice versa, departures are timed to correspond perfectly, making travel a dream. Remember, though, that it's rare to find any kind of shelter at bus stops, harbours and heliports, so have your rain gear to hand in case the heavens open.

BY BUS AND FERRY The **long-distance bus** services (☏ 34 30 30; www.ssl.fo) on the main routes are frequent and reliable. There's no need to take a taxi to or from the airport as buses also link Tórshavn with all arriving and departing flights. Full timetables are available on the website; long-distance **buses** are blue in colour.

Ferries (☏ 34 30 00; www.ssl.fo) operate on the following routes: Tórshavn–Tvøroyri (Suðuroy); Tórshavn–Nólsoy; Gamlarætt (Streymoy)–Skopun (Sandoy); Gamlarætt (Streymoy)–Hestur; Sandur (Sandoy)–Skúgvoy; Sørvágur (Vágur)–Mykines; Klaksvík–Syðradalur (Kalsoy) and Hvannasund (Viðoy)–Svínoy and Fugloy. Of the ferries, only the services to Suðuroy, Sandoy and Kalsoy take vehicles. It's not possible to book a space for a car on a ferry; you simply turn up at the quay in good time and the chances are you'll get on board. Note, too, that **you only pay for the return journey towards Tórshavn**; the outbound journey is free. Only the ferry journey to and from Mykines is payable in both directions.

BY HELICOPTER The helicopter service, operated by Atlantic Airways (☏ 34 10 60; e tyrlan@atlantic.fo; www.atlantic.fo), is incredibly good value – short hops

> **TRAVELCARD**
>
> Although you can buy individual tickets each time you hop on a ferry or bus, you'll save money with a travelcard that allows unlimited use of all buses and ferries in the country (except Mykines). The card is valid for either four or seven days and costs 500kr or 700kr respectively (discounts for children). The travelcard can be bought on arrival at the airport in Vágar from the tourist information desk in the terminal or alternatively in Tórshavn from the Farstøðin bus terminal at the harbour.

between islands can cost as little as 85kr and the single fare from the most northerly islands to the other end of the country is a mere 360kr; government subsidies are responsible and a full list of fares is available on the Atlantic website under the helicopter link. The helicopter operates on Sundays, Wednesdays and Fridays, plus on Mondays from June to August, and offers a fantastic way of seeing the islands. It is important to remember though that due to the limited number of seats on board, **you are not allowed to book a return journey for the same day** – only single tickets on separate days are allowed.

BY CAR Getting around by car has become much easier in recent years thanks to a plethora of tunnels which have been bored through the islands, reducing the need to navigate twisting mountain roads. Nearly all roads are sealed and wide enough to allow two lanes of traffic. Tunnels, however, are often single-lane with passing places; priority is always in one direction, making it the responsibility of drivers coming in the opposite direction to pull in and stop until they can safely drive on against the direction of priority. An undersea tunnel now connects the islands of Vágar and Streymoy in the west of the country and Eysturoy and Borðoy in the north. Tolls (100kr) are only payable in the Vágar to Streymoy and Borðoy to Eysturoy directions.

Rental cars have an electronic chip on the windscreen which automatically debits tunnel use back to the rental company – and you. Drivers with their own cars should follow the signs and pay at the filling station after exiting the tunnels. The Faroese drive on the right and use the traffic signs for international standards. The speed limit is 80km/h (60km/h for caravans) on country roads and 50km/h in built-up areas. Seatbelts are compulsory and headlights must also be used at all times, even during daylight hours. One of the hazards of driving in the Faroes is sheep – most of which seem to have an innate death wish compelling them to leap out onto the road as you approach. Should you accidentally hit a sheep you should call the police (☏ 35 14 48) and you will probably be liable to pay the owner compensation for the loss of an animal; in short, slow down and take it easy.

Car rental in the Faroes If you're planning on travelling around the islands under your own steam, you may want to consider hiring a car, which will cost around 500kr per day. The best car-hire bets are Avis (☏ 31 35 35; e avis@avis. fo; www.avis.fo) and Hertz/62° North (☏ 34 00 50; m 21 35 46; e hertz@62n.fo; www.62n.fo), which both have outlets at the airport for collection and drop-off.

ACCOMMODATION

Outside Tórshavn, finding somewhere to stay in the Faroes can be tricky since many of the villages simply don't have anywhere. We've listed all accommodation options in the text; however, it's always worth checking with the local tourist office who will know the very latest situation. In the capital, things are not nearly so bleak and there's a choice between three **hotels**, a number of **guesthouses** where you often have access to a kitchen to prepare your own meals, a **youth hostel** and a number of private homes offering **bed-and-breakfast** accommodation. Prices are roughly in line with what you would expect to pay in any other

northern European country. The best value-for-money options are guesthouses which allow you to cut costs by self-catering. There are also a limited number of **youth hostels** and **campsites** dotted around the islands, though both are generally only open during the summer months. Since there is no common or public land in the Faroes (unlike in the other Scandinavian countries where an 'Everyman's Right' provides free land access to all), camping is only permitted in designated areas. It is not allowed to camp in a caravan on the roadside nor is it permitted to camp in car parks, in lay-bys or at viewpoints.

EATING AND DRINKING

Similarly, the greatest choice of eating and drinking establishments can be found in Tórshavn where you will find everything from Burger King to sumptuous smorgasbord spreads of every Faroese and Nordic delicacy you care to imagine, generally served in the hotels. In the villages, though, it can often be difficult, if not impossible, to find somewhere to eat and you may well find yourself backtracking to the nearest main village to get your fill. Whilst out in the sticks, you can always rely on filling stations to hold a small selection of sandwiches and to serve up hotdogs with mustard (always very good and not nearly as tasteless as you may think) and sometimes chips. If the worst comes to the worst, look for a supermarket and go self-catering; there's generally some kind of food store in all but the smallest of villages. On board the larger ferries (operating on the routes Tórshavn–Suðuroy and Gamlarætt–Skopun), there are cafeterias serving snacks and coffee.

Faroese **breakfast**, as served in the hotels in Tórshavn, and less extravagantly elsewhere in the country, is a Scandinavian-style cold table sagging under the weight of hams, cheeses, herring, cereals, yoghurts, fruit and sometimes Danish pastries. It's a help-yourself affair and you're permitted to take as much as you like and visit the table as many times as you like. There are also limitless supplies of coffee, tea and juice. The main meal of the day in the Faroe Islands is **lunch**, which, in Tórshavn at least, throws up a variety of options. Once again, some restaurants serve an extremely good value help-yourself buffet where you can eat your fill for around 100kr. A soft drink is usually included. None of these buffets is particularly traditional and the emphasis is more on pizzas, pasta, salads or indeed Chinese-style food in certain establishments. Lunchtime in the Faroes is any time between about 11.00 and 14.00, though most people tend to eat around noon or 13.00. If you're looking to save money while in the Faroes, switch your main meal of the day to lunchtime and you'll save a packet – have a snack in the evening instead, bought from the supermarket or bakery, and you'll make your money go much further. **Dinner** can be expensive for what you get – meals are often heavily meat-orientated (rather than fish-based) with an accompaniment of (more often than not) overcooked vegetables and masses of potatoes. Sadly, due to the lack of fresh vegetables in the islands, many eateries serve veggies straight out of a can. Frustratingly for a country so influenced by the sea, it can be hard to find fresh fish on the menu. You should count on around 250–350kr for an upmarket two-course restaurant dinner, though of course you can eat in the pizzerias and ethnic restaurants of Tórshavn for around half of that.

While in the Faroes it's worth searching out and sampling some of the islands' **traditional foods**. A particular favourite is wind-dried sheep's meat, *skerpikjøt*, prepared around Christmas time and then nibbled throughout the year; virtually every home in the islands has its own *hjallur* or meat-drying outhouse. Puffin breast is also popular, and when served with a blueberry sauce, verges on the divine. Pilot whale meat and blubber is occasionally also available on the menu (particularly at a Faroese evening or on the Faroese smorgasbord served up during the summer at Hotel Hafnia in Tórshavn) though it is somewhat of an acquired taste. Look out too for roast lamb and boiled wind-dried fish, *ræstur fiskur* – two other delicacies. Popular fish dishes (should you be able to find them on the menu) include haddock, halibut, plaice and salmon.

What will push the bill up is alcohol; a bottle of wine is roughly around 250kr, a draught beer usually starts at 60kr. It's much cheaper to do your drinking at home – which is what many of the Faroese do.

BUYING ALCOHOL Owing to a strong temperance movement (and religious objections), alcohol has only been (relatively) freely available in the islands since 1992. Before then the Faroes practised a system of public prohibition and every bottle of the hard stuff (including wine) had to be shipped in from Denmark and was doled out in rations. Mercifully, the Faroes have now entered the modern age and alcohol is more readily available – albeit restricted by some bizarre legislation. Forget any notion of nipping into the nearest supermarket to buy a bottle of wine for dinner because alcohol is not available in the shops. The only place to buy any form of alcohol, be it strong beer, wine or spirits, is **Rúsdrekkasøla Landsins** (known colloquially as 'rúsan'; www.rusan.fo), a state-run monolith responsible for all things alcoholic. Opening times are limited (see relevant chapters for details) and you'll find only six of these liquor stores in the entire country; they're located in Klaksvík, Miðvágur, Saltangará, Skálavík, Tórshavn and Drelnes. In short, if you're heading out into the wilds, stock up before you leave town or you'll be left with the pathetically weak fizzy beverage sold in supermarkets, *ljóst pilsnar*, purporting to be beer yet with an alcohol content of barely 2.8%.

PUBLIC HOLIDAYS

The principal public holiday in the Faroes is **Ólavsøka** (literally 'the wake of St Olav'), held on 28 and 29 July. People from across the country flood into Tórshavn for the festivities held in honour of the islands' patron saint, the Norwegian king, Olav, who fell in battle at Stiklestad in Norway on 29 July 1030. At this time, the

1 January	New Year's Day
March/April	Easter: Maundy Thursday, Good Friday, Easter Sunday, Easter Monday
25 April	Flag Day (in celebration of the announcement on the BBC on this day in 1940 calling on all Faroese shipping to fly the national flag, Merkið, instead of that of occupied Denmark)
May	Common Prayers' Day
May	Ascension Day
May	Whit Sunday, Whit Monday
5 June	Constitution Day
28–29 July	Ólavsøka
24–26 December	Christmas
31 December	New Year's Eve

Faroes were governed by Norway and all disputes were settled there. Hence, it was natural for **Sigmundur Brestisson**, one of the great characters of Faroese medieval history and hero of the *Færeyinga Saga*, to call for the king's help to overthrow his heathen rival, **Tróndur í Gøtu**, who was frustrating efforts to introduce Christianity to the islands. Although Sigmundur failed to see off Tróndur, and was eventually slaughtered while fleeing from him, King Olav's help has been commemorated ever since in the Faroes, which adopted the day of his death as their national day. Events kick off on the afternoon of 28 July a procession through Tórshavn headed by men on horseback proudly bearing the Faroese flag. They head for the grassy area in front of the parliament where crowds assemble to hear speeches from the country's leading politicians. Next off it's the final of the summer boat races, where the year's winners will be decided in a competition to row across the harbour. A series of sporting events, public meetings and concerts follow amid much drinking and merrymaking. Often nursing severe hangovers, festival-goers are a little more restrained on the 29th, a day marked by a ceremonial procession from the parliament to the cathedral where a service is held. On returning to the parliament, a choir sings and the prime minister holds his opening speech which marks the beginning of the new parliamentary session.

SHOPPING

Absolutely the best thing to buy in the Faroes is a traditional woollen **sweater**, all of which are locally knitted in the islands. Prices vary according to design and fashion, but you can pick up a plain white jumper, popular with local fishermen, for around 750kr. For something a little more contemporary, you'll need to pay in the region of 1,000–1,200kr, though, of course, you're then moving away from the traditional to the fashionable.

However, you can pick up homemade sweaters and other woollen goods in the Heimavirki stores dotted around the islands (the best one is in Klaksvík), where you'll find a whole array of sweaters hand-knitted by local women who then receive the profits of their labours; these homemade jumpers cost around 1,000kr and are some of the warmest you'll come across. There's also something tremendously satisfying about buying one of these sweaters; not only do you know that it was

Companies such as Guðrun & Guðrun, Navia, Sirri and Snældan are the main manufacturers of Faroese knitwear, and between them they make a range of products ranging from knee-length coats made entirely of wool to mittens. Anyone familiar with the hit Danish TV series *The Killing* will know that lead character, Sarah Lund, is never seen without her trendy Faroese sweater – it's from Guðrun & Guðrun. The main outlets for designer woollens are:

Guðrun & Guðrun [44 C4] Niels Finsens gøta 13; 31 51 66; www.gudrungudrun.com; 10.00–17.30 Mon–Fri, 10.00–14.00 Sat.

Navia [44 B2] Inside the SMS shopping centre, R C Effersøes gøta 31; 73 90 92; www.navia.fo; 10.00–18.00 Mon–Thu & Sat, 10.00–19.00 Fri

Sirri [45 B5] Doktor Jakobsens gøta 18; 31 66 10; www.sirri.fo; 10.00–17.30 Mon–Thu, 10.00–18.00 Fri, 10.00–14.00 Sat

Snældan [44 B4] Niels Finsens gøta 25; 35 71 54; 10.00–17.30 Mon–Fri, 10.00–14.00 Sat.

Staðið [45 D6] Áarvegur 12; 32 17 06; 09.30–17.30 Mon–Thu, 09.30–18.00 Fri, 09.30–14.00 Sat. Stocks Sirri & Noa.

made just around the corner from where you bought it but also you're putting money directly into the local economy. There are details of the Heimavirki shops in the relevant sections of the guide text.

Since the Faroese began issuing their own **stamps** in 1975, they have become a much sought-after collector's item for their rarity. Particularly popular are designs that feature images of the Faroe Islands themselves but also the country's birds and animals. Stamp collectors will want to visit Óðinshædd 2 in Tórshavn (34 62 00; e *stamps@posta.fo; www.stamps.fo*) where the Faroese Philatelic Organisation is based. Stamps can also be bought on the internet at the above address.

For such a small nation with a limited pool of talent, Faroese contemporary **music** is surprisingly good. CDs can make an excellent souvenir of any stay in the islands and while browsing through record stores (the best one in the country is **Tutl** at Niels Finsensgøta 9C (*www.tutlrecords.com*), be sure to listen to the two Faroese artists to make the big time abroad: Eivar Pálsdóttir, a sort of home-grown Björk, and the truly wonderful and gifted Teitur, whose albums are a good showcase of his songwriting and performance talents; his style is a mix of R.E.M. and David Gray. Also worth a listen are the more traditional CDs of Faroese folk songs and chain dancing – though perhaps not to everyone's taste. Count on around 170kr for a CD. For information about tax-free shopping in the Faroes see *Customs and tax-free goods*, page 33.

ARTS AND ENTERTAINMENT

Unfortunately for visitors, much of the arts and entertainment available in the islands is in Faroese only. Cinema **films**, however, are one notable exception since they are always shown in their original language (often English); there are cinemas in Tórshavn and Klaksvík. The summer months see three **music festivals** held in the islands: one in Klaksvík, one in Norðragøta and Syðrugøta, and a third which is held in various locations across the islands between June and August. For details of the first two, the Summer Festival and G!, see pages 126 and 113 respectively, while there are full details for the third, the Summartónar festival (a celebration of contemporary and classical music) at www.composers.fo, nlh.fo and tutl.com.

As for **art galleries** and **museums**, they are pretty much confined to Tórshavn and are all detailed in the text. If you're a veritable culture vulture you are bound to leave the Faroes with your appetite barely whetted. In a small country with a population of 49,000, there simply aren't enough people to create a buzzing arts and entertainment scene. If you are heading out into the sticks during your stay in the islands, make sure you get your fill of everything the Faroese capital has to offer before moving on – and take a couple of good books and your computer with you.

CUSTOMS AND TAX-FREE GOODS

Import restrictions governing alcohol are strict and allowances are minute. The following goods can be imported into the Faroes **tax- and duty-free** by anyone over the age of 18: one litre of spirits between 22% and 60% and one litre of fortified wine, or two litres of beer with an alcohol content no higher than 5.8% and two litres of table wine. You should avoid bringing non-recyclable containers into the islands. Travellers over the age of 18 may also bring in 100 cigarettes or 100 cigarillos or 50 cigars or 250g tobacco. Perfume (maximum 50g), eau de toilette (maximum 250ml) and 3kg of confectionery are also permitted. It's possible to buy duty-free alcohol on arrival at the airport on Vágar – see page 93 for details. Special import restrictions apply to fishing gear for salmon and sea trout. Anyone intending to use such equipment in the islands must present a certificate from veterinary officials in the country of origin certifying that it has been disinfected immediately before departure to the Faroe Islands. This measure is aimed at preventing Faroese inland waters from becoming infected with diseases carried by fish outside the islands. Note, too, that it is not permitted to bring pets into the Faroes.

The good news about shopping in the Faroes is that most goods can be bought tax-free (books and homemade sweaters are two notable exceptions – their prices do not include tax anyway). The minimum purchase per store to qualify for a tax-free refund is 300kr – a sliding scale then applies with the amount of tax back increasing in line with the amount you spend, though it is usually around 15–19% of the total. You then fill in the refund cheque you receive in store with your name and address. On leaving the Faroes, you must show your purchases (do not pack them away in your hold luggage if leaving by plane) together with your passport to customs officials who will then stamp the tax-free cheque. All you then have to do is to take your cheque to either the tax refund agent at the airport or on board the *Norröna* to receive your refund in Danish kroner. If you have several cheques to cash collected from various stores, you will receive the total sum of all of them. Remember, too, that if you're travelling to Denmark with Faroese notes it can be difficult to spend them in shops there – quite simply because many Danes don't realise that the Faroese currency is in fact legal tender throughout the Kingdom of Denmark and has the same value as its Danish equivalent. It's a better idea to play safe and ask for Danish notes instead of Faroese.

MEDIA, COMMUNICATIONS AND TIME

RADIO Kringvarp Føroya (*www.kringvarp.fo*) is the collective name for both Faroese television and radio. However, unofficially, Faroese radio is still known as Útvarp Føroya, though, by any name, it's unlikely you'll spend much time listening since programming is entirely in Faroese. Broadcasting a mix of music and speech, this is the main station in the islands and the only one that can be heard right across the country; when reception is poor on FM, you can always fall back on their booming medium-wave signal on 531kHz AM, which is aimed at reaching all shipping in Faroese waters or listen online a www.kvf.fo. The other stations that are likely to be of interest to visitors are the music stations, Rás 2 (*www.ras2.fo*), Kiss FM on 98.7FM and VoxPOP on 104.1FM in Tórshavn. A much better idea is to tune into the BBC, whose medium-wave signals coming up across the sea from the north of Scotland can be heard clearly on a car radio (the body of the car seems to work as a signal booster). The stations and frequencies to aim for are: BBC Radio 5 Live on 693kHz medium wave (the strongest of all the BBC medium-wave signals audible in the Faroes), BBC Radio Scotland on 810kHz medium wave and BBC Radio 4 on 198kHz long wave. Irish broadcaster, RTE Radio 1, can also be clearly heard on 252kHz long wave.

TELEVISION Faroese television is a remarkable organisation – the mere fact that the Faroese population is so small and that over 50 transmitters and transformers are needed to get the signal out to even the most remote village makes it a wonder that the station exists at all. Kringvarp Føroya, the only station based in the islands, broadcasting in Faroese and founded in 1984, transmits about 40 hours a week, and like most public-service broadcasters its programmes cover a range of news, documentaries, entertainment, culture, sport and drama. Its news programme, however, is not on air every day due to staffing levels – only about 30 people work here full time. The company produces about one in five of all its transmissions and translates into Faroese about the same percentage of foreign programmes.

MOBILE TELEPHONES Since public payphones are few and far between, it's a much better idea to take your own mobile to the Faroes and buy a pay-as-you-go SIM card from Føroya Tele. Rates for calls both within the Faroes and abroad are reasonable and this way you'll avoid paying the costly international roaming charges you would incur with your own SIM card from home. SIMs are available from Faroese Telecom offices across the islands.

POST OFFICE AND INTERNET Found in the larger towns and villages, **post offices** are generally open Monday–Friday. On the more remote islands, you will find that they may only be open for a couple of hours a day and closed on certain days; full opening times can be found at www.posta.fo.

TELEPHONE CODES FROM AND TO THE FAROES

The international dialling code to make a call abroad from the Faroes is 00. International country codes are therefore as follows:

Australia	00 61	United Kingdom	00 44
Ireland	00 353	US and Canada	00 1
New Zealand	00 64		

When ringing from abroad, the country code for the Faroe Islands is +298. There are no local codes within the islands and all numbers consist of six digits, ie: ⸜xx xx xx.

Internet cafés have never been a big hit in the Faroes – instead, Wi-Fi is provided free of charge in hotels and guesthouses across the country. Public libraries have internet terminals for use and booking is not generally necessary. The main libraries with internet terminals are in Fuglafjørður, Klaksvík and Tórshavn.

TIME Time in the Faroe Islands is always the same as in Britain and Ireland – ie: GMT during the winter months and GMT+1 during the summer. There is, however, always one hour's time difference between the Faroes and Denmark; when it is, for example, noon in Tórshavn (and London and Dublin), it is 13.00 in Copenhagen. During the winter (November–March) when the islands return to GMT they then also share the same time as Iceland, which operates on GMT all year round. Daylight saving applies from the end of October to the end of March when clocks are put back by one hour, moving forward again one hour in spring. The dates for putting the clocks forward and back are the same as in the rest of Europe.

INTERACTING WITH LOCAL PEOPLE

The Faroese, like many of the other Nordic nationals, can on the surface seem rather reserved. It is certainly true that the Faroese aren't the easiest of people to get to know, and are often thought of by foreigners as being distant. On the whole they are straight-talking, saying what they mean with a minimum of words and fuss. Many visitors interpret this as a lack of interest in conversation or even downright rudeness, but neither is likely to be the case. In short, overt expressions of emotions and raucous conversations punctuated with wild gesticulations are not the name of the game in the Faroes – indeed, when talking, some men are very wary of even taking their hands out of their pockets. However, when the weekend comes liberal quantities of beer help people throw off their inhibitions and you may find that even the most monosyllabic fisherman can talk (and drink) you under the table. On meeting a Faroese man or woman for the first time, it is customary to shake hands – though unlike in some other countries it is not usual to shake hands again on leaving, or when you meet again, even if it is several days later. It is not the done thing to kiss on meeting – that is something the Faroese avoid at all costs. Nudity is also something the Faroese find difficult to deal with; despite signs in shower rooms in public swimming pools instructing bathers to shower without a swimming costume before entering the pool on hygiene grounds, you will often see people showering, albeit rather guiltily, with their swimwear on. If you play by the rules, you should never wear swimwear in a sauna either – also for hygiene reasons – although this rule, too, is often flouted.

GIVING SOMETHING BACK

While you're in the Faroes, why not consider buying some locally produced knitwear as a small contribution towards the local economy? All across the islands, small armies of dedicated knitters churn out woollen sweaters, gloves, hats and even shawls and coats. There's no tax added to these products so they're often cheaper than the equivalent from the more mainstream factories such as Snældan and Sirri. It's satisfying to know that you are helping local people directly, as the women knitters receive direct payment from the sale of their sweaters.

In Tórshavn you can also buy fresh fish direct from local fishermen at the stalls down by the harbour at Vágsbotnur. Though there are no set times for when a boat will appear with fish for sale, you can be sure that should you buy anything the money you pay is going directly to the skipper or crew.

Part Two

THE GUIDE

3

Tórshavn

Proudly named after the Norse god of war, Tórshavn (literally 'Thor's Harbour') is curiously built around one of the worst natural harbours in the entire country, dangerously exposed to the gales and accompanying heavy swells of the North Atlantic. Yet it was here, around AD900, on the rocky promontory, **Tinganes**, that the *ting* or Viking parliament first began meeting every summer to chew over matters of national importance, doing so uninterrupted until 1816; today this promontory is still the seat of the Faroese government. An annual market was also held here to coincide with the assembly, developing in the Middle Ages – with the introduction of the Trade Monopoly in 1579 – into a permanent trading place with warehouses for the importing and exporting of goods. Although Tórshavn's future was confirmed, population growth was slow due to restrictive land ownership laws that made farming difficult; by the beginning of the 17th century, barely 100 people lived in the settlement. In 1673 there was a further setback when a devastating fire raged across Tinganes, destroying all but two of the warehouses there. Over the ensuing centuries growth gradually increased, helped in large part by reform of land ownership rights, and by 1900 Tórshavn's population had soared to 15,000, tripling in just 100 years. Today, Tórshavn has finally come of age, blossoming into a self-confident, bustling medium-sized town with a population of around 19,800 people and all the trappings of a national, if diminutive, capital: government offices, parliament and foreign consulates are all here and the town is home to two out of five Faroe Islanders.

For orientation, take the **harbour** as your point of reference: from here, Tórshavn stretches in three directions: west up the steep hillsides behind the town centre that act as the capital's backdrop, as well as both north and south curving around the waterfront. However, it is the all-important harbour, through which the country maintains contact with the rest of the world, that remains the town's focal point and is arguably the most attractive part of town. Here a long row of converted warehouses, with façades ranging in colour from a rich ochre to bright reds and blues, reflect in the crystal-clear waters of the harbour bursting with small wooden fishing vessels; during the long summer days, the couple of cafés on the waterfront here are full of people enjoying a cup of coffee, watching the boats bob on the Atlantic swell – the classic picture-postcard view of Tórshavn. From here a warren of narrow streets and lanes leads up and over the hill on to Tinganes, winding past tiny black-tarred houses with white window frames and green turfed roofs to the grander former merchants' houses that today are home to the various departments of the Faroese Home Rule government on the very tip of the promontory looking over to Skansin fort which once protected Tórshavn harbour from marauding pirates. However, it is in and around the compact grid of modern streets north of Tinganes, dominated by the pedestrianised main drag, **Niels Finsens gøta**, where you're likely to spend most of your time. It's here that most of the town's facilities

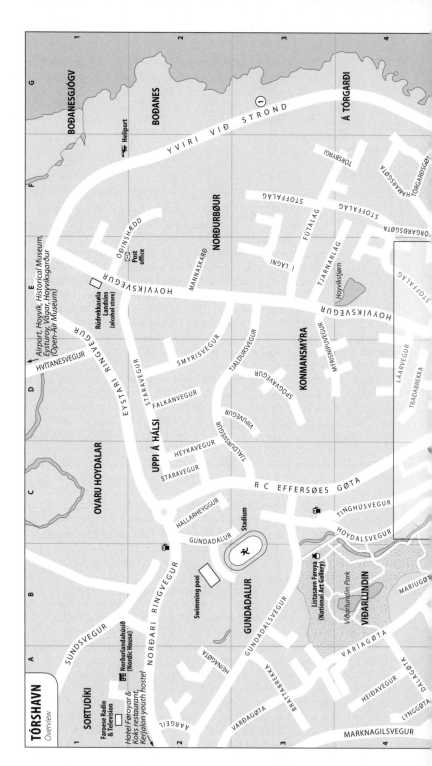

TÓRSHAVN
Overview

SORTUDÍKI

Faroese Radio & Television

Hotel Føroyar & Koks restaurant, Kerjalon youth hostel

Norðurlandahúsið (Nordic House)

BOÐANESGJÓGV

BOÐANES

Heliport

Á TÓRGARÐI

YVIRI VIÐ STROND

Airport, Hoyvík, Historical Museum, Eysturoy, Vágar, Hoyvíksgarður (Open-Air Museum)

NORÐURBØUR

ODINSHÆDD

Post office

Ríðrekkasøla Landsins (alcohol store)

TÓRSBYRGI

TORGARÐSGØTA

HÁMARSGØTA

ORÐARØSGØTA

STOFFALAG

FÚTALAG

STOFFALAG

I LAGNI

TJARNARLAG

Hoyvíkstjørn

STOFFALAG

HVÍTANESVEGUR

HOYVÍKSVEGUR

EYSTARI RINGVEGUR

MANNASKARÐ

KONMANSMÝRA

HOYVÍKSVEGUR

MÝRISNÍPUVEGUR

LÁARVEGUR

TRAÐABREKKA

STARAVEGUR

SMYRISVEGUR

FALKANVEGUR

TJALDURSVEGUR

SPØGVAVEGUR

OVARU HOYDALAR

UPPI Á HÁLSI

HEYKAVEGUR

VIPUVEGUR

TJALDURSVEGUR

STARAVEGUR

R C EFFERSØES GØTA

HALLARHEYGGUR

GUNDADALUR

Stadium

TINGHÚSVEGUR

HOYDALSVEGUR

NORÐARI RINGVEGUR

Swimming pool

GUNDADALUR

GUNDADALSVEGUR

Listasavn Føroya (National Art Gallery)

Viðarlundin Park

VIÐARLUNDIN

MARIUGØ

SUNDSVEGUR

HEINAGØTA

VARIAGØTA

HEIÐAVEGUR

DALAGØTA

LYNGGØTA

ÁRGELI

BRATTABREKKA

VARÐAGØTA

MARKNAGILSVEGUR

40

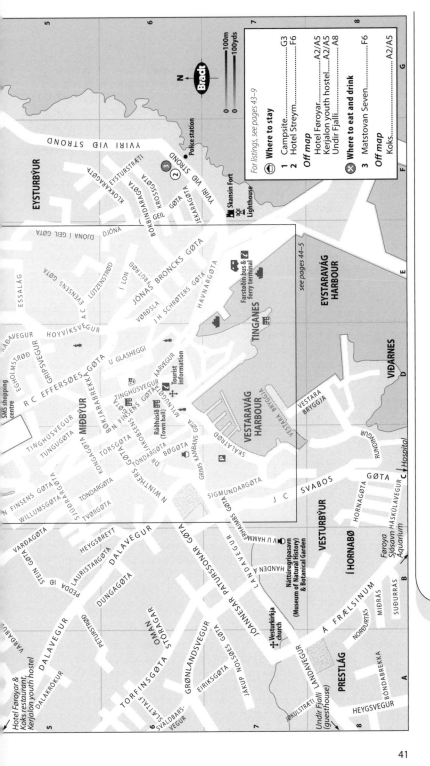

Tórshavn

3

For listings, see pages 43–9

Where to stay
1 Campsite.................................G3
2 Hotel Streym.........................F6

Off map
    Hotel Føroyar....................A2/A5
    Kerjalon youth hostel......A2/A5
    Undir Fjalli.............................A8

Where to eat and drink
3 Matstovan Seven................F6

Off map
    Koks.................................A2/A5

EYSTURBYUR

YVIRI VIÐ STROND

Police station

Skansin Fort
Lighthouse

JEKARAGØTA
GØTA
KLOKKARAGØTA
KROSSGØTA
GEIL
BØKBINDARAGØTA
EYSTURSTRÆTI

DJÓNA I GEIL GØTA
DJÓNA HÚTTRØÐ
I LON
VØRDSLA
JONAS BRONCKS GØTA
J H SCHRØTERS GØTA
HAVNARGØTA

Farstøðin hús &
ferry terminal

TINGANES

C EVENSENS GØTA
LÚTZENSTRØÐ

ESSALÁG
NADAVEGUR
EGHOLMSTRØÐ
HOYVÍKSVEGUR
R C EFFERSØES GØTA
U GLASHEGGI

SMS shopping
centre

TINGHÚSVEGUR
TUNGUGØTA
TINGHÚSVEGUR
BØKJARABREKKA GØTA
KONGAGØTA
N FINSENS GØTA
DR JAKOBSENS GØTA
TINGHÚSVEGUR
AARVEGUR

Tourist
information

MIÐBYUR

Ráðhúsið
(Town hall)

TORSGØTA
DR TØNDARGØTA
GRIMS KAMBANS GØTA

BØGØTA

SKÁLATRØÐ

VESTARAVÁG
HARBOUR

VESTARA
BRYGGJA

EYSTARAVÁG HARBOUR

see pages 44–5

VIÐARNES

N FINSENS GØTA
WILLUMSGØTA
SJÚRDARGØTA
N WINTHERS GØTA
TONDARGØTA
TVØRGØTA
SIGMUNDARGØTA

J C SVABOS

GØTA

RUNDINGUR

VARDAGØTA
STEIN GØTA
HEYGSBREYT
PEDDA ÍÐ
LAURISTARGØTA
DUNGAGØTA
DALAVEGUR
DALAVEGUR

HORNAGØTA
HORNAGØTA

VESTURBYUR

Í HORNABØ

Føroya
Sjósavn
Aquarium

HÁSKÚLAVEGUR
Hospital

PETURSTRØÐ
OMARAGØTA
GRØNLANDSVEGUR
JÓHANNESAR PATURSSONAR GØTA
STÓRAGØTA
LANDAVEGUR
BRAHAMMS GØTA

Náttúrugripasavn
(Museum of Natural History)
& Botanical Garden

U U HAMME
HANDEN Á

NORÐURTÁS
MIÐRÁS
SUBURRÁS

VESTURBYUR

VARÐABÚ
Hotel Føroyar &
Koks restaurant,
Kerjalon youth hostel

DALAKRØKUR
DALAVEGUR
SLÆTTALÍ
SVALDBARS-
VEGUR

TORFINSGØTA

EIRIKSGØTA
JAKUP NOLSØES GØTA

A FRÆLSINUM

Vesturkirkja
church

NORÐURTÁS
BONDABREKKA

PRESTLÁG

HEYGSVEGUR

JØKULSTRÆTI LANDAVEGUR
Undir Fjalli
(guesthouse)

N
Bradt

0   100m
0   100yds

41

are located: shops, restaurants and a bank are all to be found within a central area measuring no more than 1km² or so – Tórshavn is, after all, the smallest national capital in the world. From the centre of town, Tinghúsvegur streaks north, past the Faroese parliament to the SMS shopping centre and on to the forested Viðarlundin Park, one of the few plantations in the country and a favourite place for a stroll.

GETTING THERE AND AWAY

Without a shadow of a doubt, the most appealing approach to Tórshavn is from the sea; slowly turning the corner into Eystaravág bay, watching the town come into view, banking more and more steeply up the surrounding hillsides as you approach the harbour, is a truly remarkable sight. However, given the long journey times involved in reaching the Faroe Islands by ferry, most visitors opt to fly and you're more likely, therefore, to arrive at the Faroes' one and only airport, 49km west of Tórshavn on the neighbouring island of Vágar.

BY AIR Although there is often talk of building one, Tórshavn doesn't actually have an airport, just a **heliport** [40 F1] located adjacent to the campsite on Yviri við Strönd; annoyingly the capital's fog-prone location is likely to forever rule out any fanciful idea of relocating the international airport from its current location, not even on the same island as Tórshavn. Accordingly, all flights to and from the Faroes operate from Vágar **airport** (35 44 00; www.fae.fo), which has a slightly better track record when it comes to inclement weather. Following every flight arrival, a **bus** (#300; 90kr; 55mins) leaves from in front of the terminal building for Tórshavn. Alternatively, a **taxi** to Tórshavn costs 600kr per car; 190kr per person for a shared vehicle booked in advance at www.taxi.auto.fo. While you're waiting for your luggage, you may want to pop into the **duty free store**, which is open to all arriving passengers before they go through customs and represents a considerable saving on prices in the Rúsdrekkasøla stores (see page 30). Buses also leave the bus station in Tórshavn to connect with every flight departure, roughly two hours before the plane leaves; timetables are at www.ssl.fo.

BY FERRY Taking the ferry to Tórshavn certainly avoids the hassle of arriving on an altogether different island from that of your destination, but it does involve a lengthy journey across some of northern Europe's most unpredictable waters. The *Norröna* ferry and the various cargo ships that carry passengers to the Faroes all use the main eastern harbour, Eystaravág. The *Norröna* ties up right alongside the **Farstøðin bus and ferry terminal** [45 F–G7] (34 30 30), whereas the cargo ships use the berths a little further out, at the harbour entrance. From the terminal it's a five-minute walk northwest along Havnargøta to reach the town centre.

GETTING AROUND

One of the best things about Tórshavn is its wonderfully compact size. Nowhere is too far to reach on foot, and in this town of narrow streets and alleyways, you're frankly better off without a car.

Taxis can be handy if the weather is bad or if you don't feel like hiking up the hill to the Kerjalon youth hostel or Hotel Føroyar; reckon on 80–100kr from the town centre and tipping is not expected. Taxis generally wait around outside the Farstøðin terminal or at the ranks at the bottom and top end of Niels Finsens gøta. Otherwise you can contact one of the two main operators, Auto (✆ 36 36 36) or Bil (✆ 32 32 32).

TOURIST AND WEATHER INFORMATION

Tórshavn's tourist office, **Kunningarstovan** [45 D5] (✆ 30 24 25; e torsinfo@ torshavn.fo; www.visittorshavn.fo; ⏰ May–Aug 08.00–17.30 Mon–Fri, 09.00–14.00 Sat, also Jul 11.00–15.00 Sun, rest of the year 09.00–17.00 Mon–Fri, 10.00–14.00 Sat) is located in the low wooden building at Vaglið 4 which also houses the main bookshop. The friendly staff have a list of bed-and-breakfast accommodation (see page 29) but it's also a good place to pick up Faroe souvenirs such as badges, posters and stickers. Every morning the staff post the latest weather forecast up on a board inside the tourist office – always worth a look when passing.

There's a second, more modest, tourist office down at the ferry terminal which is open mid-June to August 09.00–16.00 Monday–Friday and when the *Norröna* is in port.

WHERE TO STAY

Owing to Tórshavn's modest size, the town is not awash with accommodation options, although in recent years things have dramatically improved. Outside the budget category, your choice is essentially between an upmarket hotel charging typical northern European prices for smart, comfortable double rooms, or much simpler guesthouse accommodation (where breakfast is not always included in the room rate) for around half the price.

Should you opt for a hotel, you will be treated to a lavish eat-as-much-as-you-can buffet breakfast featuring everything from herring to Danish pastries. Since Tórshavn really has only three upmarket hotels to speak of, your decision over which one to plump for should be based on whether you wish to be in the town centre or not. If you choose to stay at Hotel Føroyar for its magnificent views (see page 46), bear in mind that it is a very steep 20–30-minute walk from the town centre – a distance that seems all the further when the wind and rain are blowing you back down the hill!

TÓRSHAVN WELCOME CARD

Available for purchase from the tourist office in Tórshavn, the Tórshavn Welcome Card (*24hrs for 80kr; 48hrs for 95kr; 72hrs for 110kr*) is worth considering if you're planning to visit several museums. In addition to free entry at the national museum, Hoyvíksgarður, the aquarium and the swimming pool, it offers a number of discounts at various stores and cafés in town. Remember, though, that outside the summer months the museums are not open daily, which could make the card less attractive.

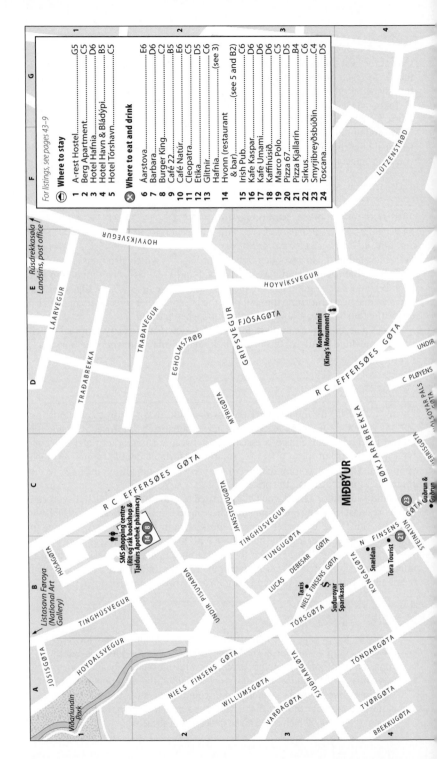

For listings, see pages 43–9

Where to stay

1 A-rest Hostel.............................G5
2 Berg Apartment........................C5
3 Hotel Hafnia.............................D6
4 Hotel Havn & Bládýpi................B5
5 Hotel Tórshavn........................C5

Where to eat and drink

6 Aarstova...................................E6
7 Barbara.....................................D6
8 Burger King...............................C2
9 Café 22.....................................B5
10 Café Natúr...............................E6
11 Cleopatra.................................C5
12 Etika...D5
13 Glitnir......................................C6
   Hafnia.............................(see 3)
14 Hvonn (restaurant
   & bar)...................(see 5 and B2)
15 Irish Pub..................................C6
16 Kafe Kaspar..............................D6
17 Kafe Umami...............................D6
18 Kaffihúsið.................................D6
19 Marco Polo................................C5
20 Pizza 67....................................D5
21 Pizza Kjallarin...........................B4
22 Sirkus.......................................C6
23 Smyrjibreyðsbúðin....................C4
24 Toscana....................................D5

MIÐBÝUR

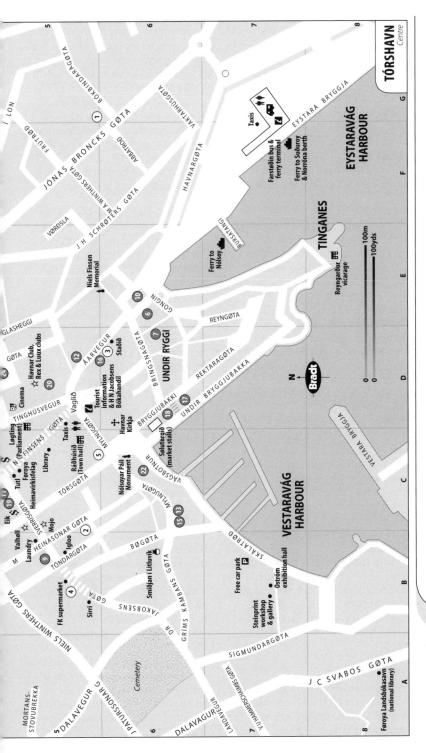

TÓRSHAVN Centre

EYSTARAVÁG HARBOUR

Taxis

Farstøðin bus & ferry terminal

Ferry to Suðuroy & Norrøna berth

EYSTARA BRYGGJA

Ferry to Nólsoy

TINGANES

Reyngarður vicarage

BÚRSTANGI

100m
100yds

Niels Finsen Memorial

① ⑩ ⑥ ⑦

GONGIN

REYNGØTA

UNDIR RYGGI

BRINGSNAGØTA

REKTARAGØTA

N

Bradt

UNDIR BRYGGJUBAKKA

☆ Havnar Club, Rex & Luux clubs
⑳ ⑫

AARVEGUR
③ ⑯ Staðið

Tourist information & H N Jacobsens Bókahandil

✝ Havnar Kirkja

BRYGGJUBAKKI
⑱ ⑰

Saluturgið (market stalls)

VESTARAVÁG HARBOUR

VESTARA BRYGGJA

Cinema

TINGHÚSVEGUR

Løgting (Parliament)

Føroya Heimavirkisfelag

Library

FINSENS GØTA

Taxis ♀♂

Vaglið

Ráðhúsið (Town hall)

MYLNUGØTA

Nólsoyar Páll Monument

⑤

VÁGSBOTNUR

MYLNUGØTA

☆ Mojo
Igloo

TORSGØTA

HEINASONAR GØTA

TÓNDARGØTA

Valhøll
Laundry

VERRISGØTA

Eik ⑲ ⑪

Tutl

BØGØTA

Smiðjan í Litluvík

Steinprint workshop & gallery

Østrøm exhibition hall

Free car park

SKÁLATRØÐ

GRIMS KAMBANS GØTA

DR JAKOBSENS GØTA

FK supermarket
④

Sirri

⑮ ⑬
②

NIELS WINTHERS GØTA

MORTANS-STOVUBREKKA

J PATURSSONAR G GØTA

DALAVEGUR

Cemetery

SIGMUNDARGØTA

J C SVABOS GØTA

Føroya Landsbókasavn (national library)

LANDAVEGUR

V U HAMMERSHAIMBS GØTA

DALAVEGUR

In addition to the places listed below, a large number of private rooms are available on a **bed and breakfast** basis with local families. Contact the tourist office in Vaglið square [45 D5] (*30 24 25;* e *torsinfo@torshavn.fo; www.visittorshavn.fo*) for their latest list. Booked through the tourist office, a double room costs **$$**, a single is **$**. The long-established tour operator, Tora Tourist, at Niels Finsens gøta 21 (*31 55 05;* e *tora@tora.fo; www.tora.fo*) also rents out self-catering accommodation.

Price codes here are per room unless otherwise stated. Single hotel rooms are not good value; they generally cost barely 200kr less than a double; guesthouse singles offer better value for money, at around two-thirds the price of a double. It is always a good idea to book in advance since accommodation is limited. If you visit during the national festivities of Ólavsøka in late July you'd be wise to book at least six months in advance or you may find everything has already been taken.

LUXURY

Hotel Føroyar [40–1 A2/A5] Oyggjarvegur 45; *31 75 00;* e hf@hotelforoyar.fo; www. hotelforoyar.fo. Rooms at this hilltop hotel complete with turf roof are the best the Faroes have to offer: Nordic chic with warm autumn colours, soft furnishings & a bathtub. Each room boasts an unsurpassed view out over the whole of Tórshavn. Although staying in this modern hotel, built into the hillside, can feel like being holed up in a bunker, it is justifiably popular: even Bill Clinton stayed here in 2007: rooms 117 & 118 are now sold as the President Clinton suite. The best breakfast of any hotel in the country is included. **$$$$** (*but w/end rates drop by around half*)

Hotel Hafnia [45 D6] Áarvegur 4–10; *31 32 33;* e hafnia@hafnia.fo; www.hafnia.fo. Recently expanded in size, rooms here are cosy, carpeted with contemporary furnishings & feature creative wall prints of stylised kissing puffins (more attractive than it sounds). Hafnia certainly beats its rival, Hotel Føroyar, in terms of downtown location, but some rooms have little or no view & can be a little small. B/fast inc. **$$$$** (*with w/end discounts*)

Hotel Tórshavn [45 C5] Tórsgøta 4; *35 00 00;* e ht@hoteltorshavn.fo; www.hoteltorshavn. fo. Perfectly located hotel overlooking the harbour whose fashion-conscious rooms boast stylish carpeting, curtains & lighting. The 9 rooms with sea views are worth the extra 200kr. B/fast inc. **$$$$**

TOP TO MID RANGE

Berg Apartment [45 C5] Magnus Heinasonar gøta 13; *31 63 01;* e apartment@ olivant.fo. 4 modern apartments with fully fitted kitchens for rent in the centre of town, sleeping 2

to 4 people. Interior décor is plain & white & there's plenty of space throughout. A sound choice if you're self-catering for a few days. **$$$**

Bládýpi [45 B5] Dr Jakobsens gøta 14–16; *50 06 00;* e hostel@hostel.fo; www.hostel. fo. A dozen dbl rooms with private facilities are available in the yellow building known as Bládýpi guesthouse, behind Hotel Havn (they're part of the same complex). Rooms are clean & comfortable though not as stylish as those in the hotel; a guest kitchen is available. **$$$**

Hotel Havn [45 B5] Dr Jakobsens gøta 14–16; *50 06 00;* e hotel@hotelhavn.com; www. hotelhavn.com. This newly opened hotel has around 20 chic & stylishly decorated rooms right in the heart of Tórshavn. Rooms feature floor-to-ceiling windows with privacy afforded by a frosted glass panel. Best of all, though, are the 2 larger rooms with balconies on the top floor, which enjoy glorious views (*350kr/650kr extra*). B/fast inc. **$$$**

Hotel Streym [41 F6] See ad, 2nd colour section; Yviri við Strond 19; *35 55 00;* e booking@ hotelstreym.com; www.hotelstreym.com. A welcoming hotel overlooking the ocean down by Tórshavn's ferry terminal, this place is a dependable choice for reasonably priced, no-nonsense accommodation near the town centre. Rooms are simply furnished & decorated in neutral colours & have compact bathrooms with heated floors. B/fast inc. (*150kr less from Oct to Mar*) **$$$$**

Undir Fjalli [41 A8] Marknagilsvegur 75; *58 99 99;* e info@undirfjalli.com; www. undirfjalli.com; ⊕ late Jun–mid Aug. Located in 2 blocks of student accommodation a 20min walk west of the town centre, the rooms here are what you'd expect: small, no-frills though perfectly adequate. All have private facilities & a kitchen is available. **$$**

BUDGET

🛏 **A-rest hostel** [45 F6] Bókbindaragøta 1; 📞 50 06 00; e hostel@hostel.fo; www.hostel.fo. An unusual place for a hostel, located in the former police station, with accommodation in the old cells (some still with bars on the windows). Dorms sleeping up to 6 people share facilities, while dbl rooms have their own bathroom. B/fast is not provided but there is a guest kitchen on site. Linen is 50kr extra. Dbls **$$**; dorms 250kr per person.

🛏 **Kerjalon** [40–1 A2/A5] Oyggjarvegur 49; 📞 31 89 00; e kerjalon@hosteltorshavn.fo; www. hotelforoyar.fo. Comfortable, modern & well-kitted

out, this superbly located youth hostel on a hilltop overlooking the capital has the same views as its expensive hotel neighbour but at a fraction of the cost. Bookings are necessary in summer as this is one of the first places to fill up – particularly when the *Norröna* is in. *65kr extra for rental of bed linen. Dorm beds 175kr pp; dbl room* **$**

⛺ **Campsite** [40 G3] Yviri við Strond; 📞 30 24 25; e torsinfo@torshavn.fo; www.visittorshavn.fo; 🕐 May–Sep for both tents & caravans (advance reservations required for May & Sep). On-site facilities include showers, toilets, kitchen, washing machine & tumble dryer. *95kr pp.* **$**

WHERE TO EAT AND DRINK

If you're arriving in Tórshavn from one of the other remoter islands, the wealth of eating possibilities in the capital will make you quite dizzy: if you're coming directly from anywhere else, grit your teeth and bear it. Mercifully, though, the range of eateries in Tórshavn has mushroomed beyond even the locals' wildest dreams in recent years. Today Tórshavn boasts an impressive range of restaurants for its size, offering everything from Mediterranean and Chinese to traditional Faroese – even Burger King is in residence. There are, however, slim pickings for vegetarians and vegans other than the ubiquitous pizza. There are some particularly good-value Monday-to-Friday eat-as-much-as-you-can **lunch deals** on offer in some places, aimed at office workers nipping out for a bite to eat. Join them, eating at lunchtime, and you'll save plenty of cash into the bargain. In short, make the most of the possibilities the capital has to offer if you're moving on into the countryside beyond. It can be virtually impossible to find a table between 18.00 and 20.00 in the popular places in Tórshavn on weekdays, which means that booking ahead is sensible. Always book a table for Friday or Saturday night, and during Ólavsøka.

Restaurants are generally open for lunch and dinner; their opening hours are included below.

EXPENSIVE

✗ **11** [45 C5] Tórsgøta 11; 📞 31 16 11; www. menu.fo/11; 🕐 11.30–13.30 & 18.00–22.00 Mon–Thu, 11.30–13.30 & 18.00–23.00 Fri, 18.00–23.00 Sat. Serving an adventurous menu including a starter of foie gras terrine with almonds & apple (*125kr*) & a main dish of venison with hazelnuts, mushrooms & blackcurrant jus (*295kr*), alongside more mainstream steaks, lamb & fish dishes, the choices are certainly commendable but prices tend to be on the high side. **$$$**

✗ **Áarstova** [45 E6] Gongin 1; 📞 33 30 00; www. aarstova.fo; 🕐 18.00–22.00 daily. A delicious & well-prepared seasonal menu featuring the freshest of Faroese ingredients is served in this

romantic & snug, low-ceilinged little restaurant, housed in a building dating from the early 1600s. They serve 3- & 5-course menus for 500kr/700kr featuring the likes of lobster bisque, rack of lamb & rhubarb compote. **$$$**

✗ **Hafnia** [45 D6] Inside Hotel Hafnia, Áarvegur 4–10; 📞 30 80 00; www.hafnia.fo; 🕐 11.30– 14.00 & 18.00–21.30 Mon–Fri, 18.00–21.30 Sat, noon–17.00 & 18.00–21.30 Sun. This place specialises in good-value lunchtime buffets of open sandwiches, soup, a main course & a dessert (🕐 11.30–14.00 Mon–Fri) for just 138kr. From Jun to Aug there is an evening fish buffet on Tue in Jun, Tue & Thu in July & Thu in Aug (🕐 18.00–21.30; 350kr). Alternatively go à la carte: the pork cheeks with mushrooms or halibut with Brussels sprouts (*both 265kr*) are especially tasty. A 3-course set menu is 445kr, 5 courses is 635kr. $$$

✘ **Koks** [40–1 A2/A5] Inside Hotel Føroyar, Oyggjarvegur 45; ☎ 33 39 99; www.koks.fo; ⏲ 18.30–late Tue–Sat. Despite the unfortunate name, this is undoubtedly the restaurant with the best views in town, overlooking the entire capital from its hilltop location, & the best food in the country – it was voted the best restaurant in the Nordic countries in 2014. Seated amid the basalt stone walls dressed with green panels, diners are treated to a surprisingly simple menu of Faroese & Nordic fare: it consists solely of a list of ingredients such as skate, sea sandwort, angelica & rhubarb, which are then prepared to perfection by expert chefs: a multi-course dinner here goes for 1,085kr. $$$

MID RANGE

✘ **Barbara** [45 D6] Gongin 4–6; ☎ 33 10 10; www.barbara.fo; ⏲ 18.00–22.00 Mon–Sat. Housed in a snug little stone building, this excellent new seafood restaurant, decked out in maritime whites & blues, is a real treat serving the likes of fresh scallops, succulent local horse mussels, monkfish & ocean perch. Mains from 135kr, 6 courses for 465kr. $$

✘ **Etika** [45 D5] Áarvegur 3; ☎ 31 93 19; www.etika.fo; ⏲ 11.00–22.00 Mon–Sat, 17.00–22.00 Sun. Tórshavn's first sushi restaurant, bizzarely housed in a former florist's (hence the long glass windows). All the classics are here for the initiated to savour: tempura prawns with grated ginger (*130kr*), pork dumplings (*78kr*) & morsels of cod (*98kr*). But there are also meat options too, such as lamb chop with lemon zest (*38kr*) & chicken meatballs in teriyaki sauce (*35kr*). $$

✘ **Hvonn** [45 C5] Inside Hotel Tórshavn, Tórsgøta 4; ☎ 35 00 35; www.hvonn.fo/vagsbotn; ⏲ 11.30–midnight Sun–Thu, 11.30–01.30 Fri & Sat. A stylish & inordinately popular Italian-American brasserie which is packed to capacity every evening. The combination of tasty food at reasonable prices is the best you'll find anywhere in the Faroes: pizzas (*88–108kr*), burgers (*130kr*), pasta dishes (*115kr*), Indian curry (*168kr*), British-style fish & chips (*198kr*), fajitas (*185kr*) & a salad bar (*75kr*) are all on the menu. On Sun, there's an excellent brunch (⏲ *11.30–14.30*) for 225kr. Booking on any day is absolutely essential. $$

✘ **Marco Polo** [45 C5] Sverrisgøta 12; ☎ 31 34 30; www.marcopolo.fo; ⏲ 11.30–23.00 Mon–Thu, 11.30–midnight Fri, 17.00–midnight Sat, 17.00–23.00 Sun. This place is trying hard to be in the same league as the hotel restaurants but isn't quite there. Nevertheless, it's worth seeking out as its prices are quite reasonable: baked salmon in puff pastry for 200kr; steaks from 195kr; pizzas & burgers from 110kr; pasta dishes from 120kr; & a 3-course menu for 380kr. If your conscience allows, there's also pilot whale steak with mushrooms, bacon & gravy for 280kr. $$

✘ **Toscana** [45 D5] Nólsoyar Páls gøta 13; ☎ 31 11 09; ⏲ 17.00–23.00 Sun–Thu, 17.00–midnight Fri & Sat. A small, cosy & intimate Italian restaurant that has become a firm favourite with the locals of Tórshavn. Serving a range of steaks (*from 275kr*), shellfish & fish dishes such as lobster & giant prawns (*from 275kr*) as well as classic pasta & spaghetti mains for a more reasonable 165kr, it's easily the best place for Italian fare in town. There's a limited number of tables & booking is essential. $$

CHEAP AND CHEERFUL

✘ **Burger King** [44 C2] Inside the SMS shopping centre, R C Effersøes gøta 31; ⏲ 10.30–21.00 Mon–Sat, 14.00–21.00 Sun. The usual array of burgers & fries (Whopper Meal is 72kr) proudly served up by Faroese teenagers speaking impeccable English. Most easily accessed by the main shopping centre entrance off Tinghúsvegur, though there is also a drive-through (⏲ 19.00–23.00 Mon–Thu & Sat, 20.00–23.00 Fri, 14.00–23.00 Sun). $

✘ **Hvonn** [44 B2] Inside the SMS shopping centre, R C Effersøes gøta 31; ☎ 32 34 24; www.hvonn.fo/sms; ⏲ 09.00–18.30 Mon–Thu & Sat, 09.00–19.30 Fri, 14.00–18.30 Sun. A good place for a quick bite to eat while shopping at SMS, the menu here is a cut-down version of that at the main Hvonn in town, featuring winners like spaghetti bolognaise for 95kr, lasagne 115kr and pizzas from 98kr. $

✘ **Kafe Kaspar** [45 D6] Áarvegur 4–10; ☎ 30 80 10; www.hafnia.fo; ⏲ 11.00–23.00 Mon–Thu, 11.30–01.00 Fri, 11.00–02.00 Sat, 14.00–23.00 Sun. Attached to Hotel Hafnia, this modern, artily decorated café is known for its great bagels – you can choose any number of fillings for around 69kr. Otherwise, there's a pesto-marinated chicken salad for 78kr, soup at 59kr, & a club sandwich & burgers both for 125kr. $

✕ **Kafe Vágsbotn** [45 C6] Bryggjubakki 3; ⊕ May–Aug 10.00–18.00 daily in fine weather. An ad hoc open-air café beside the marina, serving fresh juice, coffee & beer; there are heaters under the awnings should it a get a little chilly. **$**

✕ **Kafe Umami** [45 D6] Bryggjubakki 19; ☏ 28 47 47; ⊕ 10.00–18.00 Mon–Sat, noon–18.00 Sun. The latest waterfront addition on Bryggjubakki, this simple café with outdoor seating serves a few sandwiches & light meals, but is best known for its fresh juices & smoothies; try the tangy ginger shot with beetroot & lemon, guaranteed to put a zing in your step. **$**

✕ **Kaffihúsið** [45 D6] Bryggjubakki 14; ☏ 35 87 87; www.kaffihusid.fo; ⊕ Sep–May 09.00–18.00 Mon–Sat, Jun–Aug 09.00–21.00 Mon–Sat, noon–18.00 Sun all year round At last Tórshavn has its own modern, European-style café, complete with painted stone walls & wonderful views over the marina; there's even outdoor seating for those fine afternoons. Serving soup (72kr), pancakes (55kr), paninis (78kr), quiche (98kr) & a range of cakes, too. **$**

✕ **Matstovan Seven** [41 F6] Yviri við Strond 21; ☏ 32 35 65; ⨍ Matstovan Seven; ⊕ 11.30–21.00 Mon–Fri, noon–21.00 Sat. Run by a Chinese-Faroese couple, Tórshavn's new Chinese restaurant, located next to Hotel Streym, is worth checking out for its great weekday lunch buffet (⊕ 11.30–

14.00; 95kr), which is guaranteed to fill you up with tasty southeast Asian treats. At other times, mains such as beef in black bean sauce or fried noodles with chicken cost around 99kr. **$**

✕ **Pizza 67** [45 D5] Tinghúsvegur 8; ☏ 35 67 67; ⨍ Pizza67fo; ⊕ 11.30–13.30 & 16.30–21.30 Mon–Thu, 11.30–13.30 & 16.30–23.30 Fri, 14.00–23.30 Sat, 14.00–22.00 Sun. Pizza 67 may have vanished from towns in its home country of Iceland, but the Faroese outlet of this pizza chain is still going strong. The menu features all your favourite pizzas, pasta & burgers, including the unusual & delicious Crazy Bananas pizza (pepperoni & banana) for around 79–99kr. At lunchtime (⊕ 11.30–13.30 Mon–Thu), there's an eat-as-much-as-you-want buffet of lasagne, pizza & salad dishes for 99kr. **$**

✕ **Pizza Kjallarin** [44 B4] Niels Finsens gøta 21; ☏ 35 33 53; ⊕ 17.00–23.00 Sun–Thu, 17.00–05.00 Fri & Sat. Take-away pizzas for around 80kr depending on toppings. **$**

✕ **Smyrjibreyðsbúðin** [44 C4] Niels Finsens gøta 12; ☏ 32 16 18; ⊕ 08.00–17.30 Mon–Thu, 08.00–18.00 Fri, 11.00–15.00 Sat. Delicious take-away open sandwiches sporting mouth-watering toppings such as roast beef & fried onion or egg & prawns, for 35–69kr from this tiny bakery & café. Brunch is served on Sat (145kr) & there's a few more substantial dishes like fish & chips (99kr), too. **$**

ENTERTAINMENT AND NIGHTLIFE

For a town of its size, Tórshavn supports a surprisingly large number of pubs and clubs. Although not as frenetic as the legendary night scene in Reykjavík in Iceland, the Faroese capital can certainly hold its own. The busiest nights out are always Friday and Saturday, though that doesn't mean to say that if you go out for a midweek drink you'll be sitting alone. Chances are there'll always be someone to keep you company since fresh faces always attract attention and interest; the drinking scene in Tórshavn is extremely friendly. Clubs in the Faroes are not the sophisticated affairs you might be used to at home; emphasis is pretty much on getting drunk as quickly as possible and having a wild time.

In addition to a visit to the cinema (two screens), Tórshavn is also one of the best places in the islands to catch a traditional Faroese evening which combines a buffet of local delicacies with a chance to perfect your footwork in the ancient Faroese chain dance.

PUBS

♀ **Café 22** [45 B5] Sverrisgøta 22; ✆ 31 15 65; ◷ 11.00–midnight Mon–Thu, 11.00–04.00 Fri & Sat, 11.00–midnight Sun. Despite a change in name (formerly Tórshøll), this smelly, first-floor bar is still the graceless drinkers' den it always was. Fun if you want to get under the skin of Tórshavn, though, with plenty of drunken seadogs.

♀ **Café Natúr** [45 E6] Áarvegur 7; ✆ 31 26 25; ◷ 11.00–midnight Mon–Thu, 11.00–04.00 Fri, 13.00–04.00 Sat, 14.00–midnight Sun. More bar than café, this is one of the most popular places to come for a drink, with a good range of local brews on tap, including Gull & Black Sheep. Although the surroundings are great – wooden floors & a faintly maritime feel – it can get a bit raucous & drunken in here as the evening progresses.

♀ **Cleopatra** [45 C5] Niels Finsens gøta 11; ✆ 31 34 30; ◷ 17.00–midnight Sun–Thu, 17.00–04.00 Fri & Sat. Up a flight of rickety metal steps from the main street, this is the place to come if you fancy a cocktail or two – there's a wide range available from Harvey Wallbangers to pina coladas, each costing 55kr. Fri & Sat excluded, the clientele is generally more restrained than at Café Natúr, so it can be a good place to come for a drink & a chat.

♀ **Glitnir** [45 C6] Gríms Kambans gøta 13; ✆ 31 90 90; ◷ 11.30–23.30 Mon–Thu, 11.30–04.00 Fri, noon–04.00 Sat, 13.00–midnight Sun. An upfront karaoke & sports bar which shows the latest matches on a big screen, attracts a lot of workers from the shipyard & the trawlers. Darts & board games are available.

♀ **Hvonn** [45 C5] Tórsgøta 4; ✆ 35 00 35; ◷ 11.30–midnight Sun–Thu, 11.30–02.00 Fri & Sat. Located on the ground floor of Hotel Tórshavn (below the Hvonn brasserie), this trendy, style-conscious bar is *the* place to see & be seen in Tórshavn. It's busy most nights with the town's movers & shakers & is an altogether more sophisticated hangout than Café Natúr.

♀ **Sirkus** [45 C6] Gríms Kambans gøta 2; ✆ 32 31 35; ◷ 17.00–midnight Mon–Thu, 17.00–04.00 Fri & Sat, 19.00–midnight Sun.

A cross between a café & a bar, this quirky, alternative hangout is unique in the Faroes & is a great place to get talking to the locals; there's sometimes live music here, sometimes soccer matches on big screens. It also boasts occasional gay nights, organised by lgbt.fo.

♀ **Irish Pub** [45 C6] Gríms Kambans gøta 13; ✆ 31 90 91; ◷ 11.30–midnight Mon–Thu, 11.30–04.00 Fri, 17.00–04.00 Sat, 17.00–22.00 Sun. With black-&-white chequered tiles on the floor & seating booths, this is the Faroes' attempt at creating a real Irish pub – it falls a bit short but it's still a good & inordinately popular place for a drink.

CLUBS

☆ **Havnar Club** [45 D5] Tinghúsvegur 4–11; ✆ 31 15 52; ◷ 17.00–22.00 Sun, 19.00–midnight Wed & Thu, 17.00–01.30 or 04.00 Fri & Sat. Rough & ready, heavily male drinking club not renowned for its restrained behaviour – hold onto your hat & lose any idea that the Faroese don't know how to party.

☆ **Luux** [45 D5] Tinghúsvegur 8; ✆ 50 55 57; ◷ 23.00–04.00 Fri & Sat. This club has a minimum age of 21 & has a downstairs bar & sitting area & an upstairs bar & dancefloor. Specialises in dance music aimed at 30-somethings.

☆ **Mojo** [45 C5] Sverrisgøta 15; ✆ 50 11 05; ◷ 17.00–midnight Mon–Thu, 17.00–04.00 Fri, noon–04.00 Sat, noon–midnight Sun. A combined café & nightclub which attracts a wide cross-section of Tórshavn folk. The nightclub operates on Fri & Sat nights and there's often live music & poker nights.

☆ **Rex** [45 D5] Tinghúsvegur 8; ✆ 31 06 87; ◷ 23.00–04.00 Fri & Sat. Your best bet for a night's clubbing in Tórshavn, with 2 bars & a dancefloor. Attracting a crowd of over-18s, there's house & techno on Fri while on Sat there are live bands & a selection of '80s hits.

☆ **Valhøll** [45 C5] Tørsgøta 13; ✆ 50 11 01; ◷ 20.00–04.00 Fri & Sat. A popular bar that attracts late teens & early 20s for loud & brash party nights & billiards.

OTHER PRACTICALITIES

Alcohol store Rúsdrekkasøla Landsins [40 E1], Høyvíksvegur 67; ☏ 34 04 00; www.rusan.fo; ⏰ 10.00–17.30 Mon–Fri, 10.00–14.00 Sat

Banks Eik [45 C5] Sverrisgøta 3; ⏰ 09.30–16.00 Mon–Fri. Suðuroyar Sparikassi [44 B3] Niels Finsens gøta 31; ⏰ 09.30–16.00 Mon–Fri. Both banks have ATMs.

Bookshops H N Jacobsens Bókahandil [45 D5], Vaglið 4; ☏ 31 10 36; www.bokhandil.fo; ⏰ 09.00–17.30 Mon–Thu, 09.00–18.00 Fri, 09.00–14.00 Sat. Rit og rák, inside the SMS shopping centre [44 B2]; ☏ 60 30 30; www. ritograk.fo; ⏰ 10.00–18.00 Mon–Thu, 10.00–19.00 Fri, 10.00–16.00 Sat

Cinema [45 D5] Tinghúsvegur 8; ☏ 31 19 56; www.bio.fo

Consulates *Finland* Hoyvíksvegur 74; ☏ 31 46 50. *France* Tróndargøta 49; ☏ 21 10 57. *Germany* Bryggjubakki 22; ☏ 35 95 95. *Netherlands* Kósarbrúgvin 3, Klaksvík; ☏ 40 99 00. *Norway* Yviri við Strond 4; ☏ 31 12 60. *Sweden* Bøgøta 16; ☏ 35 17 10. *UK* Niels Finsens gøta 5; ☏ 35 99 77

Emergencies ☏ 112

Internet Býarbókasavnið town library [45 C5] Niels Finsens gøta 7; ☏ 30 20 30; www.bbs.fo; ⏰ 09.00–21.00 Mon–Thu, 09.00–18.00 Fri, 10.00–16.00 Sat, 14.00–17.00 Sun

Libraries Býarbókasavnið town library [45 C5] Niels Finsens gøta 7; ☏ 30 20 30 (see *Internet* for times, above). Føroya Landsbókasavn national library [45 A8], JC Svaboes gøta 16; ☏ 34 05 25; www.flb.fo; ⏰ 10.00–18.00 Mon–Thu, 10.00–17.00 Fri

Pharmacy Tjaldurs Apotek, in the SMS shopping centre [44 B/C1–2]; ☏ 34 11 00; ⏰ 09.00–17.30 Mon–Fri, 10.00–14.00 Sat, 14.30–15.00 Sun

Police [41 F6] Yviri við Strond 17; ☏ 35 14 48; www.politi.fo; ⏰ 10.00–15.00 Mon–Fri

Post office [40 E1] Óðinshædd 2; ☏ 34 60 00; www.posta.fo; ⏰ 09.00–17.00 Mon–Fri

Sauna & swimming pool Svimjihøllin [40 B2], Hoydalsvegur 21; ☏ 30 20 72; www.svimjihollin. fo; ⏰ 06.45–20.00 Mon, Tue, Thu & Fri, 06.45–09.00 Wed, 09.00–17.00 Sat, 08.00–10.00 & 14.00–17.00 Sun (30kr to swim, including sauna).

WHAT TO SEE AND DO

Although the centre of Tórshavn doesn't take more than a long morning or afternoon to explore, you'd be wise to allow the capital two or three days if you want to take in some of the more cultural offerings such as museums, the Nordic House and galleries. What follows below is an account of the town's attractions working inland from the areas around Tinganes and Skansin fort, which can be sampled in any order you choose.

THE OLD TOWN: UNDIR RYGGI AND HAVNAR KIRKJA

If Tórshavn has an old town, it is the delightful confusion of narrow winding lanes and passageways known as **Undir Ryggi** [45 D6] that spill south from **Bringsnagøta**, a street that cuts west to east across the Tinganes promontory between Bryggjubakki and Áarvegur. Here neat 19th-century wooden houses, their black-tarred walls punctuated by white-framed windows, nestle eave to eave under roofs of springy grass. Mercifully, these homes were spared the devastation wrought by the fire of 1673 which swept through Tinganes destroying everything in its path. Take time to amble around these alleyways in summer and you're more than likely to find children playing undisturbed in their tiny gardens and chickens wandering freely scratching for food – in fact, a snapshot of Tórshavn life that has barely changed over several hundred years. As late as the 1950s there were still some 3,500 hens and chickens registered in the town! Houses here were built purposely small and low, not simply because they were correspondingly easier to keep warm, but also because wood was a scarce commodity. Indeed, it was in Bringsnagøta that the Faroese storyteller, **William Heinesen**, once lived and scenes from this tightly woven web of lanes

3

and alleyways, where grinding poverty was such a prominent feature of life, pop up repeatedly in so much of his work. Although there's no set path to take when wandering around this area, sooner or later you're bound to come across **Gongin**, once Tórshavn's main street, today a charming narrow lane of picturesque restored houses and small stores dating from the 1800s, many sporting the typical Faroese turf roof and black-tarred walls.

Sitting squat in the middle of the churchyard on the northern side of Bringsnagøta is **Havnar kirkja** [45 D6] (⊕ *14.30–18.00 Tue–Fri*), the church that effectively functions as Tórshavn's cathedral. The term 'cathedral', however, is something of a misnomer since this unassuming wooden church is by no means the structure of soaring stone buttresses and giant steeples you may be expecting and has only functioned as the Faroes' cathedral since 1990. In fact the first known church in Tórshavn, built in 1609, didn't even occupy this spot, but was instead located further out on the Tinganes peninsula. At the time it was the largest in the country, seating around 150 people, although Tórshavn's population was barely 100. It was this first church with its choir, nave and porch that served as a model for the traditional Faroese timber church that proliferated after 1816. In 1788, it was replaced by today's unadorned white-painted timber structure topped by a grey-slate roof. Major rebuilding in 1865 added an extension to the east and heightened the belltower to make room for a clock. Though demure on the outside, the church interior is altogether more vivid, consisting of garish orange-coloured pews, white walls and blue ceiling panels dotted with gold stars and an altarpiece totally dominated by the early 19th-century painting of the burial of Christ by Daniel Conrad Blunck. Also worth a quick look are the model ships hanging from the roof; one is a model of the *Norske Løve* of the Danish East India Company which foundered in a storm in Lambavík off Eysturoy in 1707. Tradition has it that several members of the crew made the model, donating it to the church in thanks for their rescue. Look out too for the church silver, which includes an altar crucifix from 1713 and a leatherbound service book with silver ornamentation that was given to the church by the crew of another ship, the *Justitia*, in 1686.

TINGANES Marked at its northern edge by the wooden dwellings of Undir Ryggi, Tinganes [45 E8] is the tooth-shaped point of land that reaches out southwards into the waters of Tórshavn harbour, separating the commercial harbour of Eystaravág from the shipyards and marinas of its westerly neighbour, Vestaravág. Today this flat rocky outcrop is dominated by a gaggle of hulking maroon-coloured, turf-roofed structures that, quite unassumingly, are home to the **Faroese Home Rule government**. Forget any notion of security guards armed to the teeth posted outside the seat of national power; instead visitors are free to meander at will amongst these coarsely hewn former warehouses, now home to various ministries, and ponder the admirably low-key approach the Faroese take to government. Although little remains on Tinganes to indicate its medieval importance, largely due to the great fire of 1673 and several ensuing blazes, including one in 1950, the remaining structures still give the impression of the trading station that once operated here. Indeed, the most significant building on Tinganes is the **Skansapakkhúsið**, a former storage building that was erected in 1749 furthest out on the promontory on the site of an earlier small fort. In its original form, the building consisted of little more than a single timber storey atop a basement of stones glued together by mortar made from burnt sea shells, a structure typical of much of Tinganes. The addition of several floors and various extensions has given the building its present multi-storey form, grand enough today to house the offices of the prime minister.

Amble behind Skansapakkhúsið toward the flagpole close to the very tip of the Tinganes promontory and you'll find a **Viking sundial**, or 'sun rose' as it's called in Faroese, engraved into the rock. Although little is known about its origins, it's thought the sundial is linked to worship of the Norse god Thor, which took place here until the acceptance of Christianity in the islands around AD1000. You'll find the sundial roughly halfway between the flagpole and the right-hand corner of Skansapakkhúsið when standing with the building behind you; it's about the same size as a large dinner plate.

Tagged onto the side of Skansapakkhúsið, **Salurin**, **Vektarbúðin** and **Sjóbúðin**, along with **Bakkapakkhúsið** opposite, are essentially more of the same – wooden structures balanced on a base of stone and mortar, which today house the administrative offices of the prime minister and his deputy. The only two buildings to survive the 1673 fire stand on the other side of a low stone wall from here: the **Leigubúðin**, which once functioned as the Royal Rent Collection Store where the king's revenue, paid in kind, was stored, as did the **Munkastovan** (Monk's Dwelling) opposite, attached to the Bakkapakkhúsið. The unusual structure of this low thick-set turf-roofed building is noteworthy, not only because it is different from the other timber structures on Tinganes, but also because its chunky cavity stone walls are reminiscent of the building style at nearby medieval **Kirkjubøur**, reliable proof that this building dates from the early Middle Ages and is therefore the oldest building in Tórshavn. Diagonally opposite the Munkastovan, the bizarrely named **Portugálið** (literally 'Portugal', though the word is a Faroese corruption of the French *corps de garde*), erected in 1762, superseded a jail or guardhouse with cells in its basement and today still contains an inscription of the crowned monogram of King Christian V in its right wall, the 1693 date and the name of the feudal overlord of the day, Frederik von Gabel, whose family originated from Hamburg. Immediately behind here is one of Tórshavn's most impressive constructions, the **Reyngarður vicarage** [45 E8] built in 1630 in Danish style with four wings around a central courtyard. The west wing has been restored and is a fine example of Danish half-timbered design.

AROUND VÁGSBOTN: THE HARBOUR Contained between Undir Bryggjubakka and Skálatrøð, **Vágsbotn** (literally 'end of the bay') is just that: a narrow little square squeezed into the head of the harbour. This is undoubtedly the most photographed part of Tórshavn and offers perfect views of the colourful old warehouses which line Undir Bryggjubakka and the bobbing boats and yachts moored in the harbour. It's here, too, that you'll find **Sølutorgið** [45 D6], a row of metal tables where fishermen display and sell their catch. There are no set times of operation – it simply depends on when a boat arrives. From Vágsbotn it's a five-minute walk west through the car park which lines Skálatrøð to two art workshops: **Steinprent,** both lithographic workshop and gallery, at Skálatrøð 16 [45 B7] (📞 *31 63 86; www.steinprent.com;* ⏰ *09.00–17.00 Mon–Fri, 14.00–17.00 Sat*), which produces and sells a series of arty prints, and **Öström**, next door at No 18 [45 B7] (📞 *28 60 10;* ⏰ *10.00–17.30 Mon–Fri, 10.00– 18.00 Fri, 10.00–16.00 Sat*), which functions as a temporary exhibition hall and shop selling fashion accessories, stylish clothing and other knick-knacks.

SKANSIN FORT [41 F7] Beyond Vágsbotn and Tinganes, at the seaward end of Havnargøta, Skansin Fort once marked the entrance to Tórshavn harbour.

Tórshavn WHAT TO SEE AND DO

3

Dominated by a red-and-white-painted lighthouse, this small fortress was built around 1580, most probably on the orders of the great Faroese adventurer Magnus Heinason. Construction of a fort to protect the trading centre of Tórshavn was deemed necessary in the face of the steadily increasing numbers of seaborne attacks across the North Atlantic. Indeed, shortly after Skansin's completion, news reached Tórshavn of a devastating attack on the town of Hvalba on Suðuroy by Barbary pirates in 1629. The original fortification didn't last long before falling victim to the French plundering of Tórshavn in 1677; they destroyed the fort when their final demand for 100 oxen, 200 sheep, 500 pairs of gloves, 1,200 pairs of stockings and 60 nightshirts couldn't be met by the people of Tórshavn within the 12-hour deadline. Skansin was rebuilt a century later only to suffer a similar attack, this time by the British in 1808 during the Napoleonic Wars; two Faroese boat crews were dispatched by the fort commander out into the harbour – where the English brig, *Clio*, had laid anchor – to enquire what the vessel required, only to return as shields as the British mercilessly attacked the fort, without the demand for either stockings or nightshirts. Finally rebuilt into its present star shape to accommodate an artillery battery and a permanent Danish garrison of around 40 soldiers, the fort later saw the British return as it served as the Royal Navy headquarters when they occupied the Faroes during World War II. Indeed, the two guns which face out to sea from behind the fort were used here to defend the islands against German attack. Four older brass cannons from the time of the Danish Trade Monopoly can also be seen. Although there's not much more to Skansin today, it does offer some quite exceptional views out over the sea to neighbouring Nólsoy, back towards the extremities of Eysturoy and naturally of Tórshavn and Tinganes itself.

AROUND NIELS FINSENS GØTA Tórshavn's main shopping street, Niels Finsens gøta, may be a modest affair but it is here that you'll find the town's main square, **Vaglið** [45 D5], formed by the junction of Niels Finsens gøta, Tinghúsvegur, Mylnugøta and Áarvegur. The square is the location of the summer Ólavsøka celebrations (see pages 30–1) and, in addition, boasts several pleasing sculptures and statues: a bust of the Faroese poet and politician RC Effersøe, the bronze sculpture *Man and Wife* by Janus Kamban and a portrait of two workers by Fridtjof Joensen. Incidentally, the statue in stainless steel of dancing children a little further along Niels Finsens gøta was originally intended to be the centrepiece of a fountain. However, passers-by became so tired of being drenched by spurts of horizontal water whipped up by the unpredictable Faroese wind that the tap was finally turned off.

On the opposite side of Vaglið square, at the junction of Niels Finsens gøta and Mylnugøta, you'll find one of old Tórshavn's best-preserved turf-roofed wooden buildings which now houses **H N Jacobsens bookshop** (see page 51 for details), without a doubt the best store for books and stationery in town, and the Kunningarstovan tourist office. Well concealed under a row of maple trees, this three-winged structure from 1860, set in front of a well-tended garden, once served as Tórshavn's secondary school, before opening as a bookstore in 1918.

There could hardly be a greater contrast between the delicate timber façade of the bookshop and the sturdy grey-basalt slabs used to construct the **Ráðhúsið** building opposite, which today houses the offices of Tórshavnar Kommuna (the local council). Built in 1894, this rather oppressive block-like building served as a district school before conversion into a town hall in 1955. Thankfully, the impressive sculpture in front of this ugly edifice, *Traðarmaðurin* (Crofter) by Hans Pauli Olsen, depicting a naked man bearing a fantastically heavy rock, enlivens an otherwise gloomy corner.

LØGTING (THE FAROESE PARLIAMENT) Despite its dominant position at the southern end of Niels Finsens gøta overlooking Vaglið square, the Løgting [45 D5] (*www.logting.fo*), one of the smallest parliament buildings in the world, looks more like a suburban family home than the nation's principal debating chamber. Nevertheless, the Faroese parliament has been meeting in this modest timber building since its erection in 1856, although it has undergone several renovations over the years, most recently in 2000 when major restoration work was undertaken to improve the cramped working conditions of the parliamentarians inside and to recreate the building's original pale-grey exterior walls and slate roof. The ground floor is devoted to the chamber, cramped in the extreme and more akin to a town council meeting room in most other countries, whereas the first floor is given over to administration. Every year in July, the grassy lawn in front of the small flight of stone steps leading up to the parliament sees the gathering of Faroe Islanders from across the country to listen to the speeches that mark the beginning of the national Ólavsøka festivities.

KONGAMINNI (THE KING'S MONUMENT) From the parliament it's a short dog-leg walk up Tinghúsvegur, right towards Undir Glaðsheyggi, right again into R C Effersøes gøta and finally left into Hoyvíksvegur to reach one of the finest viewpoints in Tórshavn: the King's Monument [44 E3] . This basalt obelisk was erected in 1882 to commemorate the visit of Danish King Christian IX to the Faroe Islands eight years before. From the monument there are arresting views out over the whole of the Faroese capital and the island of Nólsoy; indeed, it's hard to find another place to take equally good close-up aerial shots of the town.

SMS SHOPPING CENTRE AND VIÐARLUNDIN PARK Back on Tinghúsvegur, you'll soon cross busy Bøkjarabrekka heading north out of town for the biggest shopping centre in the Faroes, SMS [44 B/C1–2] (*www.sms.fo*; ⊕ *10.00–18.00 Mon–Thu & Sat, 10.00–19.00 Fri*). Occupying what appears from a distance to be a series of vast upside-down V-shaped warehouses, this is where the Faroese come to indulge in serious retail therapy, though its relatively small scale and lack of big-city sophistication may leave you rather underwhelmed. Nonetheless, this is definitely the place to come if you're self-catering since it's also home to the country's largest **supermarket**, Miklagarður, selling everything from whale meat to chewing gum. Body Shop and Burger King are also here, alongside a bookshop, electrical store and various other purely Faroese stores. While you're here make sure to see the unusual multi-coloured glasswork that adorns the central spiral staircase, courtesy of local artist Tróndur Patursson.

If the array of delights inside the shopping centre has left you out of breath, you may wish to recuperate amid the delightful surroundings of **Viðarlundin Park** [40 B4], barely a 5-minute stroll from the main exit across Tinghúsvegur and then right into Hoydalsvegur which leads directly to the park walls. More tree plantation than park, this is the place to come to get your arboreal fix before heading off into the treeless expanses of the rest of the country. Although efforts began in the 1880s to try to create a wooded park in Tórshavn, they met with little success and most of the specimens present today are barely 100 years old. Storm-force winds tearing in from the Atlantic regularly uproot the plantation's trees and bushes in the park, making maintenance a year-round task. On a positive note, the presence of the small forest here has attracted several species of birds rarely found in the Faroes including blackbirds, redwings and collared doves as well as more common varieties such as starlings and house sparrows, which, incidentally, only arrived in the Faroes in the 1940s. Countless paths criss-cross the park and it's not difficult to find your own shady glade to relax and enjoy the crisp clean air. Following the small stream that runs through Viðarlundin up through the hilly terrain will bring you to two small ponds, noisy with ducks and geese. Here, at the highest point in the park, a monument commemorates the Faroese sailors who lost their lives during World War II.

LISTASAVN FØROYA (THE NATIONAL ART GALLERY) Housed in what appears at first sight to be a series of top-secret military bunkers hidden among the trees of Viðarlundin, the Listasavn Føroya [40 B3] (*Gundadalsvegur 9;* ✆ *31 35 79; www.art. fo;* ◷ *May–Aug 11.00–17.00 daily; rest of the year 14.00–17.00 Tue–Sun; admission 50kr*) is the Faroes' premier art exhibition. Dedicated to continually changing displays of work by local artists and sculptors, this really is the place to come to get to grips with one of the least-well-known arts scenes in Europe. Although Faroese art is still in its infancy it's easy to pick out the recurrent themes that determine much of the art that this small Nordic nation produces: landscapes, turf-roofed village houses and, above all, the many moods of the sea. The gallery, a delightfully light and airy building whose floor is composed of curiously shaped wooden blocks,

WHERE TO BUY TRADITIONAL SWEATERS AND YARN IN TÓRSHAVN

One of the best souvenirs to take away from the Faroes is a traditional woollen sweater. Originally made for fishermen to keep them warm and dry whilst at sea, high-quality hand-knitted sweaters are still made by small armies of knitters dotted up and down the islands along with all manner of other woollen items to traditional patterns and designs. You'll find a good selection in Tórshavn at the **Føroya Heimavirkisfelag** [45 C5] at Niels Finsens gøta 7 (✆ *50 87 69; www.craft.fo; 10.00–17.30 Mon–Thu, 10.00–18.00 Fri, 10.00–14.00 Sat*). A handmade sweater will cost around 950kr.

For quality Faroese wool and yarn, look no further than the knitting emporium that is **Igloo** [45 B5] at Sverrisgøta 19 (✆ *31 52 63; 11.00–17.30 Mon–Thu, 11.00–18.00 Fri, 11.00–14.00 Sat*).

For details of other stores selling designer woollen goods, including sweaters, see the *Designer Knitwear* box on page 32, though remember that anything designer is not handmade.

is divided into a handful of small rooms and corridors, making browsing painless and straightforward. Downstairs a much larger hall is often used for temporary exhibitions, concerts or lectures.

The **first exhibition hall**, just past reception on the right, is dedicated to Sámal Joensen-Mikines (1906–79), who, as his name suggests, came from Mykines. After studying art in Copenhagen between 1928 and 1932, he spent much of the rest of his life in Denmark and his style is influenced by Danish modernism. His best known work is the 1934 *Mykinesmaður* (Man from Mykines), which depicts the enigmatic face of an old man with an unkempt grey beard wearing a pointed black hat and represents classic Faroese art; his *Grindadráp* from 1960 also features a mêlée of deep reds, maroons and purples to portray the alfresco slicing up of a pod of pilot whales. As the first Faroese painter, Mikines specialised in peaceful, idyllic village portraits as well as the soaring cliff faces and crashing surf that characterise the Faroe Islands. His work has been an example to all those who have followed after him.

The **second hall** is devoted to Ingálvur av Reyni (1920–2005), the only Faroese artist to enjoy an international reputation. After studying in Copenhagen from 1938 to 1946, the artist returned to his native Tórshavn. Until the early 60s, his brightly coloured works showed influences of French naturalism, though later his style moved towards abstract expressionism. Check out his self-portrait from 1955, a fusion of reds and greens, whose stern expression exudes determination.

In the **third hall**, you'll find work by a new generation of Faroese artists, who have breathed new life into the traditional themes of landscape and nature, notably Edvard Fuglø (b.1965). His *Koloni* from 2006, for instance, depicts a colony of humanised gannets dressed in black dinner jackets, white shirts and black ties, with their heads pointing manically in different directions; whilst his *Luncheon on the grass* (2011) captures a clifftop picnic scene, with oystercatchers and puffins overflying a woman wearing nothing but a bonnet dining with two men, one with horns, the other with a ram's head.

A number of other favourites are dotted around **the rest of the gallery**. Zacharias Heinesen (b.1936) is best known for his Cubist landscapes. His *Vár* from 1987 portrays a Faroese village in spring, bound by the whites, blues and greens of land merging into sky. *World of Trolls* from 1952 by author and artist William Heinsen (1900–91) is a magnificent caricature of the board meeting of the directors of an insurance company in Tórshavn. Perhaps best of all, the unsung watercolours by the much-overlooked Ruth Smith (1913–58), in particular *Houses in Nes* (1951), which is bursting with bright, summery greens, blues and yellows and the equally appealing variation, *Á Nesi* (1952). For more on Ruth Smith see pages 156–7.

Downstairs you'll find an unusual display of glasswork and mirrors by Tróndur Patursson (b.1944) entitled *The Deep Blue*, which features a room with a glass floor and walls of mosaic-like glass tiles of blue, black, turquoise and red, designed to express the depth and infinity of sky and ocean.

NORÐURLANDAHÚSIÐ (THE NORDIC HOUSE) [40 A1] A ten-minute walk

northwest from the art gallery along Gundadalsvegur then right along the Norðari Ringvegur, passing Faroese national radio and television on the way, brings you to a building that, since its inauguration in 1983, has become a Faroese institution: the Norðurlandahúsið [40 A1] (☏ 35 13 51; www.nlh.fo; ⊕ 10.00–17.00 Mon–Sat, 14.00–17.00 Sun; admission free). As its name suggests, the Nordic House is the Faroes' link with the rest of the Nordic countries; indeed, it was one of the aims of the Nordic Council, on whose instigation the building was constructed, that it should help develop cultural links to the rest of the Nordic region through art exhibitions, film shows and lectures. However, over the years the Nordic House has grown into a fully fledged concert hall-cum-theatre-cum-cinema showcasing the many facets of Faroese culture; the concert hall alone, measuring an impressive 500m², can comfortably seat up to 400 people. The true Nordic nature of the project is encapsulated in its construction: the floor tiles are Norwegian, the furniture Finnish, the timber walls Swedish, the glass Danish and the roof Icelandic. Indeed, the very design of the house was carefully chosen to fit in with the Faroese landscape; the Soviet-style monster that is the Faroese national broadcasting headquarters, fronted by a mini-Stonehenge structure outside, looks all the more ghastly beside its sleek and stylish neighbour.

Since the Nordic House is regularly used as a venue for seminars, exhibitions, music festivals, theatre productions and film shows, there's likely to be something of interest going on when you visit. It was here, for example, that Bill Clinton spoke during his visit to the Faroes in 2007. If nothing appeals, there's always a chance to read one of the Nordic-language newspapers that are kept here (the Faroese and Danish ones are particularly useful for weather forecasts – see box, page 21 for weather terminology) or sample a tasty open sandwich with a slice of cake and a cup of coffee in the excellent café while enjoying the views over Tórshavn. Curious sheep sculptures, *Seyðafylgi*, made of galvanised iron by Bernhard Lipsøe, sit just beyond the floor-to-ceiling windows, which help to make the Nordic House such a light, airy and altogether agreeable place to while away an hour or two.

OTHER MUSEUMS

Tjóðsavn (National Museum)
No visit to Tórshavn is complete without taking in the main museum in the country, the National Museum [40 D1] (*Brekkutún 6;* \31 80 76; www.savn.fo; bus #2 and #3; ⊕ mid-May–mid-Sep 10.00–17.00 Mon–Fri, 14.00–17.00 Sat & Sun; all year 14.00–17.00 Thu & Sun; admission 30kr), located in the town of Hoyvík on the northeastern outskirts of the capital. Housed in a two-storey building looking out over the Atlantic, this is the place to come to really understand how the Faroes and the Faroese have developed over the centuries.

The basement exhibitions After paying your modest entrance fee, forsake the ground-floor exhibitions and head straight away down the staircase to your right for an eyeful of the museum's *pièce de résistance*: the medieval **Kirkjubøstólarnir pew-ends**. In a dark room lit only by soft overhead lighting, these ornately carved bench-ends, all 16 dating from the early 1400s, are truly breathtaking in their elemental beauty and showcase intricate carvings of the 12 apostles, including readily discernible images of St Peter holding the key to heaven and John the Baptist with a poisoned chalice. Justifiably regarded as the Faroes' greatest national treasure and preserved in quite a remarkable state, each piece adorned the pews of the medieval cathedral at Kirkjubøur. During extensive renovation work in the mid-19th century, all woodwork in the church was replaced and dispatched to the Museum of National Antiquities in Denmark. For over 100 years, the pew-ends remained a bone of contention between Tórshavn and Copenhagen, with frequent requests by the Faroese for this invaluable piece of their heritage to be returned to the islands ignored. However, spurred on by the success of their Icelandic neighbours in ensuring the return of several strategic medieval Icelandic manuscripts held by the Danes, the Faroese persisted and finally signed an agreement with the Danish government in the summer of 1999 for the return of around 400 antiquities and documents, including the Kirkjubøstólarnir, which returned in July 2002.

Elsewhere downstairs, check out the **skeletons** of a man, woman and child found during excavations of the church in Sandur on Sandoy in the late 1960s, dating from the 13th century. Including today's structure, a total of six churches have stood on the same spot in the village; 23 bodies were found in the nave of the second church to occupy the location. The male skeleton was over 45 years of age at the time of death, while the woman was aged between 35 and 45 and the child was less than one year old. The skeletons form part of a larger genome project and the museum is hoping to receive more information about their age in due course.

Close by you'll see **Viking-age finds** from a farm at Leirvík on Eysturoy: part of a wall stave, a door handle and a padlock have been dated to the 9th or 10th centuries. Remains of birch bark also found on the site suggest that the farm, which consisted of four buildings including a longhouse, may have had a thatched roof.

The ground-floor exhibitions Back on the ground floor, it's best to skip the tapestry made in 1963 by two local women showing scenes from the *Færeyinga Saga* and have a quick look instead at the story of the ships and shipping lines that have plied the stormy waters of the North Atlantic over the years, linking the Faroes with Denmark and the UK, in particular the handsome old steamer *Tjaldur*, which sailed up until 1922. The rest of the ground floor is given over to a frankly rather pedestrian **natural history section**, whose most engaging section is a history of the **Lítla Dímun sheep**, a subject clearly close to the heart of all Faroese. Occupying centre stage inside a glass cabinet in the centre of the exhibition are three stuffed sheep which were shot on the island in 1844 before being sent to Denmark for preservation. It is thought that these sheep belonged to the original breed of sheep brought to the Faroes by the very first Viking settlers; they were almost completely wild, difficult to manage and yielded much less meat than other breeds. Indeed, the Dímun sheep were very similar to sheep which still inhabit the remote Scottish island of Soay off St Kilda. However, the breed became extinct after these three animals were shot to make way for other imported breeds from Iceland, Shetland and Orkney.

HOYVÍKSGARÐUR (OPEN-AIR MUSEUM) [40 D1] (*same details as National Museum; see page 58*) An operating farm from the Middle Ages until the 1960s, the Open-Air Museum, Hoyvíksgarður, barely a stone's throw across Hvítanesvegur from the Historical Museum, is worth a look for an insight into Faroese farming traditions through the centuries. Hoyvík was originally a settlement of just two farmhouses and associated outhouses; the farm has been divided and reunited several times over during its existence. The museum site is composed of several small barns and storage huts gathered around the main farmhouse, a solid timber construction from 1803 designed to withstand the worst of the Atlantic storms that sweep in from **Hoyvík bay**, the farm's location. Inside, the low ceiling and solid timber walls create a snug atmosphere for the array of rooms that lead off the main living room. Close to the farmhouse, there are a number of slatted outhouses worthy of a quick peek, where mutton was left to dry in the fresh air. In the opposite direction, a path heads off through the farm down to Hoyvík bay, ending at a series of landing places. Take care to stick to the paths and not to walk on the grass.

VESTURKIRKJA CHURCH [41 A7] From the Museum of Natural History it's an easy 10-minute walk back down V U Hammershaimbs gøta and left onto Landavegur to one of the most striking landmarks in Tórshavn, the Vesturkirkja church. Its soaring copper tower, built in the form of a pyramid, can be seen across the capital and caused much controversy upon completion in 1975. The church has restricted opening hours (☉ *Jun–Aug 15.00–17.00 Mon–Fri; admission free*), although it's generally possible to visit at other times by making an appointment; ask at the Kunningarstovan in Niels Finsens gøta. The unadorned interior is dominated by a 30m-high vertical column of white stone behind the altar which reaches up into the pyramidal tower, high above the grey-slate flooring.

FØROYA SJÓSAVN AQUARIUM [41 B8] (✆ 50 51 20; www.sjosavn.net; ☉ *mid-Jun–Aug 14.00–17.00 Tue–Sun, rest of the year 14.00–17.00 Sat & Sun; admission 40kr*) From the church, a stroll down Á Frælsinum will bring you to the grey bulk of a building that is the national hospital on J C Svabos gøta. Once here, weave your way around Sandagerðisvík bay (where there's a nice stretch of sandy beach for those sunny afternoons), by taking Dr Dahls gøta south from the roundabout just beyond the hospital and then left into Rættargøta. Once over the river that flows into the bay, you'll come to the Faroes' one and only aquarium. From the church it's a 20-minute walk or so to reach here. With a collection of open octagonal tanks and regular aquaria, this is *the* place to come face to face with some of the exceptionally ugly sea life of the North Atlantic, all of it landed by local landliners and handed over to the owner, who feeds them squid. In the seas off the Faroes there are over 200 species of fish, some of which are present here: cod, saithe, catfish and conger eels, to name but a few. Curiously, in recent years several new species such as pollock have also been found in Faroese waters, and it's suspected that rising sea temperatures are largely responsible.

AROUND VESTARAVÁG HARBOUR Retracing your steps north past the hospital along J C Svabos gøta brings you to Tórshavn's **old graveyard** [45 A6] (see box, page 61). From here **Gríms Kambans gøta** leads downhill towards **Vestaravág harbour** [45 C7] passing some of Tórshavn's most elegant dwellings, a lovely place to stroll. With its huddled wooden houses and twisting corners, this street evokes much of the atmosphere of 19th-century Tórshavn. It's worth studying some of the houses closely, not least the one towards the western end of the street at **No 26** – a weathered creamy orange-and-red structure dating from 1902 with an elaborate carved roof in Norwegian style. Look out too for the turf-roofed wooden house, **Smiðjan í Litluvík** [45 B6], at the corner with Skálatrøð. A stylish gallery used by the town's artists to exhibit their work, its opening times vary according to the exhibition, so ask at the Kunningarstovan for details (see page 43). Continue along Gríms Kambans gøta and you'll eventually come back around to Vágsbotnur, the end of the bay, which marks the corner of Vestaravág harbour with the beginnings of Undir Ryggi and Tinganes. It's here that you'll find a monument to Nólsoy Páll (see box, page 69) who is remembered in the islands as the man who fought for the lifting of the Danish Trade Monopoly.

BOAT TRIPS FROM TÓRSHAVN An excursion by boat is an absolute must while in the Faroes, and arguably the best trip to consider from Tórshavn is a tour aboard the atmospheric old oak schooner *Norðlýsið*. During the summer months (roughly late May to August), there are two weekly sightseeing departures (Tuesday and Thursday) from the harbour in Tórshavn: at 09.00 the ship leaves for a three-hour tour (*300kr*) of the islands; bookings can be made by phone or online (📱 *21 85 20; www.nordlysid.com*). Also worth considering if you're around at the right time is the twice-weekly concert cruise lasting five hours (☉ *13.00 Tue & Thu; 450kr*) to the Klæmintsgjógv caves of Hestur. After sailing close to the caves onboard *Norðlýsið*, passengers are transferred to smaller boats which then sail into the caves, where special musical performances are held using the acoustics of the rock to stupendous effect. Check the website for updates.

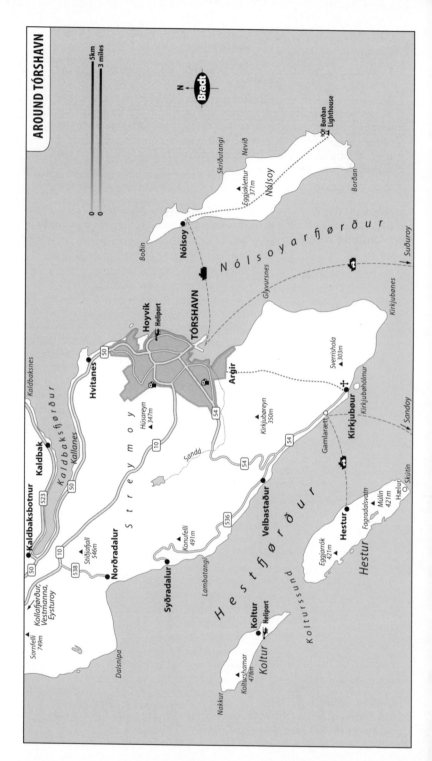

AROUND TÓRSHAVN

4

Around Tórshavn

Even if you're only staying for a short time, it's a good idea to get out of Tórshavn and see some of the surrounding attractions. Indeed, it's only upon leaving the Faroese capital and venturing into some of the smaller villages and islands that you'll fully appreciate Tórshavn's charms; life in this pint-sized town may be enviably sedate, but the place is a veritable metropolis when compared with some of the remoter villages and islands that are all totally dependent on the capital for their economic well-being. While all roads may lead to Rome, in the Faroe Islands it's Tórshavn that acts as the focal point for all buses and ferries. Travelling on the islands' superb network of public transport therefore makes day trips an absolute doddle and a refreshing contrast to the 'Big Smoke'.

The one place everybody who comes to the Faroe Islands wants to see is barely half an hour outside Tórshavn: **Kirkjubøur**. Easily the most significant settlement during the Middle Ages, the wonderfully preserved medieval **cathedral** here stands as a monument to the leading role this tiny hamlet, once the site of the bishop's see, played throughout Faroese history. However, the possibility of combining a trip to Kirkjubøur with a one-way hike up over the barren moorlands of southern Streymoy helps to make a visit here such an alluring option; you can then hop on the bus and be whisked back into Tórshavn. There's more religious history at hand in the village of **Kaldbak**, barely a 30-minute bus ride north of Tórshavn on the shores of the eponymous fjord, where the handsome **wooden church**, complete with turf roof (one of many dotted around the Faroes), dates from 1835.

Equally appealing, though for totally different reasons, is a short boat trip out to **Nólsoy**, the island immediately off Tórshavn with the flat-topped mountain, which helps make views out across the harbour so striking. The huddle of narrow streets that make up the tiny village couldn't be more different from the capital: not only are there no cars here but also life goes on seemingly as it has for decades. Wander through the village and you'll perhaps see seabirds being plucked ready for the pot and seated old men gossiping at the harbourside watching the comings and goings of the fishing boats. Nólsoy is also the place to come for hiking: an easily negotiable path leads out across the springy heathland, skirting the foot of the Eggjarklettur peak, to the old lighthouse station on the island's southern tip, from where there are dramatic views out over the Atlantic swells to Sandoy.

If, after a stay in Tórshavn, you're looking to get completely out into the wilds and take in some stunning mountain scenery along the way, you're in luck. Off Streymoy's southwestern coast, the little-visited islands of **Hestur**, and better still **Koltur**, home to just one solitary farm, are within easy reach. A ferry runs out to Hestur from the harbour at Gamlarætt, just north of Kirkjubøur and connected to Tórshavn by bus, making a total journey time of around 90 minutes. However, it's Koltur that is the real draw: painstakingly restored stone dwellings give an idea of how people once lived on the island, and the island also boasts one of the most beautiful and unusually shaped mountains in the country, the sugar-loaf Kolturshamar that can be seen for miles around. If you're looking for a quintessentially Faroese experience, it's right here.

KIRKJUBØUR

Curiously for such a historically significant site, Kirkjubøur (*www.patursson.fo*) owes its existence to two seemingly incidental things: driftwood and seaweed. Thanks to the tidal currents, the preponderance of driftwood that washes up on the shore here, matched nowhere else in the country, coupled with copious amounts of seaweed, proved invaluable for the settlement's development. In a denuded country where trees simply don't grow without man's help, driftwood was a much-prized and sought-after commodity, not simply for construction of houses but also for kindling. Seaweed, on the other hand, was used as fertiliser on the barren land to aid the cultivation of crops. In fact, it's widely believed this enabled Irish hermits, probably the area's first inhabitants, to eke out a simple existence here around AD800, brief accounts of which can be found in the work *Liber de Mensura Orbis Terrae*, by the Irish monk Dicuil.

However, their stay in the Faroes was short-lived and, as the arrival of Norwegian Vikings in their longboats became steadily more frequent, the Irish fled. It wasn't until several centuries later, around 1020, with the islands firmly under Viking control, that Kirkjubøur began to flourish. It was on the instigation of a wealthy woman known as Gæsa, daughter of the local farmer Tórhallur the Rich, who then owned half of Streymoy, that a church was first built here. With the arrival of Gudmundur, the first bishop in the Faroes around 1100, the tiny settlement's strategic role in Faroese religious life was not only assured, but was also strengthened as the Church, from its base here at Kirkjubøur, asserted its dominance by seizing land across the country. According to tradition, Gudmundur confiscated large parts of Gæsa's land as punishment for her breaking the Church's strict fasting rules.

Today, in addition to the overgrown and somewhat uninspiring remains of what's thought to be a church and graveyard to the east, up beyond the main site, the farmstead of Kirkjubøur effectively consists of three main elements: the farmhouse itself, **Roykstovan**; the present parish church, **Ólavskirkjan**, benefiting from a superb location right on the shoreline; and the reason for all the fuss: the magnificent medieval **Magnus Cathedral**, the effective seat of power over several centuries.

GETTING THERE AND AWAY Bus #5 runs six times daily (Monday–Friday only) from Jónas Broncks gøta in Tórshavn to Kirkjubøur. If you're hiking (see box, page 66), you may want to time your walk to coincide with return bus times to Tórshavn: the last afternoon bus currently leaves at 17.17; timetables are available at www.torshavn.fo.

OTHER PRACTICALITIES Since there is no overnight accommodation available at Kirkjubøur, it's best not to get stuck here. Other than a small **shop** selling woollen jumpers and other souvenirs during the summer months, the only facilities here are a toilet block and a waiting room located by the bus stop and the car park, so if you're planning a day trip it's a good idea to bring everything you need with you.

WHAT TO SEE AND DO
Magnus Cathedral It's for the impressive Magnus Cathedral (*múrurin* in Faroese, literally 'the walls') that Kirkjubøur is justifiably best known. This whopping

Gothic structure, measuring 27m long and 11m wide, was built around 1300 from rock and stone quarried from nearby hillsides at the behest of the Faroese bishop, **Erlendur** (1269–1308) and served as the Faroe Islands' cathedral until the Reformation in 1538. However, it was probably never completed and today looks pretty much as it did on the day building ground to a halt 700 years ago – roofless. It seems the bishop overestimated the capacity of the islanders to construct such a vast monument to their new God (Christianity had come to the Faroes barely 300 years earlier); in fact, depending on which story you believe, building stopped due to a bloody uprising against the bishop's extortionate taxes, or as a symbol of the poverty wrought by the Black Death in the mid 1300s. It's thought, though, that a roof may actually have been built.

Today the cathedral's stone walls, over 1.5m thick, still stand at their full height of 9m, quite a remarkable achievement given the inclement nature of Faroese weather. Whereas the long southern wall is decorated by five steeply arched windows and two smaller openings, the opposite wall has just one access point leading into the sacristy where the remains of a staircase are still visible. Although a roof once covered this part of the cathedral, an avalanche in 1772 brought it crashing to the ground, destroying the staircase, which it's believed led up into a tower; barely one or two steps now remain. Carved into the interior walls, six of the original 12 Maltese crosses are still in place, whilst on the external eastern wall a stone plaque portraying Christ on the cross with the Virgin Mary and Mary Magdalene at his side bears a weather-beaten inscription in Latin noting the fact that the cathedral is dedicated to St Magnus and St Thorlak. According to the plaque there is also, bizarrely, a secret cavity in the wall behind containing a number of ancient relics. In 1905 the plaque was indeed removed to reveal seven religious artefacts including a silk ribbon supposedly from the habit of the Virgin Mary and pieces of bone from Bishop Thorlak and Magnus Erlendsson, the Earl of Orkney who was canonised in 1135.

Following heated debate about how best to preserve the crumbling remains of Magnus Cathedral, it was decided to cover the outer walls with metal sheeting to give the stone chance to dry out. Sadly, although it's no longer possible to see the cathedral in its original state, a visit here is still incredibly worthwhile; it's only by getting close up to the cathedral that you can comprehend the sheer scale of this unfinished venture. The structure is at its most impressive when viewed with the sea behind you and the wall of windows on the seaward side slightly to your left. Since it's not known how long the drying-out process will take, the weather shield looks set to remain in place for the foreseeable future.

Roykstovan farmhouse (⊕ *09.00–17.30 Mon–Sat, 14.00–17.30 Sun; admission 30kr*)

Dating from the 11th century and formerly used as the bishop's residence, the turf-roofed Roykstovan is the oldest inhabited wooden house in Europe. The Faroese name, literally meaning 'smoke room', refers to the ancient practice of lighting a fire in a specially constructed room with a hole in the roof, which allows the smoke to escape. Built of coarsely hewn timber logs smeared in black tar, the farmhouse sits atop a basement of sturdy stone walls, in parts more than 2m thick. According to tradition, the farmhouse is of Norwegian origin and first stood in the Sognefjord before being dismantled, its logs numbered and floated across the sea to the Faroes. Today, the Patursson family, who have occupied the building for centuries and can trace their ancestors back over 17 generations to the time of the Reformation, still live here. Naturally, their home is not open to visitors but the oldest part of the building, the **Stokkastovan**, built from driftwood around the same time as the cathedral, as well as the more interesting Roykstovan itself, are open to visitors. Entrance is via the stone staircase directly opposite the cathedral; put your entrance fee in the box provided. Once inside, take the narrow staircase up into the Roykstovan which occupies the central portion of the farmhouse. Formerly a living, working and dining area all rolled into one, this long rectangular room was where the fire was set; indeed, the blackened roof timbers are now thickly impregnated with smoke from the turf fires that once burned in here. To escape the inclement weather outdoors, the entire family would gather here to comb wool, sew and make everything they needed to keep the house in good order. It was also here that they told stories and danced the Faroese chain dance around the fire, naturally for enjoyment's sake, but also as an effective way of keeping warm. Today, though, the room is smoke-free and a window covers the hole in the roof above where the fires once burned. Alongside various traditional household implements that were once used in the room (the fanciful wooden carvings are sadly 20th-century imitations), there's a bust of the Norwegian king, Sverri, who, as the illegitimate son of King Sigurd, was brought up by Kirkjubøur's bishops away from the prying public eye. The cramped room, located right up under the eaves off the Roykstovan, is where the bishops once worked.

Ólavskirkjan church
The whitewashed parish church at Kirkjubøur, dedicated to St Olav, is the oldest still in use in the Faroe Islands. Originally built sometime during the 12th century, most probably around 1111, it served as a cathedral throughout the medieval period but has since been extensively rebuilt and renovated, most notably in 1874 (to save it from falling into the sea) and 1966. Unlike the pew-ends from the cathedral, which were spirited off to Denmark, thankfully the church's exquisitely well-preserved carved Madonna, dating from the 13th century, remained

HIKING TO KIRKJUBØUR FROM TÓRSHAVN

The easy 7km hike to Kirkjubøur takes about two hours and climbs up to around 230m. From Vestaravág harbour head west along J C Svabøes gøta out towards the hospital. Beyond here the road changes its name to Velbastaðvegur, passing the new cemetery and a small industrial estate used by Föroya Bjór. Take the next left, við Sandá, to a farm and the start of the footpath to Kirkjubøur. Go through the gate which marks the end of the homefield and start climbing the hill – turn around and you'll have a fantastic view over Tórshavn and all of Nólsoy. Soon you'll start to see cairns marking two different paths – left to Kirkjubøur and right to Velbastaður. Take the much better-trodden left path and after a short while you'll come across two small lakes where there's a profusion of kittiwakes during the summer months. Still following the cairns, next you'll find a chair built of rocks; oddly for such a remote location, open-air public meetings have been held here since the late 1800s with flags fluttering, national speeches and patriotic songs filling the air. A superb panorama of Hestur, Koltur and Sandoy will come into view beyond here followed by a steady descent towards the tiny offshore islet, Kirkjubøholmur, which was once part of the main village and attached to the mainland. The ruins of a couple of houses can still be seen on the island from Kirkjubøur's heyday during the 15th and 16th centuries, when up to 50 dwellings stood here and the place counted 200 people and 5,000 sheep. The last stretch of the path descends steeply before it turns into a wider track which then leads down into the farming settlement of Kirkjubøur.

in the islands and is today held in the National Museum in Tórshavn. Despite the rebuilding, one interesting feature of the church walls remains: the bricked-up hole in the northern wall, which until leprosy died out in the mid-18th century, was used by lepers, who were not allowed into the church, to listen to the service; be prepared to hunt around a bit to locate it. Unusually for a Faroese church, this one is never locked, making it not only an easy worthwhile visit, but also a welcome haven should the heavens open. Inside the 1.5m-thick walls, you'll find a solemn white-painted interior containing pews of natural wood; the only colour is that of the striking Impressionist painting behind the altar by Sámal Joensen-Mikines of a religious scene depicting a rowing boat. During excavation work in the 1950s, a bishop's staff with a gilded head was discovered in a grave under the floor of the crypt; an uninspiring replica is on display in a glass case near the altar, whereas the original is under the safekeeping of the National Museum.

NÓLSOY

A day trip to the island of Nólsoy is one of the most enjoyable things to do whilst visiting Tórshavn. Not only do you get a superb view of the Faroese capital from the water as the tiny ferry which sails to the island steadily chugs out of the harbour, but it's also a chance to explore the floating humpbacked finger of land that you'll have become distantly familiar with while in Tórshavn, as it's an integral part of the view out to sea from all over town. Nólsoy also has the advantage of being just about the right size to tackle in a day: between ferries there's enough time to explore the village, visit the Faroes' most famous taxidermist to admire his stuffings as well as hike out through unspoilt nature to the stunningly located lighthouse on the island's southern tip. However, should you choose to stay overnight, there's also a chance to visit the largest colony of storm petrels anywhere in the world.

NÓLSOY VILLAGE Even though it's so readily accessible from Tórshavn, Nólsoy village makes a striking comparison with the capital. It's a wonderfully sedate, traditional and slow-moving sort of place where life is concentrated on the tiny harbour immediately below the couple of gently sloping streets that climb the hillside upon which the village perches. On leaving the ferry dock on the quayside, you enter Nólsoy under an archway made by the jawbones of a sperm whale, while being observed by the old men who gather on the couple of benches alongside to chew the fat and eye up the island's visitors.

Getting there and away Although sailing time from Tórshavn to Nólsoy is just 20 minutes, ferry departure times vary from day to day. In addition to two daily sailings, there are several extra trips on most days of the week, with ferries most frequent on weekdays. Ferry times are available at www.ssl.fo.

Tourist information Nólsoy now proudly boasts its own tourist office, the Kunningarstovan (✆ 32 70 60; www.visitnolsoy.fo; ⏰ Jun–Sep 10.00–17.00 daily). Located down by the harbour, it stands just to the left of the whale bone that marks the entrance to the village and is located in the building locals call Petersen's warehouse – actually one of the first shops in the village dating from 1787. There's also a small **café** here serving light refreshments and coffee.

Where to eat and drink Food is available at Nólsoy's new café, **Maggie's**, at Válagøta 26 (⏰ 17.00 until late Mon–Fri, 14.00 until late Sat & Sun; ✆ 32 71 99;

Intent on raising money to build a swimming pool on the island, Nólsoy seaman and adventurer Ove Joensen rowed single-handedly in the summer of 1986 all the way from the Faroes to the *Little Mermaid* statue in Copenhagen. After several previously unsuccessful attempts in 1984 and 1985 (bad weather forced him to turn back), Ove reached the Danish capital in just 41 days after an arduous journey alone in the North Atlantic, routing via the Shetland Islands and the Limfjord in Jutland. Tragically, just a few days before his 40th birthday and just a year after his momentous achievement, Ove slipped on the deck of his boat and fell to his death in the icy November waters off the southern tip of Eysturoy while on his way back to Nólsoy following a day's fishing; it's thought alcohol may have been to blame for the accident. His grave can be visited in the village churchyard to the south of the main village; above the poignant inscription 'the fjord is rowed', the headstone bears a black-and-white photograph of the man and his rowing boat, the *Diana Victoria*.

www.maggies.fo) including fish soup, homemade ice cream and a range of hot and cold drinks. There's also occasional live music here.

Other practicalities There's a **food store** (⊕ *mid-May–mid-Sep 09.30–17.30 Mon–Fri, 09.00–noon Sat, rest of the year 09.30–14.00 & 16.00–17.30 Mon–Fri, 09.00–noon Sat*) and a **post office** (⊕ *11.00–noon Mon, Wed & Fri*) in the food store.

What to see and do It's by the harbour that you'll find a **memorial stone** to Ove Joensen whose heroic achievements (see box, above) are celebrated every year in early August with the *Ovastevnan* – a sort of island games consisting of various sporting challenges held in the school playground, which attracts competitors from across the country; money raised goes towards the swimming pool project, which is still underway. Ove's boat is still proudly kept on the island and is available for viewing in the boatshed below the tourist office who hold the key (*admission is free but you can leave a donation*). Other than the *Diana Victoria*, there's really only one other sight in the village, the **húsini við brunn** (house by the well), an atmospheric, turf-roofed home dating from the 17th century which was originally built of driftwood. However, the eastern part of the structure is made from a single trunk of Pomeranian pine bought at auction following a shipwreck in Saksun in 1829. You'll find the house immediately behind the Kaffistovan. It's open on request through the tourist office; entrance is 30kr. While you're on the island, why not have a look inside the **Heimavirkið**, too, where you'll find a small selection of hand-crafted woollens lovingly produced by Nólsoy's knitters (⊕ *mid-May–mid-Sep 14.00–16.30 Mon–Fri, 11.00–14.00 Sat*). Ask at the tourist office for directions of how to find it.

However, the reason most people come to Nólsoy is to visit **Jens-Kjeld Jensen** (*www.jenskjeld.info*), the Faroes' taxidermist extraordinaire; everything from rabbits to gannets – you name it, he's got it stuffed. Jens-Kjeld doesn't catch the birds himself; instead, he buys them from the islanders, eats them and then stuffs them. However, there's more to Jens-Kjeld's talents than first meets the eye: not only is he the proud owner of Europe's largest private collection of bird lice – at the last count, 240 species of lice have been plucked from obscurity for your delight and delectation – but he also discovered a rare moth that is now named after him, the fabulous *Abromias assimilis jenskjeldi*. Should the urge for something stuffed strike, this is *the* place to buy: small birds cost 500kr while the mighty gannet goes for 1,800kr. It's worth remembering, though, that some countries have import restrictions on stuffed birds. Jens-Kjeld's house (*Í Geilini 37*), a yellow building on the northwestern side of the village, is the last on the road that climbs up left out of the village past the village school; look out for the sign in the window: *udstoppede fugle sælges* – Danish for 'stuffed birds for sale'. Entrance to Jens-Kjelds's workshop is 30kr and is generally possible whenever he's at home. Between June and August Jens-Kjeld also leads night-time excursions (📞 *32 70 64;* ✉ *jkjensen@olivant.fo; or book at the Kunningarstovan or Kaffistovan in Nólsoy*) to the world's largest **storm petrel colony** on Nólsoy's east coast. Tours leave the village one hour before sunset for the 60-minute walk to the colony at Suður í Dølum below the island's main peak, Eggjarklettur (372m). The trips (minimum four people) offer a unique chance to see these nocturnal birds lunge through the night sky at truly remarkable speeds as they search for food, and also to see a number of other species including

BUSINESS AS USUAL: NÓLSOY PÁLL AND THE TRADE MONOPOLY

Without a doubt, Nólsoy's most famous son is also one of the Faroes' greatest heroes: Poul Poulsen or Nólsoy Páll, as he's popularly known. Born on the island in 1766, Páll grew up during the needy years of the Danish Trade Monopoly, which forbade the Faroese to own ships and trade with foreign countries. However, the young Páll was quick to benefit from the opportunities available in Tórshavn, where he learnt boatbuilding and navigation, administration and bookkeeping. Following the American War of Independence (1775–83), when the Faroes served as a strategic base for smuggled goods across the Atlantic, Páll made his first journey overseas to America at the age of 20 to work as a ship's master. It was following his later service on board ships operating between the Faroes and Denmark that he decided to challenge the unjust monopoly. With the aid of friends, he rebuilt the wreck of the *Royndin Fríða*, which had stranded off Hvalba on Suðuroy, and set off on several trading trips to Copenhagen and Bergen; in 1805 he returned to the Faroes from Norway with much-needed smallpox vaccine, traded against Faroese coal. Páll's ship (the *Good Endeavour* in English) was the first trading vessel to be Faroese owned and operated since Viking times and hence marked a significant turning point in the commercial stranglehold the Danes had over the Faroes. However, facing opposition not only from the Danish authorities in Copenhagen but also from the Faroese petty bourgeoisie whose wealth depended on the monopoly's continued existence, Páll in 1807 took his complaint of unfair trading to Crown Prince Fredrik, who agreed that changes were indeed necessary. Although Denmark's fatalistic involvement in the Napoleonic Wars against England put paid to any agreement reached, it's widely believed that Páll's battle against Danish supremacy marked the beginning of the end of the Trade Monopoly, which was finally lifted in 1856. Tragically, it was an achievement Páll never lived to see: in the winter of 1809, at the age of 42, his ship went down whilst transporting a cargo of corn to the famine-stricken Faroe Islands, a pawn in the war between Denmark and England, with all hands lost.

4

The walking path to the lighthouse on Nólsoy's southern tip, Borðan (6km each way; allow 4 to 5 hours there and back), begins just south of the main village beyond the island's narrowest point – literally a few metres across – to the left of which lie rounded basalt rocks thrown up by winter storms; to the right is the harbour. During easterly gales the greater part of the village can be drenched with spray and it's not uncommon for the enormous Atlantic rollers to crash right over the island at this narrow isthmus. Follow the road up past the graveyard through an area known as Korndalur where you may spot several 14th-century stone ruins by the roadside. Still in the homefield, these remains are the *Prinsessutoftir*, said to be the home of the pregnant daughter of a Scottish king, who fell out with her father and fled to Nólsoy after he refused to accept her choice of husband, none other than the man who had fathered her still-unborn child. Once beyond the homefield boundary the made road turns into a path following traces of an old water pipe and eventually reaching a small reservoir. From here cairns mark the steep climb up the lower reaches of the **Eggjaklettur** peak (371m). The path soon levels out and from here on it's an easy, if somewhat soggy walk in parts, along a wide grassy plateau known as **Langabrekka**. There are some truly spectacular views from this part of Nólsoy, both up towards the northern islands as well as south towards Sandoy and – at one point – even the sugar-loaf mountain of Kolturshamar on Koltur can also be spotted. At times the cairns can be hard to pick out and it may be easier to use the two transmitters which will soon come into sight to help guide you towards the southern shore. Once beyond the small lake, Halavatn, it's a steady descent towards the main **lighthouse**, Nólsoyar Viti. At the time of its construction in 1893, the lighthouse boasted one of the largest lenses in the world at nearly 3m in height and four tonnes in weight. The two longhouses beside the lighthouse were built by the British during World War II to act as a decoy and mislead the Germans. Today, they're used solely for accommodating maintenance workers who come here every so often to keep the lighthouse in order. Unbelievably, three families with a total of ten children once lived at this remote outpost; there was even a school here which alternated classes with its equivalent in Nólsoy village. From the lighthouse a path leads down to the landing stage, Stallurin, where all goods in and out of Borðan had to be loaded and unloaded; if you choose to walk down to the landing stage, whose Faroese name 'the stall' was coined since boats here can lie side by side like horses in a stable, it will add another 800m each way to the hike. The smaller lighthouse you can see in the distance to the southwest is a much less impressive affair and not really worth the extra effort in reaching; it's this light that can be seen from Tórshavn, not that of Nólsoyar Viti. Instead sit and enjoy the views from its much bigger brother whose light can be seen from up to 30km at sea. The route back to Nólsoy village simply involves retracing your steps.

fulmars and puffins. Incidentally, Nólsoy's main **puffin colony** is just down the coast from here, beyond the next headland, Nevið, at the cliff face known as Urðin – though it's not a trip you should make in the dark. Accommodation is provided at the Kaffistovan in the village; the cost of the tour is 450kr pp, plus 350kr pp for overnight accommodation in the village.

Separated from southwestern Streymoy by the choppy waters of **Hestfjørður** fjord, the 6km² island of Hestur is home to just 15 people, most of whom live in the cluster of houses grouped around the harbour midway along the sheltered east coast. The steep hillsides which bank up behind the village are indicative of the terrain of much of the rest of the island; the peaks of **Eggjarrók** and **Múlin**, both 421m, dominate the northern and western parts of Hestur and render much of the coast inaccessible. In fact, the uninterrupted sheer cliff faces of the west coast are a haven for many species of bird, particularly guillemot, and, until it became extinct in the 1800s, the great auk was also found here in considerable numbers. From the two peaks, the land gently falls away to the south towards an area of boggy farmland known as **Hælur**, just north of the lighthouse that guards the island's southernmost point, Skútin. It's on this relatively flat tract of land, dotted by several trout-rich lakes including the poetically named **Fagradalsvatn** (literally 'lake of the beautiful valley') that most of the island's farming takes place, since the land around the village of Hestur itself is too steep.

GETTING THERE AND AWAY A trip to Hestur requires careful planning since there are very few sailings; on certain departures the ferry between Gamlarætt and Skopun calls in at Hestur. Timetables are prone to change so check carefully for the latest information at www.ssl.fo.

OTHER PRACTICALITIES Although there's no accommodation on Hestur, it is possible to camp near the lakes at **Hælur** though you should bring all provisions with you since there are no facilities on the island and nowhere to buy food. Curiously for such a small place, Hestur also has a **swimming pool** to which every inhabitant has a key; it's in the modern-looking building up behind the school, although it's not open to the public.

THE ISLAND Although three fishing boats still put out from Hestur, the island has suffered severe depopulation over the years as men have moved to Tórshavn to work on larger ocean-going vessels and earn considerably more money. However, in an attempt to stem the outflow of people, a new harbour and breakwater were built in order to operate a car ferry all year round.

Peaceful and uneventful, Hestur is the place to come if you want to experience the Faroes at their most remote without trekking up to the far north of the country: the island's charms are to be found in a stroll up and down the one and only road that runs the length of the east coast, petering out past the Hvannagjógv cleft at the lighthouse (allow one hour in each direction), or a hike up to the high land known as **Heyggjur**. Although there are no marked walking paths on the island, it is possible, with local advice, to reach the flat-topped Eggjarrók and Múlin peaks, where some really quite stunning views unfold. Up here you're well above the hills that divide Kirkjubøur from Tórshavn over on Streymoy and you have picture-perfect vistas of neighbouring Koltur, barely a couple of kilometres away across Kolturssund sound.

KOLTUR

Dwarfed by its much bigger northerly neighbour, Koltur – measuring in at just 2km² – may be the third smallest of all the Faroe Islands (ahead only of Stóra and Lítla Dímun), but it is certainly one of the most beautiful and is now a national park.

Faroese poet R C Effersøe used a true story from Koltur as the basis for one of his best-loved plays, *Magnus*. Having fallen in love with a girl from Hestur, local boy Magnus would swim on the ebb tide from the island's southernmost point, Kolturstangi, across to the Hestsboði promontory on Hestur to meet his sweetheart, returning several hours later on the flood tide which would sweep him back home. However, the girl's disapproving father finally snapped and waited for Magnus at Hestsboði with an axe threatening to kill him if he came ashore. Magnus was tragically never seen again after turning back for Koltur and swimming in the icy waters against the strong tidal current which rushes through Kolturssund sound between the two islands.

More than half of this long and skinny island is made up of **Kolturshamar**, the ice cream-cone-shaped peak soaring to a height of 478m that bears down ominously on the solitary farm here, today the only human habitation on the isle.

GETTING THERE AND AWAY Since Koltur is home to just one family, visiting the island is not really practical. However, should you be flying on the helicopter you may well land here, skimming the vertical cliff faces that make up Koltur's western coast and clipping the top of Kolturshamar en route to your final destination – a truly breathtaking experience. Schedules are available at www.atlantic.fo. Note, too, that it's not possible to stay overnight on Koltur.

THE ISLAND During Koltur's heyday in the 1900s, a couple of dozen people lived here working four dairy farms. Quite unbelievably for such a remote outpost, the islanders even had their own teacher who shuttled back and forth from Hestur to instruct the handful of children who once lived here.

Although, as time passed, just two farming families shared the narrow isthmus of fertile land at the foot of the mountain (albeit without speaking to each other following a bitter row), they deserted the island after succumbing to the bright lights of Tórshavn. Life on Koltur has always been tough, not least in winter when the shortage of fuel forced people to make the often hazardous journey through open water to Skopun on Sandoy to cut turf. Indeed, during the worst of the ferocious winter gales which sweep in unopposed off the Atlantic, the low-lying southern end of the island between Kolturshamar and the smaller hill, Fjallið, was regularly inundated by the huge waves that can crash right over tiny Koltur. Needless to say, Koltur stood abandoned for several years until new life was finally breathed back into this most inscrutable isle in the mid 1990s. The current farmer, Bjørn Patursson, and his wife, fell for its charms and moved here to resume the long farming tradition tending sheep and Scottish Highland cattle. With the help of the Faroese Museum Society, the Heima í húsi settlement on the island has now been restored to how it would have looked around the year 1000 at the time of the Settlement: the architectural style of the two main dwellings here with their sturdy stone walls and turf rooves, plus all the various surrounding outhouses and barns which formed a core part of the original site, is rooted in the longhouses built by the islands' first Viking settlers. Although the reconstruction took ten years to complete, Koltur can now boast an ancient settlement which showcases Faroese history from 1,000 years ago.

Slicing deep into the southern portion of Streymoy, **Kaldbaksfjørður** fjord and its one principal village, **Kaldbak**, are within easy striking distance of Tórshavn, making a short but pleasant excursion if time is limited. The head of the fjord, 11km to the northwest of the capital, is known as **Kaldbaksbotnur** and is today the location for several fish farms producing salmon, trout and mussels. It's from here that Route 523 swings off to the right to follow the inlet's northern shore, passing several waterfalls cascading down the precipitous hillsides, all the way to Kaldbak, a further 4km away at the mouth of the fjord. The route to reach this unspoilt village, home to around 200 people, may be circuitous but it has at least helped spare the place the fate that befell the farmstead of Sund on the opposite shore. There, the historic smallholding, reputed to be one of the most beautifully located in the entire country, was levelled to make way for an industrial development that never saw the light of day.

GETTING THERE AND AWAY Kaldbak is best visited as a short day trip from Tórshavn. City bus #5 (journey time around 30 minutes) runs here from the capital six times daily (Monday–Friday); timetables are available at www.torshavn.fo.

KALDBAK As pleasant as Kaldbak may be, the real reason to come here is not to see the village itself, but to visit one of the oldest timber churches in the country. Enjoying a superb location right on the fjordside inside an immaculate dry-stone wall, the black-tarred walls, white window frames and turf roof of this **church** were constructed in 1835, making it one of only ten such structures in the country and undoubtedly one of the easiest to reach from Tórshavn. What makes this church stand out from the others is the unusual carving that decorates the screen dividing the choir from the nave. It appears that the craftsmen who carved this particular screen ditched the stylised patterns they'd been given of the much-favoured tree of life, which adorns several others elsewhere in the country, and actually created their own designs and patterns, including a number of violins. Ask any local person to be let into the church and they'll point you in the direction of the warden who has the key.

Although there's little else to see or do in Kaldbak, before leaving make sure to glance across the fjord to the southern shore and pinpoint the waterfall virtually opposite Kaldbak; this point is known as **Kallanes**, literally 'calling point', and it's from here that people would shout across the fjord to get messages to the villagers, hence saving a lengthy journey around the head of the fjord.

KALLANES: THE NEW GATEWAY TO EYSTUROY

In September 2015 initial work began on the construction of a new **sub-sea tunnel** which, on scheduled completion in 2019, will link the Tórshavn area with southern Eysturoy, significantly reducing the journey time between the capital and Runavík on Eysturoy and, accordingly, also Klaksvík in the northern islands. The new tunnel will be around 7.5km in length and will link **Kallanes** on Streymoy with both the western and eastern shores of Skálafjørður on Eysturoy. From Kallanes the tunnel will first come ashore on Eysturoy just south of Strendur before continuing underwater again to emerge just west of Runavík. Currently, the distance from Kallanes to Runavík is around 58km, routing via the Kollfjarðar tunnel and the bridge across to Eysturoy at Oyrarbakki. Once the new tunnel opens, the driving distance is expected to be under 10km.

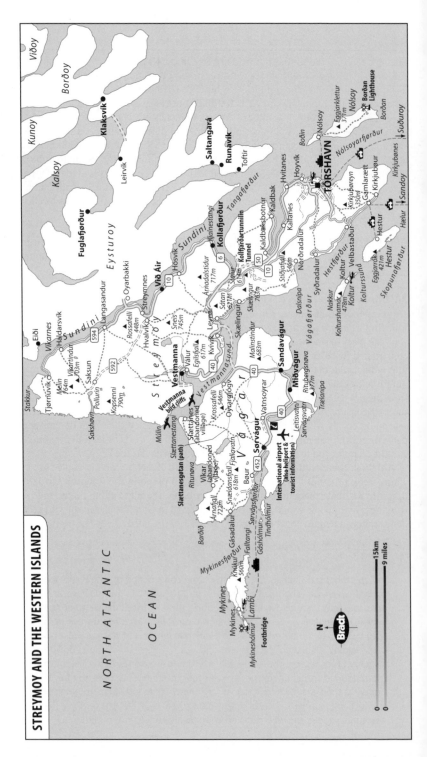

STREYMOY AND THE WESTERN ISLANDS

5

Streymoy and the Western Islands

The largest and longest of the Faroe Islands, measuring around 50km from Tjørnuvík in the north to Kirkjubønes in the south, **Streymoy** is named after the strong current, *streymur* in Faroese (*oy* is simply a shortened form of *oyggj* meaning 'island'), which rips up both the west and east coasts at speeds of up to 20 knots, slowing any vessel in its path. Located at the heart of the country and sheltered to a large extent from the elements by its neighbours, Vágar to the west and Eysturoy to the east, this was the first of the islands to be settled. Geographically, Streymoy can be divided neatly into two portions, the deep waters of **Kaldbaksfjørður** acting as a natural barrier. Emerging north of the fjord from the Kollafjarðar tunnel, which links the less rugged southern area of the island around Tórshavn with the more mountainous central and northern sections, an altogether different landscape unfolds. This part of Streymoy is essentially a land of deep valleys and craggy peaks; in fact, the western and northern coasts are almost perpendicular bird cliffs. Several of the mountains in the far northwest of the island are well over 700m high: **Melin** (764m) and **Kopsenni** (790m) both dominate the landscape for miles around. Although Streymoy is home to around 20,000 people, only one person in five lives outside Tórshavn, making large parts of the island virtually empty. Indeed, large parts of the western side of the island are totally uninhabited; villages tend to be concentrated on the flatter, more fertile eastern side of the island, which forms an almost straight line between Tjørnuvík and Kollafjørður.

Now linked to its bigger brother to the east by a tunnel under the choppy waters of Vestmannasund sound, **Vágar** is an altogether less dramatic island than Streymoy, though that's not to say it's without charm. In fact, what makes this island particularly appealing is the abundance of excellent walking paths that criss-cross the relatively flat centre of the island dominated by the lake, **Fjallavatn**. Vágar's other much larger lake, known as both **Leitisvatn** and **Sørvágsvatn** depending on who you're talking to, is one of the Faroes' most unusual natural features. Shaped like a twisting snake, this sizeable body of water is bound along its length by two equal hillsides yet by just the merest sliver of land at its seaward side, over which the impressive Bøsdalafossur waterfall cascades into the Atlantic below.

Beyond Vágar, **Mykines** is the most remote of all the Faroe Islands and certainly the most beautiful. Shaped like a favourite old cap with the Faroes' most westerly extremity, **Mykineshólmur** islet, as its peak, this enigmatic island can often be cut off for days during bad weather. Indeed, it's the tremendous erosive power of the Atlantic that has sculpted the island's highly indented coastline, gnawed into countless craggy inlets over the centuries. From behind the turf-roofed houses that make up the solitary village here, the land rises steeply in ever-changing shades of green through the tussocky outfield of Djúpidalur valley up to the heights of Knúkur peak (560m) with its sweeping views. However, it's for its rich birdlife that

Mykines has deservedly become a traveller's favourite; if you haven't yet seen a puffin, the chances are you will here, because hundreds of them nest in burrows in the clifftops either side of the deep Hólmgjógv cleft which divides Mykines from Mykineshólmur.

WHERE TO GO

Like much of the rest of the Faroe Islands, Streymoy is blessed with a network of good roads which links even the most remote village with the capital in around an hour or so. Heading north from Tórshavn, **Kollafjørður** is the first stop, where the traditional timber church, dating from 1837, is immediately visible by the roadside. Although there's little else to see in the village, Kollafjørður is also the starting point for an enjoyable coast-to-coast hike up over the curiously named Sátan peak (621m) to the village of **Leynar** on Streymoy's western shore. Rounding the head of the fjord, the road now clings to the shores of Sundini, the narrow sound separating Streymoy from Eysturoy, *en route* to the former whaling station at **við Áir**, today a fish research centre, and the charming village of **Hvalvík**, home to another timber church, and a parting of the ways. From here, Route 592 heads northwest through the lonely Saksunardalur valley, to its namesake, **Saksun**, one of the most worthwhile destinations in the country. Stunningly set in a natural circular amphitheatre high above a tidal lagoon, this remote outpost is home to a fascinating museum recounting farming traditions over the centuries; there's also a pleasant walk to be had down to the lagoon and the shore. Back in Hvalvík, the main road continues north to the Faroes' only octagonal church, a most unusual sight, in **Haldarsvík**, before arriving in gloriously pastoral **Tjørnuvík**, a village as typically Faroese as they come with old wooden houses overlooking potato allotments down on the sandy beach.

Heading west from Tórshavn, Route 40 branches off left just beyond the Kollfjarðartunnilin tunnel bound for **Kvívík**, with its handful of Viking-age remains, and **Vestmanna**, a workaday fishing village, on Streymoy's west coast. Although not especially attractive in itself, Vestmanna is the departure point for one of the best excursions in the country: a trip to Vestmanna **bird cliffs**, which ranks as the highlight of any trip to Streymoy. Small boats wind their way under rock arches and around stacks to provide you with an unparalleled view of the sheer cliffs teeming with seabirds.

Although Vestmanna was once linked to Vágar by ferry, all traffic between Streymoy and Vágar now passes under rather than over Vestmannasund sound thanks to a tunnel, which opened in 2002. On reaching this often overlooked island, Route 40 winds its way past the uneventful villages of Sandavágur and Miðvágur heading for yet another *vágur* (Faroese for 'bay'), **Sørvágur**, the best base on the island and also the home of the airport. It's from here that the main network of walking trails extends northwards towards Fjallavatn lake. West of here, the hamlets of **Bøur** and all-but-forgotten **Gásadalur** (before a tunnel was built in 2004 the last village without a road connection), offer a plentiful taste of off-the-beaten-track Faroes.

However, it's **Mykines** that really steals the show. A must for any visitor to the islands, this remote outpost is quite simply the best of all the Faroes and you should allow it plenty of time, not least because the unpredictable weather out here often cancels ferry and helicopter departures. Brooding and sombre on occasions, alluring and seductive at others, this is the most verdant of all the islands and, without a doubt, the most enjoyable destination in the entire country. Spend a few days here exploring the delights of Mykines's rolling hills and precipitous cliffs; take a stroll out amid the puffin burrows of **Lambi**; cross the suspension bridge over to the islet of **Mykineshólmur** and gaze out at the open Atlantic from the lighthouse at the Faroes' most westerly point and you'll soon see what all the fuss is about.

GETTING AROUND

With the exception of Mykines, Saksun, Bøur and Gásadalur, all destinations in this chapter are reachable by **bus**. When travelling between Tórshavn and Tjørnuvík you should make connections at **Oyrarbakki** which is served by #400 operating between Tórshavn and Klaksvík.

In addition to the #400, Tórshavn city buses also operate to Kollafjørður.

KOLLAFJØRÐUR AND AROUND

Kollafjørður is a textbook example of a linear village, houses and the odd shop strung out in a long line along the main road which hugs the northern shore of the fjord of the same name. Although home today to around 800 people, the original settlement consisted of no more than a handful of dwellings tightly clustered around the timber church, which is still the focal point of the village. Built in 1837, a couple of years later than its near-identical neighbour in Kaldbak, the church shows the classic construction techniques of black-tarred walls, white windows, turf roof and white clocktower. There are generally subtle differences between all the wooden churches in the Faroes and the Kollafjørður example is no exception: the windows support an upper arch divided into three glass panes by radial bars. Admittedly, it's not a line that's going to make it onto your postcards home, but if you're passing, the church – and its windows – are worth a quick stop. Once you've seen the church, there's no real reason to tarry and it's probably wise to push on round the head of the fjord towards Hósvík.

THE COAST-TO-COAST HIKE: KOLLAFJØRÐUR TO LEYNAR

Stretching northeast from the head of Kollafjørður fjord, the narrow valley of Kollafjarðardalur marks the starting point of the 4.5km hike (allow 2½ hours) over the hills to Leynar on Streymoy's western coast. The path begins at the Búnaðardepilin farming centre between the northern exit of the Kollafjarðar tunnel (which is served by buses #100, 300, 400 and city bus #4 from Tórshavn) and the roundabout where the road splits left for Vágar and right for Eysturoy. Follow the middle of three rivers, the Brekká, from the farming centre up the hillside heading for the cairn in front of you; the going is a little steep at this point. The path takes you over the old mountain road from Tórshavn, the Oyggjarvegurin (Route 10), towards the next cairn and on towards Skælingsvatn lake. According to legend a horse-like creature once lived in this remote mountain tarn, which is also the meeting point for several walking trails. There are good views from here of some of Streymoy's tallest mountains: to the south Skælingur (763m), once mistakenly thought to be the island's highest; north to Sátan (621m), named after its resemblance to a haystack); and southeast to Stalur (614m). Now, following the cairns, it's downhill all the way to Leynar with some good vistas of Vágar and, a little later, of Koltur, out ahead of you. From Leynar bus #100 runs back to Tórshavn.

PRACTICALITIES Opposite the church at Við Sjógv 68, **Café Chill** (📞 *47 14 71;* ⏰ *17.00–22.00 Sun–Thu, 17.00–02.00 Fri & Sat*) is a pleasant little bar and bistro, which has also an outdoor terrace. The mainstay here is pizzas but with a little cajoling you might persuade them to stretch to a steak. Friday is pub quiz night. Below the restaurant, there's a **food store** (⏰ *10.00–22.00 Mon–Thu, 08.00–22.00 Fri & Sat*) where you should ask about the key to the church.

HÓSVÍK Rounding Kjalnestangi point at the head of Kollafjørður fjord, Route 10 now meanders along the western shore of Sundini sound, across which there are clear views of neighbouring Eysturoy. In fact, the next settlement along the road, Hósvík, was once the transit point for all traffic from Streymoy bound for Eysturoy and the northern islands. However, with the opening of a bridge across the sound further north at Nesvík, the ferry which once shuttled over to Selatrað on the opposite shore was taken out of service. During Viking times, Hósvík was known as Tórsvík, after the Norse god Thor, and was the site of a pagan worship place. However, with the introduction of Christianity the *hof*, as it's known in Faroese, was converted into a church which stood until the time of the Reformation. Today though, other than the waterfall which tumbles down the hillside behind Hósvík, there's little else to see.

THE VIÐ ÁIR WHALING STATION A couple of kilometres beyond Hósvík, you'll come across the former whaling station, Við Áir, which was built by the Norwegians in 1905, who operated it for 30 years. It is the only one of the original seven whaling stations built in the Faroes in the early 1900s whose buildings have not been demolished and only one of three such stations still standing anywhere in the world (the other two are in South Georgia and Australia). Located beside two rivers that reach the sound here (*Við Áir* means 'by the rivers'), the rusting reds and greens of the derelict corrugated iron buildings and winding gear may look like a Hollywood film set today, but until 1958 this place was buzzing with life. Harpooned sperm, fin and sei whales were offloaded from ships onto the slipways to be unceremoniously sliced up al fresco ready to be turned into fish oil, prepared for fodder for export or sold as meat to ships and local households. The station was still used intermittently during the 60s and 70s and the last whale came ashore here in 1984. Until the early 60s, whaling contributed significantly to the industrialisation of the Faroes and accordingly, there are now plans to turn the site into an open-air museum to preserve what was once an important part of Faroese culture; see www.savn.fo for the latest details.

HVALVÍK A further 6km north of Hósvík and home to around 200 people, Hvalvík (literally 'whale bay') nestles around the expansive mouth of the Stórá river, the Faroes' biggest river and renowned for its excellent salmon fishing; it's thought the village is named after the countless whales that have been stranded on the estuary sands. Undoubtedly one of Streymoy's prettiest villages, Hvalvík benefits from being set back from the main Route 10, straddling instead the minor road that leads off to Saksun. It's the **traditional houses**, painted in subtle shades of red, yellow and green, that help to make the centre of the village so charming, dominated by the **timber church** that has been the focal point of Hvalvík since its construction in 1829. The oldest of all the wooden churches in the islands, this one was built of pine bought from a ship that was stranded in nearby Saksun in 1829; earlier the same year the church that originally stood here was destroyed by a ferocious storm. Inside, the pulpit, which the church acquired in 1790, is quite something; built in 1609, it was originally used in the old church in Tórshavn until it was seized by French pirates

From the centre of Hvalvík a 10km hike (allow 3½ hours) leads up through the remote mountain valley of Bjarnadalur over to Vestmanna on the western Streymoy coast. The trail begins where the Myllá river enters the village, roughly halfway along the village's one main road. Follow the north bank of the river through a gate and along a fenced track that's been used over the years for herding cattle. Look out for a cairn located after the Hvalvíkgjógv cleft. From here the path continues upwards towards **Eggjarmúli hill** where you meet the overhead electricity cables which serve Vestmanna and lead all the way there. From this point there are superb views of Saksunardalur valley running to the northwest. Next you'll come across a cairn built on top of a large rock known as **Kellingarsteinur**. At the next cairn you have a choice: the right path takes you on to Vestmanna, whereas the trail cutting off to the left leads down to Kvívík. You now walk through Bjarnadalur valley between the twin peaks of Moskursfjall (624m) to the north and Loysingafjall (639m) to the south, about which there are several tales. One account is of a girl from Vestmanna who was found high on the mountain by a shepherd after she'd disappeared from home, claiming she'd been led there by a ghostly figure dressed in white, whereas the other story concerns a young milkmaid who fell into the Gjógvará river hereabouts and was carried away down a waterfall. She was eventually found on the mountain wretched and naked and living in fear of the *huldufolk*, the Faroes' hidden elves and spirits.

Emerging from the valley at the Fossá dam, you again have two choices, though this time both paths lead to **Vestmanna**: either you can follow the road off to the left and walk down to an area known as á Fjørð, or you continue straight on, passing around the dam, still following the cairns and the Gjógvará river (of milkmaid fame) which then leads down into the village.

There's public transport to both ends of this hike: bus #400 runs to Hvalvík from Tórshavn and service #100 runs from Vestmanna back to Tórshavn.

---

during a raid in 1677. In fact it's said that slashes to the woodwork were caused by the pirates' swords. Certainly, the church with wild flowers growing in its turf roof is of striking elemental beauty, and its setting is wonderfully enhanced by the shady grove of trees decorating the churchyard behind.

Moving on from Hvalvík presents two opportunities. Route 592 to **Saksun** loyally follows every twist and turn of the wide but shallow Stórá, before finally crossing it at the point where the river reaches the valley bottom after tumbling down to sea level from the mountains above. The road then picks up the course of the Dalá river as it traverses the longest valley in the Faroes, **Saksunardalur**: a wonderful switchback ride through the austere beauty of the valley marked at its northern end by the popular fishing lake, **Saksunarvatn**. Alternatively, Route 10 continues north to what the Faroese claim is the only bridge across the North Atlantic, the 220m-long Brúgvin um Streymin, which now carries all traffic heading over to Eysturoy. At this point, known as Nesvík, Route 10 swings east to Norðskáli, on the opposite side of the bridge, whereas Route 594 sticks to the shores of Sundini on its journey north to Streymoy's last two settlements, **Haldarsvík** and **Tjørnuvík**.

SAKSUN Barely 30 people today live in Saksun, a wonderfully remote hillside village strung out along the banks of the Dalá river close to Streymoy's northwestern

Streymoy and the Western Islands   KOLLAFJØRÐUR AND AROUND

5

tip, which has become a favourite summer day trip for many Faroese. The setting is austere in the extreme: high rocky knolls bear down on the tiny settlement on three sides, creating the impression of a natural amphitheatre. The western end of the village overlooks the **Pollurin tidal lagoon**, a circular body of water virtually enclosed by sheer craggy cliff walls over which the Gellingará river tumbles into the lagoon.

Getting there and away Since the withdrawal of the (albeit limited) bus service to Saksun, your only choices to get here are to either drive or hike from Tjørnuvík or Haldarsvík (see box, page 82), which are both connected by service #202 to Oyrarbakki and ultimately Tórshavn.

19TH-CENTURY TIMBER CHURCHES

If you come to the Faroes looking for ancient architectural monuments such as those found in other European countries, you'll return home sadly disappointed. As in neighbouring Iceland, the main building material of the Middle Ages was untreated wood, which simply didn't withstand the rigours of time and climate and rotted away. However, as the economic circumstances of the islands improved in the early 19th century, building techniques were refined and a design of church was perfected which was more able to withstand the salty air and damp conditions that prevail in the midst of the North Atlantic. Between 1829 and 1847, around a dozen traditional timber churches were built across the country. Based on the same design, the churches are composed of double timber walls, which sit on top of a foundation of solid rock which is always painted white. In contrast, the walls are covered with black tar as protection against the weather and support a turf roof. Although the turf was originally laid on a layer of straw or birch bark imported from Scandinavia, a synthetic base is now used instead; all Faroese timber churches have turf roofs except those in Nes and Strendur, whose roofs are made of slate and cement tiles respectively. A low wooden belltower which can be either parallel or perpendicular to the main entrance hall is found at the western end. A small staircase leads up into the tower and to a balcony which extends over the rear of the nave from behind the main door. Time has given the nave, plain in the extreme and usually made of unpainted scrubbed pine, a warm golden colour. Accessed through a second door, the nave consists of fixed wooden pews either side of the aisle which leads to a carved screen which stands in front of the altar and the font. The latticework adornments to the choral wall generally consist of various forms of crosses, flora and decorative patterns and were made by the same carpenters and boatbuilders who constructed the churches themselves. Normally the northern part of the choir is partitioned off by a wall forming a sacristy giving direct access to the pulpit, which in all Faroese churches is located on the northern side. Although all these churches are locked against theft, if you ask around in each village you'll eventually come across someone who keeps the key; you'll find the oldest-surviving examples in Hvalvík (1829), Norðragøta (1833), Strendur (1834), Kaldbak (1835), Kollafjørður (1837), Oyndarfjørður (1838), Sandur (1839), Nes (1843), Funningur (1847) and Porkeri (1847). Sunday service is usually held at either 11.00 or noon.

The village At the entrance to the village, on the northern end of Saksunarvatn lake, there's a choice of roads: the left turn takes you down amongst the jumble of farm buildings and houses that make up the minute centre of Saksun (a track continues from the end of this road toward Pollurin), whereas the main road crosses the river and continues in a relatively straight line, on the eastern side of the river, to the **village church** and the **Dúvugarðar museum** (m 21 07 00; www.savn.fo; ☉ mid-Jun–Aug 14.00–17.00 daily; admission 30kr), an excellent snapshot of life on a Faroese farm from the Middle Ages to the early 20th century. Located by the main roadside opposite the church, the long stone walls and turf roof of the sturdy Dúvugarðar farmhouse are immediately apparent: around 300 years old in parts, this was the main building on the farm and was inhabited until World War II. After passing through a small outer porch you enter the main room, the *roykstova*, which traditionally served as an all-purpose kitchen, workroom and living room centred on the open fire that once burned in here on the dirt floor, which has been preserved. Smoke escaped through a hole in the ceiling, which also provided the only source of daylight in the room. Alcoves in the walls served as beds for the farm workers. Although the present construction dates from around 1820, an older *roykstova* stood on the same spot. Next door, the *glasstova*, so called because it was often the only room in a house with a window, was used as both sleeping quarters for the farmer and his wife and a parlour where guests would be entertained on Sundays and holidays. This room was heated by an oven which was filled with embers through a hole in the wall behind the main fire in the *roykstova*. About 160 years ago, to coincide with the construction of the church in Saksun in 1858, an extension was made to the *glasstova* to provide living accommodation for the local priest who resided in Kvívík. Naturally known as the *prestastova*, or priest's room, the extension consisted of a kitchen, bedroom, dining and sitting room though it was only used when the priest visited once every two months or when the house was full of guests. Throughout the farmhouse you'll find examples of old tools and implements that once formed part of daily life: everything from weighing scales marked up in the former imperial Faroese measures to special combs for preparing wool for spinning. Although a handful of other smaller buildings are open to the public, such as a meat-drying hut and a turf shed, it's worth remembering that they are all still in use by the current farmers, Jógvan and Richa, and you should show due consideration when wandering around their property.

Opposite the museum, the **stone church** enjoys one of the most dramatic positions in the whole of the islands, standing proud high above the Pollurin lagoon from inside a turf-topped stone wall. Although a small chapel once existed in Saksun, it only survived until the Reformation after which people had to trek 2 hours over the mountains to neighbouring Tjørnuvík to attend church. In fact, the timber in today's church was shipped west around the headland from Tjørnuvík to help rebuild a church for the village. Unusually, one of the walls is composed almost entirely of vast rectangular windows allowing a generous view of the unadorned interior; unpainted pine walls, floor and roof create a picture of total simplicity.

Pollurin tidal lagoon While you're in Saksun it's worth making the effort to walk down to the lagoon, from where it's possible to continue on to the open sea. The best approach is from the western side of the Dalá river – remember, though, that you should not walk through fields of fresh grass (a precious resource for the two farms on this side of the river) when heading down to the lagoon; stick to the path and follow the river. At low tide it's possible to walk along the sandy shore of the lagoon around the headland which marks the neck of Pollurin round to the

5

To reach the beginning of the walking trail (2 hours) that leads from Saksun up over the Melin peak (764m) to Tjørnuvík and Haldarsvík on Streymoy's eastern shore, you need to press on from the Dúvugarðar museum to the farm at the main road. Once here, look for the stable block and you'll see a nearby fence; this is where you start. Cross the fence and follow the cairns and you'll begin to climb the steep hillside up behind Saksun heading slightly towards the northwest. At around 400m, the path splits to work around the base of **Melin**, giving you a choice. The left route heads north for Tjørnuvík along the eastern side of the Frammi í Dal valley, marked at its head by the Tjørnuvíksskarð pass; you pass through before heading gradually downhill southeast of the **Heyggjurin Mikli** peak (692m) for the steep grassy hillsides that form the backdrop to Tjørnuvík. The alternative path cuts off right for the Skipá river which descends back towards the Dúvugarðar farm; once over the river the path continues towards Haldarsvík by climbing through Skipádalur valley to the **Víkarskarð** pass squeezed in tight between the peaks of **Víkartindur** (703m) to the west and **Gívrufelli** (701m) to the east. The climb is now over and it's now a pleasant and gradual descent along a path known as Saksunarvegurin down to Haldarsvík. See page 83, for details of buses back to Oyrarbakki.

sea. At high tide, it's best to follow the path a little higher up the hillside; the surf crashing against the narrow sandy inlet to Pollurin is quite a remarkable sight.

HALDARSVÍK Back in Hvalvík, Route 10 continues north to the bridge over to Eysturoy and the junction with Route 594 which heads out to Streymoy's northernmost settlements, Haldarsvík and Tjørnuvík. Although the road is well surfaced, it is extremely narrow in parts, predominantly after the small cluster of houses that is Langasandur, around which there are several large fish farms. Roughly halfway along its length, the Faroes' highest **waterfall** comes cascading down to sea level; connected to Víkarvatn lake high on the hills of the Vatnfelli peak above the road, the Fossá river falls majestically from a height of 140m over two rocky outcrops before passing under the bridge carrying Route 594 and finally reaching the waters of Sundini sound. There's a stopping place just after the bridge should you wish to pause and admire the spectacle. Beyond the falls, it's just another 3km further to **Haldarsvík**, an average-sized fishing village home to around 160 people.

Most of the 50 or so brightly coloured houses here are tightly clustered around the small harbour, which provides superb shelter from the currents in Sundini, and the Kluftá river which flows down through the village from the hills above in a series of wide and lazy cascades. However, it's the highly unusual **octagonal church**, the only one in the country, that grabs your eye as you pass through the settlement. Built in 1856 on the instigation of the local Danish priest, Pruts, the curiously shaped white stone walls, heightened in 1932, are certainly an unusual sight. Inside the plain whitewashed interior, it's the striking painting by Tórshavn artist, Torbjørn Olssen, behind the altar that immediately catches the eye: sandal-wearing apostles at the Last Supper portrayed in sharp angular shapes and a mêlée of blues, greens, reds and yellows. The keyholder lives in the house opposite the church beside the main road as it climbs out of the village; she works at the kindergarten in the centre of the village.

Up on the hill behind the church, there's a contemporary monument erected in 1982 to all those who have lost their lives at sea; the work of Fridtjof Joensen, who intended it to symbolise eternity, the sculpture consists of stainless-steel arches twisting over a revolving metallic globe.

There are no facilities in Haldarsvík. For details of bus services, see *Getting there and away*, below, for Tjørnuvík.

TJØRNUVÍK

On leaving Haldarsvík and rounding the Víkarnes headland, excellent views open up across Sundini to Eiði on the northwest tip of Eysturoy. As you drive this narrow stretch bound for end-of-the-road Tjørnuvík, it's easy to see why it was one of the last sections of the road network to be built; the soaring sides of Hægstafjall (470m) reach virtually all the way to the shore leaving little room for any form of path; indeed the track that connected the two villages before the road was so steep and treacherous that it demanded a steady nerve to avoid a precipitous drop into the sound below.

At the head of a deep fjord that slices into the northern Streymoy shore, Tjørnuvík enjoys the most stunning setting of any settlement in the Faroe Islands. Surrounded on three sides by towering mountain walls and opening out to the sea on its eastern edge across the narrow fjord, the village lies in what the Faroese call a *botnur*, a glacial circular valley formed during the ice age, where the roar of the sea combined with the rushing waterfalls that descend behind the village is exhilarating.

GETTING THERE AND AWAY AND PRACTICALITIES Both Haldarsvík and Tjørnuvík have a limited bus service with most departures scheduled for the afternoon (timetables are available at www.ssl.fo), linking them to each other and Oyrarbakki for connections to and from Tórshavn. For details of the hike between Tjørnuvík (and Haldarsvík) and Saksun, see box, page 82. Other than a small **handicrafts store** hidden away at the back of the village and the **public toilet** at the entrance to Tjørnuvík, there are no facilities here.

THE VILLAGE Tjørnuvík's steep hillsides have been responsible for a couple of natural disasters over the centuries: in 1633 and 1868 rockfalls virtually destroyed

LINKING THE VIKING WORLD: TJØRNUVÍK'S ANCIENT BURIAL SITE

Although Tjørnuvík's greatest attraction is, arguably, its enchanting location, there's also one other thing of interest in the village: a **Viking burial site**. Excavation work on the poorly signed site, which lies beside a series of hay-drying racks and before the small car park and toilets on the right-hand side of the road, took place in the 1950s and astonishingly uncovered 12 graves that had been dug into an area of shifting sand. The bodies inside, all sadly in a poor state of preservation, were found lying on their backs; only in one case, that of a young woman, was it possible to verify the sex of the skeletons. Various everyday articles such as a fragment of a knife, a bronze buckle and a boat nail were also found, but it was a ring-headed bronze pin, common in the northwest Atlantic during the Viking period, that enabled archaeologists to date the finds to the 10th or early 11th century. This pin, which is of Celtic origin, is proof that links existed between the various Nordic settlements to the south in the British Isles and those in the Faroe Islands; today the finds are kept by the National Museum in Tórshavn and what remains in Tjørnuvík is a collection of moss-covered stones arranged in the shape of individual graves.

5

the tiny settlement, which even today barely counts 70 inhabitants. A network of dykes and stone walls behind the village now offers protection from falling rocks and enables the rich farmland at the foot of the mountains to be cultivated for hay and vegetables. Potatoes are also grown in the patchwork of allotments that lines the black-sand beach at the head of the fjord; incidentally, from here there are some superb views of the **Risin** and **Kellingin** sea stacks that lie just off the north coast of Eysturoy. Behind the beach a couple of narrow roads wind past a dozen or so turf-roofed old timber houses of the village and make a pleasant stroll; it's here, at the back of the village, that you'll find a small handicrafts store selling a few homemade woollens and knick-knacks. If you're looking for remarkable views of Tjørnuvík's dramatic location, you'll find the descent into the village, after rounding the mouth of the fjord, provides the best place for photographs.

WEST TO KVÍVÍK AND VESTMANNA

With your own transport, it's worth considering taking the old mountain road, Route 10, north from Tórshavn for some fantastic views of several fjords and the mountains that form the backbone of this part of southern Streymoy. Although today the **Oyggjarvegurin**, as it's known in Faroese (literally 'island road'), is simply an alternative way of heading north from the capital and avoiding the Kollfjarðar tunnel, until 1992, when the tunnel opened, it was the only way in and out of Tórshavn. From its starting point just west of the Nordic House on the Norðari Ringvegur, the road climbs steeply up towards Hotel Føroyar and the couple of transmitters perched on the rocky hill behind, before swinging right and reaching a flat plateau at around 300m above sea level. From this exposed stretch of road there are superlative views east down over Kaldbaksfjørður. Here, high in the mountains at the head of the fjord, the Danes maintain a military base over which a giant red-and-white flag flies in the wind. Just beyond here, a left turn leads up to **Sornfelli** peak (749m), the site of the giant radar dishes that are NATO's early warning station in the Faroes. The mountain is also a favourite destination for the people of Tórshavn who come up here during the long light summer evenings to enjoy the fantastic views out over the surrounding islands. Incidentally, the fjord you can see stretching away to the east from here is **Kollafjørður**. Beyond here the road begins the gradual descent into the Kollafjarðardalur valley ahead; at its end it forms a T-junction with Route 40 which leads west to Kvívík, Vestmanna and the tunnel across to Vágar.

KVÍVÍK Twenty-eight kilometres northwest of Tórshavn, Kvívík sits prettily in a deep narrow valley formed by the Stóra river which flows through the middle of the village on its way down to the sea. The houses here, painted in eye-catching shades of blue, green and red, are tightly clustered either side of the river in two tiny streets. The white-walled village **church** and its neighbouring **graveyard**, encircled by a perfect dry-stone wall and a grove of gnarled and twisted trees, look out over the tiny harbour beyond where a handful of small fishing boats bob on the Atlantic swell.

Getting there and away Bus #100 runs from Tórshavn via the Kollfjarðar tunnel to Kvívík (continuing to Vestmanna; timetables are available at www.ssl. fo) roughly hourly. Most departures in and out of Kvívík must be booked ahead (\ 34 30 30), otherwise the bus doesn't make the detour down into Kvívík from the main road, simply driving straight on to Vestmanna. There are no longer any facilities in Kvívík.

In 1942, remains of a **longhouse** and **byre** were discovered close to the church at the foot of the village on the western side of the river. The knee-high remains, covered with turf, consist of a dwelling house and a cowshed alongside which both date from the late Viking period, around the 10th to 11th century. The main building, 21m long by 6m wide, has characteristically curved walls made of boulders, earth and gravel. The roof would have been made of birch bark and grass sods and supported by two parallel rows of posts, whose remains can be seen in the ground. In the middle of the floor area there was once a sizeable fireplace, around 7m in length. The byre is unique in the Faroe Islands since no other similar building from the Viking period has been discovered to date. Virtually identical to the longhouse in construction though it was split into two rooms, one was used as a storage barn, the other was divided into two rows of stalls for up to 12 cows opposite each other. During the excavations several tools were found which help to give a picture of what life was like at this time and serve as proof that the people who lived here not only spun wool but also wove the yarn: loom weights, spindles, ropes made of local juniper and a number of ornaments and decorations from the Kvívík site are now kept by the National Museum in Tórshavn.

The village It was here in Kvívík church that a decisive step was taken towards making Faroese the official language of the Church: before a shocked congregation, **Venceslaus Ulricus Hammershaimb** (1819–1909) gave his New Year's Eve sermon in 1855 in his native tongue (instead of Danish as had been the common practice until then) amid scenes of shock and uproar. In fact, the young minister was so taken aback by the indignant reaction of his flock, who considered the lowly Faroese tongue not worthy of the great words of God, that he didn't dare repeat his experiment. It took the best part of another century until the Scriptures were finally translated into Faroese and an official Faroese Bible was published in 1961.

VESTMANNA It's a further 13km from Kvívík on to Vestmanna, a busy modern fishing village that curves around a superbly sheltered natural harbour on Streymoy's western shore. Although there's little to see in Vestmanna itself, the village attracts thousands of visitors every year since it's the departure point for boat trips to the nearby **bird cliffs** (see page 88). A veritable giant in Faroese terms, Vestmanna is the second-largest town on the island (after Tórshavn) and home to around 1,200 people, many of whom work in the fish factory or down on the docks at the western side of the harbour. In fact, the dockside area is relatively new, created by landfill to provide room for a couple of new quays and much-needed building land. The narrow strip of land between the harbour and the hills behind soon proved too limited for the rapid development that Vestmanna has seen in recent years; a filleting plant, fish farm, plastics company and building construction firm are just some of the businesses represented. Vestmanna is also the location for the Faroes' main **hydro-electric power plants** which use the waters of the Fossá river, which flows through the eastern part of town, to provide electricity for Streymoy including Tórshavn, Eysturoy, Vágar, Klaksvík and Suðuroy. Four dams high on the hills above the town (visible from the walking path between Hvalvík and Vestmanna; see box, page 79) help to maintain the flow of water to the power stations.

5

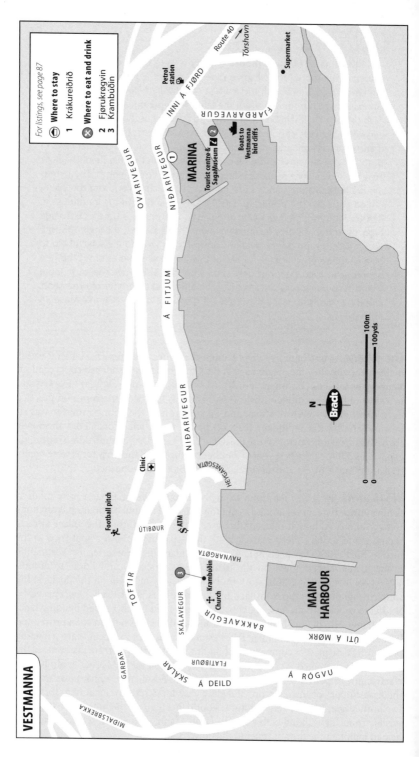

VESTMANNA

For listings, see page 87

Where to stay
1 Krákureiðrið

Where to eat and drink
2 Fjørukrógvin
3 Krambúðin

Route 40
Tórshavn

Supermarket

Petrol station

INNI Á FJØRD

FJARÐARVEGUR

MARINA

Tourist centre & Saga Museum

Boats to Vestmanna bird cliffs

ØVARIVEGUR

NIÐARIVEGUR

Á FITJUM

NIÐARIVEGUR

HEIGANESGØTA

N

Bradt

100m
100yds

Clinic

Football pitch

ÚTIBØUR

ATM

HAVNARGØTA

MAIN HARBOUR

ÚTI Á MØRK

GARÐAR

TOFTIR

SKÁLAVEGUR

Krambúðin

Church

BAKKAVEGUR

Á RÓGVU

MIÐALSBREKKA

SKÁLAR

Á DEILD

FLATIBØUR

Getting there and away Bus #100 runs between Vestmanna and Tórshavn calling at Kvívík on request (↳ *34 30 30*) roughly every one to two hours; timetables are available at www.ssl.fo.

📍 **Where to stay and eat** *Map, page 86.*
For smart guesthouse accommodation, look no further than **Krákureiðrið** (↳ *76 47 47*; e *info@krakureidid.com; www.krakureidrid.com;* **$$**) just above the marina at Niðarivegur 34 where all six rooms share facilities but are bright, airy and clean; there's also a guest kitchen and washing machine. This place is used as student accommodation during term time so it is only available from late June to mid-August.

Thanks to its relative size, Vestmanna is one of the few settlements on Streymoy outside Tórshavn to boast any form of eatery or drinking hole. Inside the Vestmanna Tourist Centre, the **Fjørukrøgvin** (↳ *47 15 00*; **$$**) restaurant serves a lunch buffet of salad and soup for 98kr as well as a selection of tasty fare including steaks (*198kr*), fresh fish (*160kr*) and chicken and chips (*125kr*). It shares the same opening times as the tourist office (see *Other practicalities*, below). Otherwise, there's a small café inside the handicrafts store, **Krambúðin** (↳ *42 42 10*; ⊕ *May–Aug 14.00–17.30 Mon–Sat*), a little further along the main road beside the western harbour at Bakkavegur 23 (see below).

Other practicalities There are just about enough tourist facilities in Vestmanna to make the village a practical second base on Streymoy after Tórshavn. As you descend into Vestmanna, you'll see the **Vestmanna Tourist Centre** (its name is emblazoned in huge white lettering on the roof) by the harbour. Inside there's an information desk (↳ *47 15 00; www.puffin.fo;* ⊕ *May–Sep 09.00–17.00 daily*) where you can book boat trips to the bird cliffs as well as buy the odd Faroese souvenir or two. Handicrafts are available from **Krambúðin** (⊕ *May–Aug 14.00–17.30 Mon–Sat*), a sturdy, timber structure beside the stream at Bakkavegur 23, where items from the Norðstreymoyar Heimavirkisfelag are available for sale.

Vestmanna also has an **ATM** outside the Vestmanna Kommuna building at Bakkavegur 8 and a new supermarket by the harbour (⊕ *09.00–22.00 Mon–Sat*), at Fjarðarvegur 12.

What to see and do Sadly Vestmanna's glory days are now gone; until 2002 all road traffic to and from the airport (as well as to other parts of Vágar, and, for that matter, Mykines) was forced to pass through the **town** since its regular ferry connections across the sound to the diminutive harbour at Oyrargjógv were the only means of reaching Vágar. The new sea tunnel, though, has put paid to all passing trade and Vestmanna now finds itself at the end of the road; to cross to Vágar you must backtrack all the way to the mouth of the tunnel near Leynar, east of Kvívík.

Although Vestmanna can trace its origins back to pre-Viking times – its name is thought to come from the Irish monks or 'west men' who first settled here some time before AD1000 – there's little sign of this ancient heritage visible today, other than the paltry nondescript remains of a Viking-age house from around the same period close to the Gjógvará river in the western part of the village. In fact, Vestmanna, benefiting from its south-facing location for the growing of crops, remained a quiet agricultural backwater until the lifting of the Danish Trade Monopoly in 1856. Then, with the purchase of a number of wooden fishing vessels or sloops from England, the people of Vestmanna began to turn their attention to the sea and indeed haven't looked back since.

SagaMuseum (⊕ *May–Sep 09.00–17.00 daily; admission 90kr/75kr if you also go on the bird cliff tours on the same day*) A good place to get to grips with the Faroes' stirring Viking past is at the excellent SagaMuseum, housed on the first floor of the tourist centre. Featuring superbly realised, life-size replicas of the characters from the *Færeyinga Saga* and taking its cue from the similar saga museum in Reykjavík in Iceland, the walk-through museum recounts Faroese history from the time of the Settlement through to the late 1600s. Indeed, all the big names are here, including **Sigmundur Brestisson** and **Tróndur í Gøtu**, who are the key figures in the saga: Tróndur opposed the introduction of Christianity to the Faroes and put a curse on Sigmundur, who was promoting the new religion. Take a headset guide from reception, walk up the stairs into the museum and let your imagination do the rest – though be prepared for the bloodthirsty nature of early Viking life.

Vestmanna bird cliffs One of the best excursions anywhere in the Faroes is a boat trip to the Vestmanna bird cliffs and grottoes. Known as the **Vestmannabjørgini** in Faroese, these soaring cliffs, roughly halfway between Vestmanna and Saksun to the north, provide safe nesting places during the summer months (roughly May until late August) for thousands upon thousands of seabirds, attracted by the vast shoals of fish that gather here in the plankton-rich waters of the North Atlantic. Rising up to 600m above the turquoise hues of the churning sea below, the cliffs are characterised by their numerous clefts and green blankets of luxuriant grass and mosses. The boats that sail out here give you an unparalleled view of the cliffs and the birds – notably puffins, razorbills and guillemots – as they weave in between the numerous sea stacks and in and out of narrow straits bound by sheer rock walls (look up and you may well see sheep grazing quite undisturbed on the clifftops) and dark echoing grottoes where the sound of the squawking birds and dripping water is amplified to unnerving proportions.

Getting to the bird cliffs Two local companies work together to run tours lasting a couple of hours to the bird cliffs (❧ *47 15 00;* e *puffin@olivant.fo; www.puffin.fo; 275kr*). Try to take a tour onboard the *Froyur* if you can: she has comfortable seating, large windows offering superb views, and a covered upper deck that allows you to escape the worst of the weather should the heavens open during the tour (which is quite likely).

Between May and September sailings operate daily, though departure times vary according to demand; you'll find the latest times when you make a booking on the website or call the tourist office in Vestmanna.

THE WESTERN ISLANDS: VÁGAR AND MYKINES

VÁGAR The third-largest of the Faroes, with an area of 178km², Vágar is generally the first island you see when approaching the country by air. The terrain, although less dramatic than that of Streymoy and the northern islands, is certainly varied: broad green valleys, patches of cultivated land around the villages that are clustered on the south coast and dozens of small rivers flowing down from rounded hilltops. The highest point is **Árnafjall** mountain (722m) in the extreme northwest, whereas the centre of the island is dominated by a long valley running north–south where the island's two main lakes are found. Although Vágar isn't going to be the highlight of any trip to the Faroe Islands – it simply doesn't have enough attractions for that – it does have vast expanses of untouched wilderness, especially around the uninhabited north of the island, which offer first-class hiking, and it's to that end that most people

above left   The ruins of medieval Magnus Cathedral in Kirkjubøur, surrounded by wildflowers (AH/VFI) pages 64–5

above right   The interior of Tórshavn's cathedral, known locally as the Havnar kirkja, located in the historic Tinganes district (KC/VFI) page 52

below   The church in Viðareiði dates back to 1892 (ÓF/VFI) page 129

above   Combine spectacular hiking and birdwatching on a trip to Mykines, the most westerly island in the Faroes (EC) pages 97–101

left   Child wearing traditional Faroese dress (AH/VFI)

below   Marvel at the age-old tradition of rappelling over the cliff edge to collect birds' eggs (AW/C) page 146

above   Flag Day celebrations take place on 25 April each year (ÓF/VFI) page 155

right   A kelp-strewn beach near Søltuvík on Sandoy (JP) page 143

below   The famous free-standing rock stacks, Drangarnir, near the uninhabited islands of Gáshólmur and Tindhólmur (AR/S) page 95

top right The Faroese starling (*Sturnus vulgaris faroensis*) is an endemic starling subspecies (AL) page 56

top left, Seabirds are the most abundant fauna
middle on the islands, and oystercatchers
& bottom (*Haematopus ostralegus*), northern gannets (*Morus bassanus*), shags (*Phalacrocorax aristotelis*) and Arctic terns (*Sterna paradisaea*) are frequently seen (*bottom* F/VFI and MV) pages 4–6

above Hardy and adaptable, the friendly Faroe pony (*føroyska rossið* in Faroese) is a common sight throughout the islands (GA/S)

right Pilot whales (*Globicephala melas*), or *grindhvalur* in Faroese, are the only whales still hunted in the islands — all meat is shared equally among the islanders at the end of the hunt (SS) pages 6–7

below left In AD567, St Brendan spoke of his travels to the 'Island of Sheep' — today, there are approximately 80,000 of these woolly ungulates in the Faroes, twice the population of people (ÓF/VFI) page 8

Below right Seals can be seen basking in the shallow waters at Søltuvík (AJ/S) page 143

above   **Puffins can be spotted perching on the cliffs of Mykines** (ÓF/VFI) pages 100–1

below   **Stunning coastal scenery on the picturesque island of Vágar** (KC/VFI) pages 88–97

FAR AFIELD, AND YET SO CLOSE …

In picturesque surroundings, far away from the treadmill of reality, Gjáargarður is the most charming hotel in the Faroe Islands.

Enjoy the idyllic village of Gjógv or go hiking in the impressive countryside.

Back at the hotel, a lovely dinner awaits your fresh and uplifted spirit.

Gjógv is ideally situated – enjoy local attractions or go sightseeing by car. The northern islands are less than an hour away, as is Tórshavn, the cosy historic capital.

With our friendly service and hospitality, you are guaranteed an unforgettable stay.

Welcome to Gjáargarður

Guesthouse of Gjógv
FO-476 Gjógv, Faroe Islands
Tel. +298 42 31 71
info@gjaargardur.fo
www.gjaargardur.fo

GJÁARGARÐUR
Guesthouse of Gjógv

come here. However, Vágar is also of interest for two other reasons: it's the location of the Faroes' only airport, and it has a ferry connection to Mykines.

From the Vágatunnilin (100kr per car; fee payable only in the Vágar–Streymoy direction), as the tunnel which links Streymoy with neighbouring Vágar is known, Route 40 climbs up the steep hillside *en route* to the island's first main settlements, the adjoining villages of **Miðvágur** and **Sandavágur**. From here the road, the only one on the island, hugs the southern shore, skirting **Leitisvatn/Sørvágsvatn lake**, as it heads west towards the airport and the neighbouring village of **Sørvágur**, from where the boat sails to Mykines. Although there's not much beyond Sørvágur, the road continues west out to the hamlet of **Bøur** and ultimately through the tunnel to Vágar's westernmost settlement, **Gásadalur**. On the deserted north coast, there are traces of two now-abandoned villages, **Víkar** and **Slættanes**, both of which can be reached on foot (see page 97).

Miðvágur and Sandavágur
Sitting snugly around the head of the tooth-shaped Vágafjørður fjord, the twin villages of Sandavágur and larger Miðvágur are essentially one and the same place and home to around 2,000 people; we've given an account of Miðvágur first, since that's where the services are, then Sandavágur. The fjord here is regarded as being the best place in the whole of the country to trap pilot whales; numerous sandbanks and a long sandy beach make it difficult for the whales to swim back out of the bay at low tide. However, local tradition has it that the women of the village don't start preparing their husbands' dinners the day of the *grindadráp* (see pages 15–16) until the whales are driven past the Presttangi headland at the southern entrance to the bay; once past this point there's no escape.

Getting there and away Bus #300 runs from Tórshavn to both Sandavágur and Miðvágur roughly hourly (timetables are available at www.ssl.fo) before continuing on to the airport and Sørvágur.

Where to stay and eat Miðvágur is home to a great little guesthouse, all decked out in 1950s decor and stuffed full of furniture from the period: **Gamla Hotellið** at Jatnavegur 31 (✆ 33 24 08; e info@magenta.fo; www.magenta.fo; $$$), the main road through Miðvágur. Lovingly restored by the ebullient Marita, whose attention to detail is second to none, this former hotel stood empty for 30 years before opening its doors again. There are just a handful of rooms, sharing facilities, though each is equipped with a washbasin. Guests also have access to a delightful sitting room – once again decorated with everything from china to embroidery from the 1950s.

Miðvágur also boasts one of the Faroes' few youth hostels, **Á Giljanesi** (✆ 21 98 99; e giljanes@giljanes.fo; www.giljanes.fo; $), complete with an adjoining **campsite** (*100kr pp*). Situated to the east of the harbour entrance on the Giljanes promontory at á Hillingartanga 8, the youth hostel is also, unusually, open all year. A long, rectangular building with 30 or so beds, the cell-block-like rooms (choose one overlooking the harbour rather than the car park) are spartan to say the least, but if you're looking for somewhere to stay on Vágar (*a dorm bed costs 220kr; dbl room 480kr*) you'll find this place considerably cheaper than the uninspiring hotel at the airport. There's also a kitchen on site for self-catering.

Other practicalities Inside Gamla Hotellið, opposite BankNordik, **Café Magenta** (✆ 33 24 08; ⊕ *May–Aug 07.00–22.00 Sun–Thu, 07.00–16.00 Fri & Sat;* $) serves breakfast, coffee, cakes, pastries and a dish of the day. Located a couple of doors down from the museum at Leitisvegur 48, **Nest** (✆ 30 88 88; ⊕ *17.00–*

The long-awaited tunnel beneath Vestmannasund sound linking Leynar on Streymoy with Fútaklettur on Vágar, and importantly the Faroes' one and only airport, finally opened in November 2002. Although initial construction work began in the late 1980s, the ensuing financial crisis soon brought the ambitious venture to a standstill and during a period of 11 years the tunnel remained little more than a big hole in the ground. Then, in September 2000, the Faroese parliament announced that building work would recommence. Inspired by a similar undersea project north of Reykjavík in Iceland, Faroese contractors began work five months later on the 4.9km-long tunnel, 2.5km of which lie under the sound at a depth of around 100m. The tunnel has not only reduced journey times between Tórshavn and the airport by over an hour and cut the distance by 10km, but it has realised that great Faroese dream: to drive virtually the entire length of the central islands from Gásadalur in western Vágar to Viðareiði in northern Viðoy in one go. An under-fjord tunnel between Leirvík and Klaksvík, which opened in 2006, completed the missing link. Two new tunnels are now planned to link the Tórshavn area with southern Eysturoy (see page 73), and with Sandoy (see page 141), due to open in 2019 and 2021 respectively.

23.00 Sun–Thu, 17.00–midnight Fri & Sat, 13.00–23.00 Sun; $), is open for pizzas (*75–95kr*), and burgers (*55kr*). Although there are no other restaurants in either Sandavágur or Miðvágur, there is a Bónus **supermarket** (⏲ *09.00–22.00 Mon–Sat*) next door to the museum, while the **alcohol store**, Rúsdrekkasøla Landsins (⏲ *14.00–17.30 Mon–Thu, 12.00–17.30 Fri, 10.00–13.00 Sat*) is beside the roundabout at Skaldavegur 5. You'll find Eik **bank** with an ATM at Jatnavegur 16 (⏲ *09.30–16.00 Mon–Fri*), **BankNordik** (no ATM) at Jatnavegur 26 (⏲ *10.00–16.00 Mon, Wed & Fri, 10.00–17.00 Thu*) and the **post office** (⏲ *11.30–noon*) at Jatnavegur 28, all beside the main road through Miðvágur.

What to see and do   Located inside the Miðvágur tourist office at Leitisvegur 58, **Føroyska Krígssavnið (Faroese War Museum)** (*www.ww2.fo;* ⏲ *May–Sep 14.00–17.00 Sat & Sun; rest of the year by appointment on* ☎ *22 19 40; admission 50kr*) is a must for anyone with even the vaguest interest in the war years in the North Atlantic. British soldiers occupied the strategically important (Danish) Faroes, as part of what was known as Operation Valentine, in April 1940 immediately after the German invasion of Denmark and Norway, leaving once the war was over. The Germans never attempted a full-scale invasion of the Faroes and the biggest problem was drifting sea mines which resulted in the loss of several Faroese fishing boats and their crews. The museum kicks off with a series of atmospheric black-and-white photographs of the British soldiers (there were around 5,000–6,000 stationed here in total) but also includes other items such as gas masks and various wartime letters and documents. The most tangible reminder of the British presence, other than the airport which was built by the soldiers, is the Faroese love of battered fish and chips, Dairy Milk chocolate (which is not available in Denmark) and British tea. While you're here, do try to watch the moving 30-minute DVD *Thurid's War* (in Danish and Faroese only) which recounts the story of young Faroese girl, Thurid Poulsen, who falls in love with a British soldier, Samuel Bingley, from Barnsley in Yorkshire. The couple had a child together but tragically Bingley was killed in March 1945 after returning to the front.

Opposite the roundabout, at the junction of Skaldavegur and Jatnavegur, the smaller of the two graveyards you can see (the one on the right) is the **Commonwealth War Graves Cemetery** (always open). Surrounded by a white stone wall, it contains the graves of 14 servicemen from Britain, Australia and New Zealand – the youngest, a pilot aged just 20 from London – who lost their lives in the Faroes during World War II; the Luftwaffe made a number of raids on the islands in 1941–2.

Once the site of the island *ting*, Míðvágur was also the residence of the priest of the western islands who lived in the building known as **Kálvalíð**, high above the town and now a museum (*Kálvaliðvegur 41;* ☎ *33 24 55;* ⏱ *on request; admission 30kr*). Built into the hillside, the walls of this curious turf-roofed house are made of local rock and blend effortlessly into the greens and greys of the surrounding countryside; there's just one tiny window at the front for daylight. Inside the building are just two plainly decorated rooms and a cow stall. The oval-shaped stone wall beside the structure was once used for hay storage. To get here, take the turn right up the hill after passing the sign announcing your arrival in Míðvágur. The path beyond the museum marks the beginning of an easy walk over the hill to Vatnsoyrar, a diminutive settlement at the northern end of the Leitisvatn/Sørvágsvatn lake where Route 40 veers sharply left for the airport and the only settlement in the country not located on the coast; the land here has been reclaimed from the boggy marshland where the lake petered out.

The villages Of the two, it's **Sandavágur** that has the more interesting history: a runestone found by chance in 1917, now housed inside the garishly painted **wooden church**, provides proof that the area was inhabited from at least the late Viking period. The inscription on the stone reads: 'Thorkæl Onundarson, East Man [ie: from Norway] from Rogaland was the first to build on this site.' Thankfully the farmer who discovered the stone in one of his fields and planned to smash it up, not realising what it was, was thwarted by a young farmhand who first came across its inscription and called in expert advice. Later excavations in the area uncovered the foundations of a dwelling house suggesting that there was indeed a settlement here in the early Middle Ages. Beside the football pitch and just across the main bridge into the village, there's a slab of a **monument to V U Hammershaimb**, the minister who's credited as the creator of the modern Faroese literary language; he was born in 1819 on the local farm, á Steig, which from 1555 to 1816 was the seat of the *løgmaður*, the highest authority in the country. After collecting countless ballads and folk stories (in various dialects) from across the country, Hammershaimb made it his life's work to write them down and give them a standard written form that would make them accessible to people right across the islands, no matter what their dialect. The man and his achievements are certainly impressive; sadly, though, the basalt block erected in his honour is anything but.

From the village there's a pleasant walk out to the wonderfully named **Trøllkonufingur**, meaning 'witch's finger', a craggy clifftop (313m) that stands guard over the entrance to the fjord to the east of Sandavágur. Although the path to the cliff is straightforward enough, climbing it is a completely different matter. According to local legend, the peak has only been scaled once: during the royal visit in 1844 of Crown Prince Fredrik, a young Faroese man did in fact manage to reach the summit in order to wave to the prince as he sailed past below. Tragically, when he returned to the peak to collect a glove he had inadvertently left behind in the excitement, the man lost his footing and was killed. To get to Trøllkonufingur, take the first left when heading from the monument to the church to reach the road above you. This road turns into a track, passing a couple of holiday homes, and soon heads out along the grassy slopes of the fjordside and over a river. From here there are good views not only of the imposing clifftop, but also of southern Streymoy, Koltur and Hestur.

Vága floghavn (Vágar airport; FAE)

It's another 8km west of Miðvágur until Route 40 reaches the airport (for the linguistically minded, the form *Vága*, without a final r, is not a spelling mistake but signifies a genitive plural (ie: Vágar's airport). Originally built by the British Royal Engineers during World War II as a

---

HIKING ALONG THE SHORE OF LEITISVATN/SØRVÁGSVATN LAKE

A kilometre or so west of Miðvágur, Route 40 meets the shore of the Faroes' largest inland lake, bizarrely known by several names: Leitisvatn and Sørvágsvatn, though most local people simply call it Vatnið, literally 'the water'. Over 6km long, this body of water, renowned for its extensive stocks of fish, makes a worthwhile walk of around an hour. At the point where the road meets the lake shore you'll see a couple of boathouses and small huts which were once used for storing peat. From here follow the bank southwards (the going can be pretty boggy in parts) and you'll have good views of the two peaks which hem the lake in on either side: Ritubergsnøva (376m) to your left and Borgarheyggjur (252m) across the water on your right. As you pass Ritubergsnøva, take care not to stray too close to the headland in front of you. Here, the promontory, Trælanípa, falls precipitously into the sea from a height of 142m, marking the southernmost extent of the lake; during Viking times, slaves who were no longer capable of heavy labour were simply flung off the clifftop to their death on the rocks below. Close by you'll see the Bøsdalafossur waterfall, which carries the lake into the ocean after flowing over an area of basalt rock at the water's southern point. The ruins that you can see here are of buildings constructed by the British during World War II. Immediately offshore, the larger of the two free-standing rock stacks you'll spot is Geituskorardrangur, a pyramid-shaped point of basalt standing 115m above the sea. From here, it's possible to cross the Bøsdalaá river, which flows out of the lake by using the stepping stones. From here you can walk up to the 115m peak which stands on the cliff edge. To return simply retrace your steps along the eastern shore. It's possible to take a 3-hour sightseeing trip on the lake on board a houseboat contraption that looks rather like a floating caravan (33 31 23 or www. lakeside.fo for reservations; May–Aug 10.00, 14.00 & 18.00 daily; advance booking required; 350kr pp).

As a symbol of national pride, it's hard to beat Atlantic Airways, a plucky little airline serving a home market of barely 48,000 people yet flying to half a dozen countries. Founded in 1988, the Faroese carrier aimed to break into the lucrative Faroes–Denmark market and carry transfer passengers to Copenhagen, one of northern Europe's biggest airports and Scandinavia's main hub. Until then, the Faroe Islands were served only by the Danish airline, Maersk. By the mid 1990s, business was booming and the airline opened a new route to Iceland, with services to Scotland and Norway following soon afterwards. Amid great patriotic jubilation in February 2000, Atlantic doubled its fleet (from one plane to two!) and two years later carried more than 100,000 passengers for the first time in its history. In late 2004 Atlantic became the sole carrier to the Faroes when Maersk left the route. In March 2012, the airline realised a long-held ambition and took delivery of an Airbus 319, and two more similar planes followed the year after. Following the extension of the runway in 2011, allowing the Airbus to operate in and out of the Faroes, the number of destinations now reachable directly from the islands has soared – the new planes can even reach New York. See pages 23–4 for contact details.

military landing strip, the site was selected because it was hard to see from the sea; proximity to Tórshavn never featured in the equation. The British also constructed the island's one main road, today's Route 40 (incidentally, the only road in the Faroes where driving on the left-hand side was permitted; British vehicles then switched to the right-hand side when they reached Streymoy). This was once the most heavily guarded part of the country, with up to 8,000 servicemen stationed here at any one time; the local population was just 2,000. Until 1944, civilians were forced to carry identity papers on Vágar and visitors from other islands had to seek permission from the military authorities before visiting. After the war the airport was modernised and extended but it has already proved too small for today's needs. Presently, it contains a cafeteria, ATM, tourist information desk (\ *33 34 55; www.visitvagar.fo;* ⏱ *in connection with flight arrivals & departures*) and car-hire outlets before security, and a restaurant, gift shop and duty-free airside. The airport is also used as the departure point for the Atlantic Airways helicopter service, which serves the islands (see pages 27–8 for details).

Getting there and away Bus #300 runs here roughly hourly (timetables are available at www.ssl.fo) from Tórshavn. The bus schedule is designed conveniently to connect with flight departures.

Where to stay and eat If you need to stay at the airport, there's a comfortable hotel, **Hotel Vágar** (\ *30 90 90;* e *hv@hotelvagar.fo; www.hotelvagar.fo;* **$$$$**), right outside the terminal next to the car park. To walk here from the terminal, turn left on exit, walk along the front of the terminal building and then follow the perimeter fencing to the hotel in front of you. The hotel has been partly renovated and the downstairs rooms are decorated in neutral, autumnal colours and contain stylish Scandinavian furniture (these rooms also have good views of the runway). There's also a restaurant (**$$**) at the hotel, **Hvonn**, serving a very good-value lunch buffet (⏱ *noon–15.00 Mon–Sat; 115kr*) while on Sun (⏱ *11.30–14.30*) there's brunch for

Streymoy and the Western Islands   THE WESTERN ISLANDS: VÁGAR AND MYKINES

5

93

225kr. In addition, it serves pizzas (*from 98kr*), burgers (*from 110kr*), pasta dishes (*from 95kr*) and steaks (*195kr*) – all daily until 21.00.

Sørvágur So close is the airport to the town of Sørvágur that the western end of the runway is virtually in local people's back gardens. In fact, it's just another 2km from the airport to Vágar's second-largest town, with around 1,000 inhabitants, which lies at the head of a 5km-long narrow fjord, Sørvágsfjørður. Unlike its eastern neighbours, though, the bay here is not suited to trapping whales since the sea bed is especially uneven. Sørvágur is a pleasant enough place to stroll around, its handful of streets supporting several small stores, and sooner or later you'll come across the local museum, **Sørvágs Bygdasavn** (*Ovarivegur 23;* m *25 37 57; www.bygdarsavnid. com;* ⏁ *on request; admission 30kr*), on the southern side of the harbour, which contains some quite inventive items from the village's past: inflatable buoys made of whale stomach lining, old spoons made of melted-down rams' horns and a couple of gaffs used during the *grindadráp* (see pages 15–16). Incidentally, the name of this museum is yet another mutant form of *vágur*: here, *-vágs* is the genitive singular.

There's not much more though to Sørvágur, since all local services and activity are concentrated in the airport terminal, leaving the town itself with little more than a **filling station** and an **ATM**.

However, the main purpose for coming to Sørvágur is to take the ferry to **Mykines**, which leaves from the main harbour just beyond the museum and the filling station. Remember, though, that bad weather often delays and even cancels the sailings of the boat to Mykines, so it's wise to check the latest situation (✆ *34 30 30*) before finding yourself stuck in Sørvágur. Bus #300 runs here roughly hourly from Tórshavn, terminating at the filling station.

🏠 ***Where to stay and eat*** *Map, page 95.*

Thanks to Sørvágur's new 70s-retro guesthouse, **Hugo**, perched above the fjord at Bakkavegur 2 (✆ *23 21 00;* e *make@make.fo; www.make.fo;* **$$$**), it's now possible to stay in the village. The spick and span rooms share facilities and have stunning views out over the water. In summer, **Café Fjørðoy** (⏁ *May–Sep noon–21.00 Tue-Sat, 14.00–20.00 Sun;* **$$**) downstairs serves coffee, cakes, bagels, quiche, pancakes and some delicious local salmon, too.

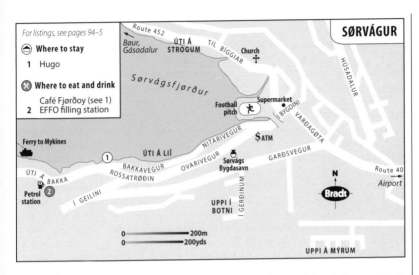

For listings, see pages 94–5

SØRVÁGUR

🏠 **Where to stay**
1   Hugo

✖ **Where to eat and drink**
    Café Fjørðoy (see 1)
2   EFFO filling station

Route 452
Bøur, Gásadalur
ÚTI Á STROGUM
TIL BØGGJAR
Church ✝
HÚSADALUR
Sørvágsfjørður
Football pitch 🏃
Supermarket
Í BYGDINI
VARÐAGØTA
Ferry to Mykines ⛴
ÚTI Á LIÍ
NÍTARIVEGUR
$ ATM
Sørvágs Bygdasavn
GARÐSVEGUR
ÚTI Á BAKKA
BAKKAVEGUR
ROSSATRØÐIN
OVARIVEGUR
N
Route 40
Airport
Petrol station
Í GEILINI
UPPI Í BOTNI
Í GERÐINUM
Bradt

0 — 200m
0 — 200yds

UPPI Á MÝRUM

Otherwise, the only place to eat in Sørvágur is at the snack bar (🕐 *noon–21.00 Mon–Sat, 16.00–21.00 Sun*) inside **EFFO filling station** down by the main quay, which sells a limited number of sandwiches and snacks as well as burgers and fish and chips for around 35–75kr.

There is, however, a well-stocked **supermarket** (🕐 *07.00–22.00 Mon–Fri, 08.00– 22.00 Sat*) in the centre of the village at Í Bygdini 3, a 20-minute walk or so from the terminal building.

West to Bøur and Gásadalur It's now worth making every effort to reach **Bøur**, just 4km west of Sørvágur along the main road, one of the Faroes' prettiest villages. This really is quite a small place, as barely 50 people live here, though as you wander around you'll notice the profusion of flowers that are cultivated in the locals' gardens, which give the village such a charming appearance. The focal point is undoubtedly its **church**, dating from 1865 and built in traditional Faroese style, beautifully located beside a cascading waterfall; the ceiling inside is painted a delicate eggshell blue whilst the pews are canary yellow.

This huddle of tarred wooden houses with turf roofs, snuggled up against the sheer mountainside behind that rises to a height of over 500m, is not only picture-postcard perfect but it also enjoys one of the best ocean views of any settlement in the islands. From its vantage point at the mouth of Sørvágsfjørður, Bøur looks out over the steep grassy slopes on the opposite side of the fjord, several free-standing rock stacks, **Drangarnir**, as well as the uninhabited islands of **Gáshólmur** and **Tindhólmur**. Named after the peak (*tindur* in Faroese, hence 'mountain island') that rises precipitously to 262m, this tiny island was, amazingly, once inhabited, though today it is used only for grazing sheep. The larger island rising out of the sea beyond Gáshólmur is majestic **Mykines**, an island that looks so tantalisingly close but can be frustratingly far away when the unpredictable currents and eddies of Mykinesfjørður, which separates the island from Vágar, are at their worst.

Getting there and around There is no longer a bus service to Bøur, so the way to reach here is to walk or drive. Bøur is best explored on foot since the narrow lanes that weave between the tiny houses are off limits to cars; you can park at the entrance to the village.

Gásadalur Beyond Bøur things get pretty remote. Until recently, Gásadalur, 9km northwest of Sørvágur, was the only Faroese settlement not accessible by road since it was considered too costly to blast through the rock and connect Vágar's most remote outpost, home to barely a dozen people, with the rest of the country. However, following a generous government rethink, engineers did just that in February 2003 and the 1.7km-long tunnel to Gásadalur is now reality, bringing the hamlet's blissful isolation to an end. At the entrance to the village, there's a car park where visitors are encouraged to leave their vehicles to explore the settlement on foot – carefully noting the signs instructing you to keep to the paths and not to trample the hay growing in the surrounding fields. The gaggle of colourful houses that comprise this remote community are grouped together on the only area of flat land for miles around on the gently sloping western side of the valley formed by the Dalá river, which plunges into the sea in the form of a waterfall. Unusually for a Faroese village, there is no church here; services instead are held in the **school**. The sea, 150m below the houses, crashes and surges into the craggy inlet that is Gásadalur's window on the world. Beginning from the top left of the village, there's a pleasant short **walk** of around 20 minutes to be taken by following the yellow and red marker posts, which leads out to the cliffs and up to a wooden bench where you can stare at the crashing waves below and from where you have tremendous views of the east coast of Mykines.

As a result of its off-the-beaten-track location, life here has changed little over the years and the settlement is still a fine example of rural island life. Indeed, until the tunnel finally broke through, the only (overland) way to reach Gásadalur was on foot using the old mountain mail route trodden by the local postman three times a week. Although it is possible to land a boat at the small point of land known as Reyðastíggjatangi just off the village, sea conditions and the offshore reefs often

HIKING FROM BØUR TO GÁSADALUR: THE OLD MAIL ROUTE

One of the most enjoyable, if difficult, hikes (allow 2 hours one way) anywhere in the Faroes stretches around 3.5km from the road out of Bøur down to Gásadalur, following the old mail route which rises to a height of around 430m. The path starts 3km west of Bøur just before the point where the new tunnel begins. From here continue along the coast, sticking close to the edge of the mountain, taking extreme care not to get too close to the cliff edge. Here, you'll have superb views of the fjord, the islands **Gáshólmur** and **Tindhólmur**, and further in the distance, Mykines. The path now starts to climb the southern side of **Rógvukollur** mountain (464m) up towards a large stone known as *líksteinurin*, literally 'the body stone', which was used as a resting place by the men whose job it was to carry coffins along the path for burial in Bøur; Gásadalur only got its cemetery in 1873. The climb up to this point is rather steep and difficult going at times. The path now turns inland a little to pass along the northern side of the next peak, Krúkarnir (414m). Beyond here, you'll come to what's known as *risasporið*, 'the giant's footprint', an impression in the rock which, legend has it, was formed when a local giant decided to jump from this point across to Mykines. Just beyond here you see an intensely green valley open up before you with a handful of houses in the distance; 300m below you; this is Gásadalur. From here it's a zigzag downhill all the way to Gásadalur, though beware of loose stones on this stretch of the path, which is rather steep. The path ends close to the entrance of the new tunnel.

make this treacherous. In reality, Gásadalur's only link with the outside world has been the helicopter service to and from Vágar airport.

Hiking in northern Vágar: the Slættanesgøtan trail
One of the best hiking circuits (allow two days in total) in Vágar leads from **Gásadalur** east along the north coast past the now-uninhabited village of **Víkar** to the island's northern tip, **Slættanes**, opposite Vestmanna on Streymoy. Amazingly enough, this remote outpost once had a population of 80 people; it was occupied until 1964, when its isolated location became too much for the elderly people who remained here and it, too, was abandoned. Experts considered it too expensive to run power cables out here and connect the handful of houses to the national grid, thus today Slættanes consists of just six summer houses and a landing stage. This trail, known as **Slættanesgøtan** (literally 'the Slættanes road'), passes through an area of outstanding natural beauty (the pasture on the floodplain around Víkar, for example, is exceptionally rich) and offers solitude in plenty; indeed, this isolated route was once the only way to reach these two remote settlements. From Slættanes, the path then leads south across the centre of the island, past Fjallavatn lake, for **Sørvágur**. This hike is certainly demanding and you should bring all provisions with you and be prepared to camp at Slættanes before moving on the next day down to Sørvágur along a much more straightforward path.

Gásadalur to Slættanes From Gásadalur, take the path along the valley up behind the village, following the river and climbing all the while, and in about 1½ hours you'll come to the pass (553m) which looks down on abandoned **Víkar**; this tiny place was only inhabited for around 60 years until 1914, when many of the men from the village were drowned in a fishing accident. Although it is possible to continue down to Víkar from the pass, it's a steep and rocky descent, and an even harder climb back up again. At this point there are sweeping views of the wild and barren north coast of Vágar. Now, turn right and follow the ridge east past a couple of rock clefts, after which point the path begins to descend into a valley bound by two peaks, Klubbin (352m) on the right and an unnamed hill on the left (322m). Beyond the peaks, the track descends towards sea level and **Viðvík bay.** Continuing east from here can be boggy, but persevere and cross the Reipsá river emptying from Fjallavatn lake, sticking close to the sides of the mountain, Klubbin (455m) (though not the same as the Klubbin in Viðvík bay). Now head up through a valley and cross one branch of the Botnáin river that flows down through it. At 426m you'll reach the mountain pass, Skoradalshálsur, from where it's a gradual descent down towards Slættanes, keeping to the northern side of the Grøv river.

Slættanes to Sørvágur After spending the night in Slættanes, it's possible to continue south along the path known as Slættanesgøtan towards Sórvágur. From Slættanes, walk south around the foot of the hill, Eggin, passing Skáadalur valley coming down from the Skoradalshálsur pass and continue climbing up towards the point where the path divides on the slopes of the Tungufelli peak (563m). Take the right turn (the left one leads to Oyrargjógv and beyond towards Míðvágur) and the path begins to descend towards the southern end of Fjallavatn lake. From here it's a straightforward hike south, over relatively flat ground, crossing the Sjatlá river, towards Húsadalur valley and the Kirkjuá river which mark the approach to Sørvágur.

MYKINES
Mykines really is something special. Geographically the Faroes' most westerly (and driest) outpost, this rugged isle, barely 10km², is certainly the most

enigmatic of the 18 Faroe Islands and the one that ranks, time and again, as the absolute favourite among Faroese and visitors alike. Looking down the fjord from Sørvágur its craggy cliffs and hills rise precipitously out of the sea in a wall of lush green, turquoise and steely grey, the winds hurrying the clouds across the sky, changing the island's aspect as frequently as the light. Depending on the prevailing weather conditions, Mykines can seem bright and inviting or, at other times, sombre and threatening. Approaching across the turbulent waters of the **Mykinesfjørður**, which separates the island from Vágar, Mykines can appear totally inaccessible, the south coast a remarkable series of unapproachable sheer cliffs and rocky clefts. High above this wall of rock, the peak, **Knúkur** (560m), bears down over the eastern end of the island, from where two rocky valleys, Borgardalur and Kálvadalur, tumble down to the sea drained by several serpentine rivers. As the land falls away to the west of the mountain, the rocky outcrops of the interior give way to a luxuriant valley of the deepest green that leads down gently to the island's only **settlement**. Some 150m below the village, hemmed into an alarmingly narrow cleft full of jagged reefs, the landing stage is regularly battered by the crashing Atlantic surf and surging waves; arrival in Mykines is not only an adventure but also something of an unpredictability, since, with southwesterly winds, the ferry may not be able to steer into the tiny harbour despite having sailed from Sørvágur with that very intention. It's not unknown for the island to be cut off for days, even a week or so, during particularly stormy weather. Charming though Mykines village is, it's the tremendous profusion of summer birdlife that is the real draw here. Seemingly everywhere you look there are birds: in the air, on the cliffs and hiding in nesting burrows on the hillsides. Indeed, the western point of the island beyond the harbour, known as **Lambi**, is a favourite location for puffins who gather here in uncountable numbers between mid April and mid to late August to hatch and rear their young – Mykines is the only place in the Faroes where they are protected and cannot be hunted. Beyond here, a narrow footbridge leads across to the neighbouring rectangular islet, **Mykineshólmur**, where the rock stacks, Píkarsdrangur and Flatidrangur, and surrounding cliffs are home to the Faroes' only colony of gannets. The gannets are present between late January and October, after when the young birds migrate to Morocco for the winter, the older ones preferring to winter out at sea closer to the Faroes.

Incidentally, the correct pronunciation of the island's name is 'mitchiness' and not 'mikiness'; armed with this fact you're bound to impress the locals.

Getting there and away

In theory, Mykines can be reached by **boat** from Sørvágur between May and August and then again during the second and third weeks of October (when the sheep slaughter is underway). Sailings are extremely popular and it is essential to **book in advance** to guarantee a seat onboard. There are usually two daily sailings, but bear in mind that they are often cancelled. During one of my previous visits to Mykines, for example, the boat hadn't sailed for a week due to bad weather and even the helicopter was cancelled, leaving me stranded for several days. According to the timetable at least, the **helicopter** is scheduled to fly out from Vágar to Mykines once daily on Sunday and Wednesday and twice on Friday (also once on Monday between September and May). Helicopter times are at www.atlantic.fo and the boat times are at www.ssl.fo.

Where to stay and eat

The main accommodation option on Mykines is **Kristianshús** (☏ 31 29 85; m 21 29 85; e mykines@olivant.fo; www.mikines.fo; **$$$**), overlooking the village stream, and one of the first buildings as you enter the town from the harbour. Run by Katrina Johannesen (born and bred on Mykines) and her husband, Esbern, this glorified hostel has just four snug and cosy rooms upstairs reached by a set of steep wooden steps (rooms 3 and 4 have sea views). Although space here is limited (be prepared to hit your head in the bathroom which is tucked up right under the eaves), it is a friendly place to stay and is also the only place to provide food: breakfast (included in the room rate) and evening meals (*around 150kr*). Although, it's strictly only open from May to the end of August, the chances are that Katrina will open up for you out of season as well. In the adjacent house, towards the harbour, there's a small kitchen which guests can use. The rooms in this rather spartan structure are also let out during the summer months. In addition, the **tourist office** at the airport also rents out a couple of houses in the village – details are at www.visitvagar.fo where reservations can also be made. Reckon on around 1,150kr per room per night. Mykines also has a small **campsite** (*50kr*) up behind the village (*use of Kristianshús showers 40kr; kitchen 80kr*), which provides the only other place to stay. Since accommodation is limited, you should be sure to book in advance, particularly during July and August which are the busiest months on Mykines; May and June are considerably quieter.

Other practicalities There is no general store on the island so it's imperative to bring all provisions with you – and bear in mind that you may get stuck here longer than you anticipated if the weather closes in. For details of boat and helicopter transport to Mykines, see *Getting there and away* on page 98.

What to see and do
Mykines village Undoubtedly one of the prettiest villages in the Faroes, the tiny settlement of Mykines, home to just 13 people, is wonderfully photogenic: brightly painted wooden houses interspersed with traditional tarred and turf-roofed structures huddle together either side of a mountain stream which trickles down between them from the hillsides behind. There are no roads here, just a couple of footpaths that wind among the houses and up to the 19th-century **church** at the top of the village whose graveyard is overrun with shoulder-high angelica. Built of sturdy white stone walls and topped with an unruly grass roof, the church is still used for services by the islanders, though the priest from Vágar does manage to make it over to the island twice a year to add a bit of authenticity. In his work *Barbara*, novelist Jørgen-Frantz Jacobsen puts the legendary appalling weather on Mykines and ensuing delays in boat traffic to good use: when the local minister finally manages to return to Vágar, after being stranded on Mykines for 11 days, he discovers his wife has run off with another man. It may only be a plot in a novel but during one of my recent visits to Mykines reality bore an uncanny resemblance to fiction: both the priest from Vágar and I were stranded by truly atrocious conditions. Indeed, during stormy weather, foam from the crashing waves below the village is blown high up over the houses and into the outfield beyond, giving the impression that you're witnessing a snowstorm.

When the church was built in 1879, around 200 people lived on the island, making a living from farming the land and fishing. Amazingly, by the 1960s, although there still was no electricity, the village boasted a school, meeting hall, a handful of shops and even a small hotel. However, Mykines's remote location, far from the bright lights of Tórshavn, has always made life here difficult and the island has often been threatened with depopulation. Today barely a dozen people live here year-round, and as you wander around the village, you'll see that many of the houses are closed up, used only as holiday homes during the short summer months. Indeed, it's during the summer that Mykines is at its liveliest, not only with tourists but also with returning islanders keen to keep their former family homes in good repair.

Although there are no sights as such in the village, sooner or later you'll come across a small **dam** in the stream at the back of the village, roughly on a level with the church. In jest, locals claim it's their swimming pool, and, indeed, it is possible to have a quick dip here, though preferably when the sun is shining to avoid hypothermia after getting out of the icy water! A stroll in the opposite direction will take you past the electricity generating station out towards the harbour, where a set of steep concrete steps and a slipway lead from the couple of boat houses on the clifftop down to the **landing stage**.

Hiking to Mykineshólmur From the electricity generator, a path runs alongside the field behind, up the hillside you can see in front of you. Follow it to the top (it's quite steep) where it reaches the north coast of the island. Continue past a **stone memorial** on your left and a grass-covered, cone-shaped hill on your right until about 100m further on your right you come to some rocky steps. The monument was erected in 1939 in memory of nine fishermen from Mykines who drowned when their trawler *Neptun* went down off Iceland five years earlier, and their names are commemorated on a plaque inside the village church. Once through a wooden gate, the path continues on the cliff side itself – a section of the cliff has been cut away to make this possible. It can be quite slippery here if it's wet, although there is a rope to steady yourself. From this section of the path there are breathtaking views of the sea below and of the cliffs further to the east (behind you). The path now weaves back towards the southern side of the island and begins to descend steeply towards the footbridge over the cleft to your right. This area is known as **Lambi** and it's full of puffin burrows; in the summer months the birds are everywhere and you should tread carefully so as not to cave in their burrows and twist your ankle in the process. You should now walk over the narrow footbridge, known rather grandly as **Atlantarhavsbrúgvin** (bridge over the Atlantic) which spans the Hólmgjógv cleft between Mykines and its smaller neighbour, **Mykineshólmur**. From its sheer northern coastline, around 130m above

FALLING SEABIRD NUMBERS

One of the first things you'll notice when you come to the Faroes in summer is the large number of birds. Millions of birds come to the islands every summer to breed; over 300 species have been recorded, of which 50 breed annually here, whilst another 60 are regular visitors. Indeed, over past centuries, seabirds have played a major role in providing the Faroese people with a nourishing source of food. However, things are changing. Numbers of seabirds such as puffins, kittiwakes, guillemots and Arctic terns have fallen dramatically during the past decade. It's not known exactly what has caused the decline, though many factors such as a lack of food, changing sea currents and global warming have been suggested as possible reasons. Though puffins are currently protected in parts of the Faroes, it's widely expected that a total ban on hunting puffins is imminent. Curiously, not all seabird species are subject to declining numbers: gannets, fulmars, shags and black guillemot are faring much better. Mykines is one of three of the Faroe Islands to be given special protection under an international treaty which obliges governments to safeguard areas that are especially biologically diverse; the other two islands are Nólsoy and Skúvoy.

sea level, the tussocky terrain of this rectangular islet slopes steeply to the south. Once over the bridge you have a choice of paths: either you head diagonally up the hillside and then west along the clifftops of the north coast to the **lighthouse**, or you stay close to the southern shoreline and walk west towards the slipway that leads down to the landing stage, keeping south of the lighthouse-keeper's house, and then follow the river up the hill to reach the lighthouse. The grass on Mykineshólmur is reputed to be the richest in the country; indeed, when the island was more extensively farmed than today, the cattle that grazed here were said to produce the tastiest meat. Amazingly, three families once lived on the island's westernmost extremity, though two of the three homes were later moved to Tórshavn and rebuilt in the street, Fútlalág, leaving the solitary red building, formerly the lighthouse-keeper's quarters, to function today as a weather station for the Danish Meteorological Institute (data can be found at www.vedrid.fo under the *veðrið á bygd og í bý* link; the site is in Danish only). Built in 1909, the lighthouse here, anchored to the ground by steel cables, is one of the most important lighthouses in the country since it warns approaching shipping that has sailed for days across the Atlantic without obstruction that the Faroes lie ahead. From here, there are views all the way down to the north coast of Suðuroy on a clear day. Southwest of the lighthouse, the free-standing rock stacks, **Flatidrangur** (27m) and the slightly taller **Píkarsdrangur** (36m), together with the cliffs below the lighthouse, are home to the Faroes' only gannetry. The westernmost point in the Faroe Islands is now in front of you: the flat rocks, furthest in the distance and a little northwest of the stacks, are **Knikarsboði**, the last or first part of the Faroes depending on your point of view. If you don't dawdle you can hike out there and back in around 2 hours, but it's better to give yourself time to watch the puffins and other birdlife and enjoy the views, so allow perhaps double this. Remember, too, that the lighthouse is often buffeted by strong winds and the surf here can crash high up on the cliffs.

Other hikes: Knúkur peak and around Rising to a height of 560m, and frequently obscured in low cloud, the **Knúkur peak**, topped by a couple of transmitters, dominates any view of Mykines. By following the farm tracks at the top of the village out through the outfield and then up the hill beyond, it's possible to reach the peak in around an hour or so. From here there are superb views over the eastern end of Mykines, which can't be seen from the village itself, as well as the islands of Vágar, Koltur, Streymoy and even Suðuroy in clear weather. It was just west of the peak itself that Icelandair flight FI701 crashed in thick fog on 26 September 1970, killing eight people. The Fokker 27 ploughed into the Mykines mountainside, believing it was on course for the airport at Sørvágur, after flying up to the Faroes from Copenhagen and Bergen, bound for Reykjavík. Search and rescue efforts were hampered by the atrocious weather and emergency teams were forced to land their boats below treacherous Kálvadalur from where it was a perilous ascent to reach the crash site to look for survivors; amazingly, 26 people did survive. The wreckage of the stricken aircraft was later buried by the islanders and remains hidden at the foot of Knúkur to this day.

From Knúkur there are two further hiking options. With care it's possible to descend into **Borgardalur valley**, the easternmost part of the island, by first heading southeast along the ridge for **Heðinsskorarfjall mountain** (433m). Following the cliffs it's a difficult descent into the valley, best undertaken without a heavy rucksack. Heading in the opposite direction from Knúkur, following a line of rock ledges, it's a straightforward walk north to the top of **Korkadalur valley** from where there are views of what the islanders call the *steinskógir*, a long line of basalt columns rising to around 60m in height, a veritable stone forest, as the Faroese name suggests.

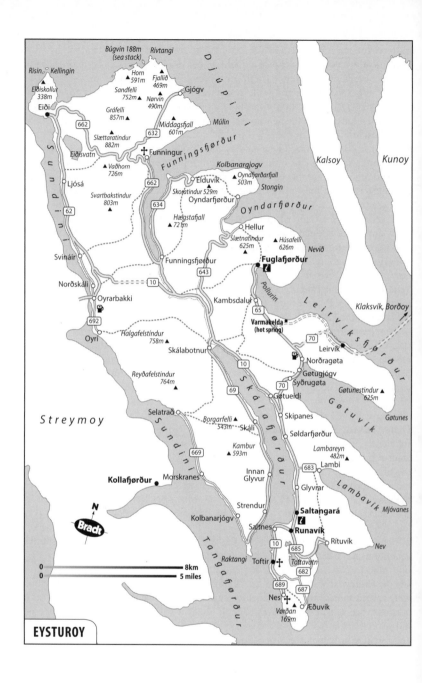

Búgvin 188m Rívtangi
(sea stack)

Risin Kellingin

Horn 591m Fjallið 469m
Elðiskollur 338m Sandfelli 752m Gjógv
Eiði Nørvin 490m
Gráfelli 857m
662 Middagsfjall 601m Múlin
Slættaratindur 882m 632
Funningur
Eiðisvatn Funningsfjørður
Vaðhorn 726m Kolbanargjógv
662 Elduvík Oyndfjørðarfjall 503m Stongin
Svartbakstindur 803m Skoratindur 529m
Ljósá Oyndarfjørður
634 Oyndarfjørður
62 Hægstafjall 721m Hellur
Sundini Slætnatindur 625m Húsafelli 626m Nevið
Svináir Funningsfjørður Fuglafjørður
Norðskáli 643
10 Pollurin
Oyrarbakki Kambsdalur Klaksvík, Borðoy
692 65
Oyri Hálgafelstindur 758m Varmakelda (hot spring)
Skálabotnur 70 Leirvík
10 Norðragøta
Reyðafelstindur 764m 69 Gøtugjógv
70 Syðrugøta
Gøtueiði Gøtunestindur 625m
Streymoy Selatrað Skipanes Gøtunes
Borgarfelli 543m Skáli Søldarfjørður
669 Kambur 593m Lambareyn 482m
Innan Glyvur 683 Lambi
Kollafjørður Morskranes Glyvrar Lambavík Mjóvanes
Strendur Saltangará
Kolbanarjógv Saltnes Runavík
10 685 Rítuvík Nev
Raktangi Toftir Toftavatn
682
689 687
Nes
Vørðan 169m Æðuvík

0 _____ 8km
0 _____ 5 miles

N
Bradt

Djúpini
Kalsoy
Kunoy

Leirvíksfjørður
Gøtuvík
Skálafjørður
Sundini
Tangafjørður

EYSTUROY

102

6

Eysturoy

The second-largest island in the Faroese chain, at 266km², Eysturoy is also one of the most densely populated, serving as home to around 11,000 people. Connected to its bigger neighbour, Streymoy, to the west by the bridge over Sundini sound (and by tunnel from 2019), it's thought Eysturoy was the second island in the Faroes to be settled, its name, 'eastern island', suggesting that settlers came here from the west, ie: Streymoy. Today most settlements are concentrated in the south of the island, where **Runavík**, with around 3,800 inhabitants, weighs in as the Faroes' third-largest town after Tórshavn and Klaksvík.

The surrounding countryside is dominated by the country's longest fjord, **Skálafjørður**, which virtually cuts the southern half of Eysturoy in two, reaching deep into the heart of the island. Although the scenery hereabouts is undoubtedly attractive, rich pastureland and low rounded hills gently sloping down to the fjordside, it's the mountainous north of the island which is the main geographical and geological attraction. Here, three majestic peaks, **Vaðhorn** (726m), **Slættaratindur** (882m) and **Gráfelli** (857m), bearing down over the scattering of local villages, and the imposing giant rock stacks **Risin** (71m) and **Kellingin** (69m) off the island's north coast, certainly provide a dramatic backdrop to this peaceful and remote northern corner of the island. East of here, Eysturoy's other great fjord, **Funningsfjørður**, slices deep into the island, reaching within 7km of the head of Skálafjørður, leaving a flat narrow isthmus of land between the two fjords, the location of some fantastic hiking. Although Eysturoy has several attractions in its own right, it's also a transit route for all traffic heading for Klaksvík and the northern islands through the new tunnel at **Leirvík** on the east coast.

WHERE TO GO

Northern Eysturoy is dominated by the the imposing rock stacks, Risin and Kellingin, situated just north of the magnificently located village of **Eiði** nestling between two hills on a narrow isthmus at the island's northwestern tip. However, the island's most picturesque villages – **Gjógv**, best known for the dramatic rocky cleft which forms the harbour, and nearby **Elduvík**, whose huddle of brightly painted homes looks out dreamily over the swelling waters of **Funningsfjørður** – are within easy reach on the opposite, eastern shore. **Elduvík** is also the starting point for the hike over the mountaintop to **Oyndarfjørður**. On the opposite shore of the eponymous fjord, another hike leads through a mountain pass and down into **Fuglafjørður**, an attractive fishing village with a busy harbour. For more cultural and historical attractions, **Norðragøta** with its timber-framed old farmhouse, now a museum, and **Leirvík**, which boasts Viking-age remains of four farm buildings dating from the 10th century, are both worth seeking out. The shops are the main reason to travel south along Skálafjørður to the cluster of settlements around Runavík. Incidentally, if you're looking for knitwear, Eysturoy is a good place to start; one of the Faroes' main outlets is located here: Navia in Toftir (see page 117).

GETTING AROUND

Eysturoy is blessed with a good and efficient **bus** network thanks to its relatively dense population. Operating directly from Tórshavn, #400 is the backbone of the service, linking the capital with Oyrarbakki, Syðrugøta, Norðragøta, Leirvík and Klaksvík, whilst the #410 runs from Fuglafjørður through Leirvík to Klaksvík. From Oyrarbakki, #201 runs to Funningur and Gjógv whilst #200 operates to Eiði. Bus #481 provides a service between Skálabotnur (at the head of Skálafjørður) and Oyndarfjørður and Hellur, while #440 runs around Skálafjørður.

NORTHERN EYSTUROY

OYRARBAKKI TO EIÐI Barely more than a filling station and a straggly road junction, **Oyrarbakki** is inordinately important to the Faroese public transport network. This dot on the map just over the bridge from Streymoy is the connecting point for a good few bus services. Despite the flurry of buses that stop off here, there's little reason to break your journey here and the settlement is best used as a starting point for the trip to Eiði along Route 62, a distance of around 11km. Clinging to the eastern shore of Sundini, the road provides excellent views of the Fossá river on the opposite shore, before passing the hydro-electric power station fed by the waters of Eiðisvatn lake above the hamlet of Ljósá, the only settlement along the entire road.

Sandwiched between two hills on a narrow isthmus of land, with a battered shoreline to the east and the precipitous end of Eysturoy to the west, **Eiði** (pronounced 'eye-yuh') enjoys a magnificent location, gently climbing the hillside above the open waters of Sundini sound below. This diminutive fishing village is home to around 700 people – and one of the most windswept football pitches in the world.

 Where to stay and eat The only place to stay in Eiði is the pleasant **guesthouse** Eysturi í Túni (m *21 31 94;* **$$$**), located in a white wooden building overlooking the harbour at Eysturi í Túni 8, where the room rate also includes breakfast.

Other practicalities Down in the village on the main road, a few doors down from the museum, at Heimtún 12, the Samkeyp **supermarket** (⏱ *08.00–22.00 Mon–Sat*) sells food and a few other bare essentials. All buses stop next to the church at the entrance to the village.

What to see and do
Eiði village During the 19th century, this little place was second in size only to Tórshavn, making a tidy income from fishing, an industry that remains Eiði's mainstay today; the fish factory down by the harbour provides most of the villagers with employment. Walk down to the northern shoreline, past the football field and Tjørnin lake, and you'll get a glimpse of the two sea stacks, **Risin** (71m) and **Kellingin** (69m), that have become one of the most photographed of all the Faroes' natural attractions and are the main reason to come here. According to legend, these are the remains of a giant and giantess who had come to the Faroes to tow them north to Iceland. However, things didn't go quite as smoothly as they had hoped and when the female giant climbed up nearby Eiðiskollur mountain to attach a rope, the

mountain cracked (the crack is visible today), delaying matters, which finally came to an end when daylight turned the two giants into stone. With your own transport there's also a good viewing point, with a free telescope, up on the hills to the east of Eiði; simply follow Route 662 up towards **Gjógv** and high up on the plateau you'll come to a small lay-by on your left after about 5 minutes or so.

The centre of the village is a muddle of narrow lanes and streets and best not explored by car. Instead there is parking next to the sizeable **church**, a stone structure dating from 1881 with a marvellous painted interior of creams, yellows, browns and blues. Model sailing boats dangle from its ceiling – a common Faroese tradition, probably pre-Christian in origin and said to bring luck to local sailors. Close by, in a little walled garden, there's a poignant monument dedicated to all those who never came back from the sea. While you're here, have a look inside the homestead **museum** (⊕ *Jun–Aug 16.00–18.00 Sun & Mon; at other times by appointment on* ✆ *42 35 97; admission 30kr*) known jointly as Eiðis bygdasavn and Látralonin – it's the turf-roofed building to the right of the supermarket, near the junction of Lækjuvegur and Heimtún. Originally used as a farmhouse until the 1950s, it contains a wonderful jumble of gifts donated to the museum, ranging from women's cotton knickers to a loom and various woodworking tools.

Hikes around Eiði From the village it's an easy hike of a couple of hours around the waters of **Eiðisvatn lake**, a couple of kilometres east of the village and reached by retracing your steps along Route 62 until just before the Breidá river, where a lane leads to the lake itself. Sitting at a height of 130m above sea level, there are some good views to be had and the lake can be a pleasant place on a sunny dry day for a picnic.

In the opposite direction, an enjoyable walk of around 2 hours begins at the hotel, before heading for the steep grassy heights of **Eiðiskollur mountain** (343m), whose flat summit is marked by a broadcasting mast and the ruins of a watchtower from World War II. From here you have great views down onto the Risin and Kellingin sea stacks below.

GJÓGV

Although bus services have improved, it can still be tricky to get to and from Gjógv (pronounced 'dyeggv') by bus in one day, but the surrounding scenery is worth the effort. With your own transport, the drive on to Gjógv is superlative and one of the most dramatic routes in the islands. From Eiði, Route 662 slowly climbs up onto the high moors to the east of the village, heading for the Faroes' highest mountain, **Slættaratindur** (882m).

Beyond here, and after a couple of hairpin bends, the road meets the junction with Route 632, which swings off left to descend gently through the rich pastureland lining the long, straight valley created by the Dalá River.

Getting there and away Since getting to Gjógv requires perseverance, it's probably best to spend a night here to make your journey easier. Bus #201 runs here from Oyrarbakki, where connections can be made to and from Tórshavn; check timetables carefully at www.ssl.fo.

Where to stay and eat Gjógv is one of most enjoyable places to stay in the Faroes. **Gjáargarður guesthouse** (*see ad, 2nd colour section; Dalavegur 20;* ✆ *42 31 71;* e *info@gjaargardur.fo; www.gjaargardur.fo;* ⊕ *Mar–Oct to individuals, groups only at other times;* **$$$**) is easily spotted by its large turf roof and Swiss-chalet-style appearance. It's one of the first buildings you'll come to when descending the valley towards the village; note, too, that prices fall by 100kr from October to April. No matter what type of accommodation you're looking for, you're sure to find something here to suit: regular double rooms (called standard rooms) with private facilities in the main building or much larger, tastefully appointed en-suite doubles (called superior rooms), complete with their own sitting area, in a low-rise structure behind the main building. Although there are no self-catering facilities, the guesthouse does have its own **restaurant** (⊕ *07.30–21.00 daily; $$*), serving meals throughout the day such as a lunch platter of salmon and potato salad (*129kr*), pancakes with rhubarb jam (*45kr*) and an evening meal with dessert (often lamb or fish) for 195kr. Between May and September there is also a good-value buffet on Sunday evenings (*225kr*). Plus, at the top of the gorge (see below), beside the steps, the guesthouse runs a café, **Gjáarkaffi** (*Jun–Aug 11.00–18.00 daily*) with a great open-air terrace overlooking the gorge, serving coffee, waffles and ice cream.

What to see and do

Gjógv village This quiet, pastoral village, dauntingly closed in by mountains and with a harbour set in a deep natural gorge in the rock, is one of the Faroes' most charming – and most visited. In Faroese, *gjógv* means 'cleft' or 'gorge', and when viewed from the walking paths that lead out on clifftops above the harbour, it does indeed appear as if the entire village is clinging to the edge of this 200m-long natural gorge. A set of 69 steep concrete steps leads down to the head of the inlet where often a couple of rowing boats are tied up on the slope. In rough seas boats are winched out of the water to prevent them from smashing into the rocky walls of the cleft. At night, the gorge is spotlit with coloured lights to stupendous effect. Nestled either side of the Dalá river, which flows right through the village, the majority of Gjógv's houses are modern in appearance, although a couple of older wooden turf-roofed structures can still be seen close to the steps down to the harbour. A village grocery store operated in one of these buildings for over 100 years until it closed in 1992.

Faroese cultural evening Between mid-June and mid-August the guesthouse holds a Faroese cultural evening with room for up to 80 people. Advance booking is necessary for the event, which takes place on Wednesday evenings, costing 395kr per person. The price includes an evening buffet with plenty of local specialities, live traditional music and the chance to learn some steps from the Faroese chain dance.

Hikes around Gjógv Ask the guesthouse for advice about hiking: the easiest hike (around 1 hour return) begins immediately behind the guesthouse and leads up through the steep field that ends at the cliff edge. Alternatively, a good day's hike from the village leads over to the hauntingly beautiful highland valley, **Ambadalur**. To get there, take the pass between the two mountains, **Fjallið** (469m) and **Nøvin** (490m), which form the western wall of the Dalá valley above the village, and then descend into the valley following the course of the Róvá river. The lonely shoreline here is dominated by the towering hulk of the Faroes' highest free-standing sea stack, **Búgvin** (188m). With care it's possible to walk back to Gjógv by following the coast eastwards around Fjallið mountain and back towards the harbour, providing stunning views of the severe form of **Kalsoy** across the choppy stretch of water known as Djúpini. Just to the east of Fjallið you're likely to see a profusion of seabirds which gather on the cliff ledges here, predominantly puffins and fulmars.

The other thing to do in Gjógv is to stroll from the harbour past the couple of circular outdoor water tanks used for salmon breeding towards the village **church** dating from 1929, standing guard over the rocky coastline beyond. The lack of adornment of the church, simply painted white and green, belies its importance in the islands' history. It was here that the first consecration service was held in Faroese, marking a major milestone in the acceptance of Faroese, not Danish, as the national language. Behind the church you'll see a small fenced garden containing a small number of shrubs and plants. Inside is a stirring sculpture of a mother and her two children staring longingly out to sea, their expressions wretched with anguish; the names of all the local fishermen who lost their lives at sea are etched on plaques here. In 1870 half the adult male population of Gjógv drowned when two eight-man boats went down.

FUNNINGUR AND ELDUVÍK From Gjógv, it's 5km back up through the Dalá valley to the junction with Route 662, which overlooks the funnel-shaped fjord **Funningsfjørður**, and its main settlement, picturesque Funningur, just 4km, four hairpin bends and 300m below, at the foot of the steep hillside that now opens up before you.

Getting there and away Although Funningur can be reached by **bus** #201, connections are poor and it's much more practical to get here by **car**. There is no public transport to Elduvík and no accommodation or facilities in either of the villages.

What to see and do
Funningur The main reason to come here is to see the **timber church**, which enjoys pride of place in the centre of the village beside the Stórá river, which empties into the fjord after its precipitous journey down from the heights of Vaðhorn peak high on the mountain plateau above. Built in 1847, the church closely follows the traditional late 19th-century design with its wooden interior. Inside, make sure to see the now rather battered wooden carving of Christ. The figure, which has sadly already had its head glued back in place, was once placed on the altar, though now it's kept on the benches nearby. There's also a silver font in the church dating from 1735. Although Funningur is probably the oldest settlement in the Faroes – in fact Grímur Kamban, the islands' first settler, is thought to have once lived here – there's little to show today for this historical claim to fame. Indeed, once you've seen the church there's little reason to tarry and it's best to press on southwards along the new stretch of road leading to the head of the fjord. This route provides the only access to Funningur during the long winter months when the steep descent from the junction above the village is too treacherous to attempt.

From Elduvík it's possible to hike to Funningsfjørður (and on to the main Route 10) or, alternatively, around Skoratindur peak to Oyndarfjørður.

It's a well-trodden path of around 7km to **Funningsfjørður** following the course of the Stórá up through its valley to its source (parts of this can be quite boggy) before making a steep descent into the settlement. From here it's just a further 2km to pick up buses along Route 10 (#400 Tórshavn to Klaksvík).

From Elduvík a second path, known as **Sniðgøta**, begins close to the foot of Skoratindur, on the eastern edge of the village, and leads along the fjord shore hugging the sides of the mountain until it reaches the inland end of the cleft in the coastline, **Kolbanargjógv**. Although the path is not difficult, care should be exercised at all times since it is very narrow and barely 50m above the sea below; in fact this was the route taken by the people of Elduvík to church on Sunday mornings before the construction of their own church in 1951. From the cleft it swings southeast and skirts the western edge of **Oyndfjarðarfjall mountain** (503m) before descending into **Oyndarfjørður**. This path should not be attempted in bad weather or during the winter months.

Funningsfjørður The village of Funningsfjørður, named after the fjord on which it sits, is a modern settlement gathered around a tiny harbour established primarily to serve the fish farms which are found in the superbly sheltered waters at the head of the fjord. From here there's a choice of roads: Route 634 swings north to follow the fjord out to pretty Elduvík whilst Route 662 continues for another 2km to meet up with the main road across Eysturoy, Route 10.

Elduvík Having reached the head of Funningsfjørður, it's worth retracing your steps to the mouth of the fjord along Route 634 to reach one of the Faroes' most idyllically located villages, Elduvík. Tucked away around a couple of small headlands, the village is quite invisible from Funningur on the opposite side of the fjord, giving the place a wonderfully isolated air. Barely 15 people live in the dozen or so houses here, painted in cheery shades of red, blue and green, which nestle at the foot of two peaks, Skoratindur (549m) and Múlin (244m). Although Elduvík is a dying village, there are still a few people who farm the land here and in summer you'll see that the lower slopes of the mountain are still used for hay production. Although most of the buildings here are relatively modern, there are still a couple of low-ceilinged wooden houses with turf roofs located close to the Stórá river that flows through the village.

OYNDARFJØRÐUR AND HELLUR At the mouth of the fjord bearing its name, Oyndarfjørður has a certain unkempt charm about it. Centred around a productive harbour, this little place of around 150 people is reached along Route 643 which cuts northwards for 10km from the main Route 10 near to the head of Skálafjørður fjord; the only other way in is the hiking route from Elduvík (see box, above) or the path from Fuglafjørður into Hellur (see page 109), which lies opposite Oyndarfjørður in the same fjord. Arriving in your own car, it's best to park on the edge of the village because it can be difficult to find somewhere to park in the narrow lanes that make up the central part of the settlement.

Oyndarfjørður Although it's possible to spend an hour or so wandering around the village admiring the brightly painted wooden houses and their luxuriant gardens or watching the comings and goings in the harbour, the main attraction here is the peculiar *rinkusteinar* (rocking stones) which can be found at the entrance to the village, below the junction of Víkavegur and Ovarivegur. From here a signed path leads down to the water's edge, where you'll come across two large rocks right by the shoreline. Quite bizarrely these massive boulders move with the slightest wave; a metal chain is attached to the larger of the two rocks – watch carefully and you'll see the chain move and the whole thing rock.

Back in the village, take a stroll to the **timber church**, dating from 1838, down by the shore. Although it is constructed to the same design as the other wooden churches in the islands, it is curious that this one does not have black-tarred walls. Instead its white-painted walls and green windows make a refreshing change, as does its blue choir screen.

Hellur Hellur, across the fjord from Oyndarfjørður and little more than a tight cluster of houses huddled together at the foot of the Rustarkambur peak (483m), is best visited as the starting point for the enjoyable 9km **hike** to Fuglafjørður (allow 2 hours one way) up through the Fuglfjarðarskarð pass (353m) between the mountain and the much higher Slætnatindur (625m) to the south. The path, known as Sjúrðargøta, is named after a giant and a local farmer's son who both shared the same name. Legend has it that Sjúrður the giant came to Oyndarfjørður from Suðuroy to test his strength. However, the giant was no match for the superior strength of the farmer's son, who beat the giant at his own game and was richly paid by his father for his efforts. Although the initial ascent out of Hellur is quite steep, the going becomes easier as you approach the pass, marked by two large **cairns**. According to an old custom, it is usual to throw three small stones at the cairns as you pass whilst saying out loud 'In the name of the Father, and of the Son and of the Holy Ghost' to protect you from getting lost and to bless the trip. Beyond here the path passes *malunar hav* (Malan's rock) – named after a pregnant local milkmaid who, astonishingly, managed to lift the rock to prove her strength when teased by her friends for failing to keep up with them on the walk – before finally descending into Fuglafjørður.

Hellur (and Oyndarfjørður) are served by bus #481 from Skálabotnur; Fuglafjørður is connected to Klaksvík by #410, though there are no facilities in either village.

FUGLAFJØRÐUR Tucked away at the head of a superbly sheltered fjord off Pollurin bay, a wide, open expanse of water on Eysturoy's east coast, Fuglafjørður is one of the Faroes' busiest fishing ports. Dominated by the three surrounding mountains, Slætnatindur (625m), Húsafelli (626m) and Borgin (571m), which bear down on the tiny village below, Fuglafjørður benefits from one of the best natural harbours in the country and boasts a fish-filleting factory, shipyard, oil depot and even a plant that produces state-of-the-art trawl nets for boats across the islands. A total of 20% of all Faroese exports pass through the harbour here. Although the population is barely 1,500, the town appears bigger than it really is, with several shops, a number of eating places, a library and even a tourist information office; altogether an agreeable place to spend an afternoon.

Getting there and away The **bus** (service #410) arrives and leaves from beside the tourist office and runs directly to Klaksvík via Leirvík. Change in Norðragøta for Tórshavn.

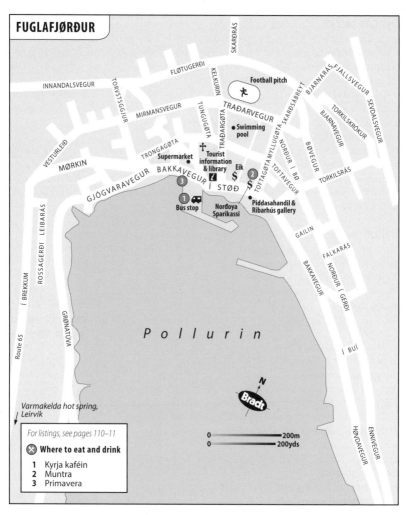

FUGLAFJØRÐUR

SKARDRÁS
FLØTUGERÐI
KELKURIN
FJALLSVEGUR
BJARNARÁS
SKARÐSABREYT
INNANDALSVEGUR
TORVSTSGJUR
TORKILSKRØKUR
BJARNAVEGUR
TORKILSRÁS
SEVDALSVEGUR
Football pitch
TRAÐARVEGUR
MIRMANSVEGUR
TUNGUGØTA
TRAÐARGØTA
Swimming pool
TOFTAGØTA
MYLLUGØTA
NORÐUR Í BØ
BØVEGUR
VESTURLEIÐ
TRONGAGØTA
Supermarket
Tourist information & library
Eik
$
TOFTAVEGUR
MØRKIN
BAKKAVEGUR
Í STØÐ
$
GJØGVARAVEGUR
Bus stop
Norðoya Sparikassi
Piddasahandil & Ribarhús gallery
GAILIN
FALKARÁS
LEIBARÁS
ROSSAGERÐI
BAKKAVEGUR
NORÐUR Í GERÐI
Í BREKKUM
P o l l u r i n
Í BÚI
GRØNATUVA
Route 65
N
Varmakelda hot spring, Leirvík
Bradt
HØVDANEVGUR
ENNIVEGUR

For listings, see pages 110–11

❌ Where to eat and drink

1   Kyrja kaféin
2   Muntra
3   Primavera

0   200m
0   200yds

🏠 **Where to stay and eat** *Map, above.*

The tourist office keeps an up-to-date list of the private rooms available; there are no hotels or guesthouses as such (see *Other practicalities*, opposite).

Eating in Fuglafjørður, surprisingly, throws up several options. The oldest restaurant in the Faroes, **Muntra** (*Toftagøta 1A;* ⏲ *noon–22.00 daily;* $) is a dependable place adjacent to the tourist office and run by the amenable Poul, who's been feeding the masses here since 1972; indeed, this is the place to meet local fishermen, who come here for a big feed. Accessed by a door at the rear of the building and up the stairs, this eatery not only has great views over the harbour but also some good-value dishes: fish/chicken and chips (*90kr*), a decent Asian fish soup (*78kr*), steaks (*210kr*) and burgers (85kr). Across the road, **Primavera** (*Bakkavegur 16B;* 📞 *44 44 46;* ⏲ *17.00–22.00 Sun–Thu, 17.00–23.00 Fri & Sat;* $) serves a good range of pizzas and burgers for around 100kr, though it's only open in the evenings. Check out, too, the new **Kyrja kaféin** (⏲ *May–Sep 11.00–20.00 Mon–Thu, 10.00–21.00 Fri & Sat, 14.00–18.00 Sun; rest of the year noon–18.00 Thu–Sun;* $), down by the harbour, behind Primavera. This snug little café, with bright red walls and soft chairs, is a great place for a drink or a bite to eat: dish of the day is 65kr; salads go for 55kr; soup is 40kr; and they also serve a brunch of eggs, bacon, yoghurt and fruit on Sat (*noon–14.00*) for 110kr.

Other practicalities For self-caterers there's a well-stocked **supermarket** (⊕ *07.30–22.00 Mon–Sat*) adjacent to the tourist office on the main road at Karvatoftir 2, where you'll also find postal services.

There are two **banks** in Fuglafjørður: Norðoya Sparikassi (*Í Støð 7;* ⊕ *09.30–16.00 Mon–Wed & Fri, 09.30–18.00 Thu*) and Eik (*Í Støð 5;* ⊕ *09.30–16.00 Mon–Fri*); both have an ATM.

The friendly **tourist information office** (✆ *23 80 15;* e *infoey-f@olivant.fo; www.visiteysturoy.fo;* ⊕ *09.00–noon & 13.00–17.45 Mon–Fri, 09.00–noon Sat*) is located in the town's **library** on the main road. Here you'll find a wealth of information about the surrounding district and also a map to help you find the hot spring. The library, open the same hours as the tourist office, has free **internet access**.

What to see and do Fuglafjørður can trace its history back to Viking times. Excavations in the 1950s turned up remains of a farm on the beach at the mouth of the Gjógvará river in the western part of the town. The foundations of a hall dating back to the 10th century together with a collection of man-made objects such as pieces of pottery, glass beads and soapstone disks were uncovered during the excavations. Although little is known about the town before the Black Death in the middle of the 14th century, there is a tale of a man known as Rádni í Lon who owned a *knorr* (a simple wooden boat) and would regularly brave the stormy seas to sail across to Norway laden with goods for sale. Quite remarkably, the spot where he beached his boat for the winter, **Karvatoftir**, can still be seen; ask at the tourist office (see above) for precise directions.

For details of the **hike** to Hellur, see page 109. The path from Fuglafjørður can be found by taking the road up the hillside from beside the tourist information office and then following the road which passes to the west of the town's football pitch.

Arts and craft centre At Í Støð 14, diagonally opposite the tourist office, **Ribarhús** and **Piddasahandil** (✆ *44 44 27; www.ribarhus.com;* ⊕ *15.00–17.30 Mon–Fri, 11.00–13.00 Sat;*) together make up the town's engaging arts and craft centre. Housed in a sturdy stone building dating from 1887, Ribarhús is an airy exhibition hall that puts on changing displays of local art, while the adjacent Piddasahandil sells quality woollens and handicrafts. If you're here during the restricted opening hours, be sure to pop in for a browse – the range of handicrafts is the best on Eysturoy.

Varmakelda The Faroes' one and only **hot spring**, *varmakelda*, is located on the shore of Pollurin about 4km south of the town. The source, which has a year-round constant temperature of 18°C, is not really warm enough to bathe in but is certainly pleasant enough to dangle your feet in on a cold day. Although the tradition of meeting here on Midsummer's Eve to dance the night away on the flat rocks nearby has all but died out today, there is an attempt to revive it. To get here from Fuglafjørður, first retrace your steps along Route 65, passing the new settlement of Kambsdalur on the way, until you come to a turn on the left. Take this road (actually the old road to Leirvík) which leads out to the southern shores of Pollurin and after a kilometre or so you'll come to a rock with the name *varmakelda* marked on it. Here take the walking path leading off towards the shore and you'll see the spring just to the left of where the track ends at the shore; the tourist information office has a map showing the route.

LEIRVÍK From Fuglafjørður it's just 6km south to the entrance to the tunnel that carries Route 70 through Ritafjall mountain (639m) and a further 3km into Leirvík, from where a sub-sea tunnel leads to Klaksvík beneath Leirvíksfjørður. Opened in 2006, the tunnel measures 6.3km in length and is rather bizarrely adorned with multi-coloured lighting designed by artist Tróndur Patursson, at the halfway point. A toll (100kr) is payable for travel in the direction Klaksvík to Leirvík. Both tunnels are often busy with lorries and other traffic since all produce bound for and coming from the northern Faroes (including every bottle of beer made at the Föroya Bjór brewery) must travel through Leirvík.

Getting there and away Buses #400 and #410 run here from Tórshavn and Fuglafjørður respectively.

Other practicalities Overnight accommodation in Leirvík is limited to a basement flat sleeping four people with private facilities at Garðsvegur 16 (*www.visiteysturoy.fo;* **$$**). **Snacks and light meals** are available at the EFFO filling station, which also sells a few staples.

What to see and do Leirvík's main attraction lies at the entrance to the village, beside the main road and close to the filling station: the knee-high remains of four buildings belonging to a **Viking-age farm**. Excavations on the site, known as **Toftanes**, between 1982 and 1987 revealed that the stone foundations of the structures date from the 10th century. The main building, a longhouse with walls 20m in length, is characteristic of the period because it has double-built curved walls and was divided into two: the western half was used as a sitting area while the other half was a cow byre. Remains of a 5m-long fireplace in the middle of the sitting area and the intricate paved stairway by the main door can still clearly be seen, though the five pairs of roof supports close by are modern interpretations. Traces of ash and charcoal found behind the main house suggest that the small structure here was used as a fire-house. Today, the house walls stand five or six boulders high, covered in a layer of grass sods, giving a good impression of the layout of the site. Archaeologists also unearthed a good number of household implements used by the people who once lived here: bronze needles, stone weights for fishing and pieces of pottery all now kept by the Historical Museum in Tórshavn. A second dig in the 1990s uncovered one of the Faroes' best-preserved monuments: the **remains of a chapel** with an ancient burial place. Closed down at the time of the Reformation, this site, known as Bønhústoft and located in a field in the village, is known to contain other such remains.

NORÐRAGØTA AND SYÐRUGØTA Spreading a kilometre or so along Route 65 from the entrance of the Leirvík tunnel to the head of Gøtuvík bay, **Norðragøta** is another example of a Faroese linear village, but one that can trace its history back to the days of the *Færeyinga Saga*. According to the saga, which recounts the rivalry and ritualised violence amongst the islands' early settlers, it was here that one of the key men in Faroese history, the powerful chieftain Tróndur í Gøtu, once lived. Converted to Christianity with a sword held at his neck, Tróndur is credited with building the Faroes' second church, which once stood at nearby Syðragøtu before being moved to the site of the current **timber church**, dating from 1833 and one of the oldest in the country. The church stands at the centre of half-a-dozen superbly preserved **timber houses** resplendent with their black-tarred walls and turf roofs; inside one of them, the Blásastova (a former farmhouse dating from 1835), you'll find the **Gøtu Fornminnissavn** (*Homestead Museum;* m *22 27 17;* ⊕ *Jun–Aug 14.00–16.00 Mon, Tue, Fri, Sat & Sun; admission 50kr*) which provides a detailed and exemplary insight into Faroese life during the 19th century. The interior of the Blásastova has been lovingly restored to its original condition, including a traditional *roykstova*, and now contains a plethora of antique furniture and household and farm implements that would once have been used here; the entrance fee includes a guided tour lasting one hour.

Other practicalities Although there is no café or restaurant in either of the Gøtas, there is a **supermarket** (⊕ *08.00–23.00 daily*) at the junction of víð Ánna and í Kongsbø, opposite the football pitch.

SOUTHERN EYSTUROY

SKÁLAFJØRÐUR AND AROUND At 13km in length, Skálafjørður is the longest fjord in the Faroe Islands, cutting deep into the heart of Eysturoy and all but joining up with Funningsfjørður to the north. The valley that separates the two fjord systems, barely 6km long and given over to the course of the Fjarðará river, is appropriately known as millum fjarða, 'between the fjords'. The superb protection the fjord offers to shipping was put to good use during World War II when the occupying British forces chose to set up a naval base here. The underwater ridge that runs between **Strendur** and **Saltnes** at the narrow mouth of the fjord, a mere 25m below the surface, meant the inlet was effectively off-limits to German submarines as a result. Today, around 5,000 people live here, concentrated in a series of small towns and villages at the fjord's southern tip. Although undeniably scenically dramatic, the Skálafjørður area is unlikely to be the highlight of a trip to the Faroes and the settlements that line its shores are predominantly modern affairs with little to offer the visitor other than a fair array of shops and restaurants, something singularly lacking in other parts of the island. The main places of interest are the woollen mill at Strendur, on the western shore, and the adjoining villages of **Toftir** and **Nes** on the eastern bank, known particularly as the location of the Faroes' international football ground. Until the completion of the subsea tunnel (see page 73), any visit to both banks will inevitably involve backtracking to the head of the fjord, Skálabotnur, and then continuing along the opposite shore.

SKÁLI AND STRENDUR Taking the head of the fjord at Skálabotnur (little more than a road junction, a couple of houses and a salmon farm) as your starting point, follow Route 69 down the fjord's western shore to reach the first settlement on this side of the water, **Skáli**. As you drive along this 6km stretch of road you'll notice that both sides of the fjord are totally uninhabited and it's only as you draw closer to Skáli that signs of habitation start to appear. This unkempt little hamlet consisting of a couple of streets of nondescript suburban dwellings owes its existence to the extensive harbour facilities, indeed the biggest in the country, which were developed along the fjordside during the late 1980s and early 90s. Tragically, the shipbuilding and repair businesses here went bankrupt during the ensuing financial crisis, and today the shipyard is all but empty; occasionally the odd Russian trawler puts in for repairs (paying in part in fish for the work carried out) though Skáli's heyday looks to be gone for good. A further 7km on, passing the pretty little timber church dating from 1834 in the hamlet of Við Sjógv, you'll reach the elongated settlement of **Strendur**, which guards the western entrance to Skálafjørður. Once visited predominantly for its spinning and knitting mill, Snældan (now closed to the public, but see box, page 32), Strendur also enjoys wide open views of Tangafjørður fjord, which separates southern Eysturoy from Streymoy, and indeed across to its sister settlement, Toftir, on the eastern side of Skálafjørður.

Getting there and away Bus #440 operates fairly frequently (roughly half-a-dozen services a day) from Skálabotnur through Skáli to Strendur, with the odd service continuing on to Selatrað (*by request only on* ✆ *34 30 30*) for the youth hostel (see below). Timetables are available at www.ssl.fo.

🏠 **Where to stay and eat** Although there is no accommodation in Strendur, a bed for the night is barely 10km further along Route 69, which now swings northwest and hugs the eastern shore of Sundini sound as it heads for **Selatrað**, the site of an ancient *ting*. The **youth hostel** (✆ *31 10 75*; e *info@skoti.fo*; *www.skoti.fo*; ⊕ *mid-Jun–mid-Aug*; **$**) and adjoining **campsite** enjoy a wonderful location at the foot of a terrace of steep hills looking out over the sound to Hósvík on Streymoy; the hostel has a kitchen for self-caterers. Around 65 people live in Selatrað today and the youth hostel certainly brings life to a peacefully uneventful settlement that has seen busier days; during the 1960s one of the two ferries linking Eysturoy and Streymoy put in here from Hósvík putting tiny Selatrað on the main road to and from Tórshavn.

HIKING FROM SKÁLABOTNUR TO SELATRAÐ

It's also possible to hike between Skálabotnur and Selatrað (7km) via the mountain pass, **Millum Fjalla** (344m), in around 3½ hours. From Skálabotnur, the path begins a couple of kilometres south of the junction of Routes 69 and 10, at a stone quarry along Route 69 for Strendur. Here, you should climb the steep slope in front of you, passing through some quite rocky terrain known as **Ennisstíggur**. Beyond here the path then runs straight for several kilometres (though at times the ground can be quite marshy) offering good views, in clear weather, of the surrounding mountains as far afield as Slættaratindur (882m) near Eiði. After passing through the Millum Fjalla pass between the **Reyðafelstindur** (764m) and **Borgarfelli** (543m) peaks, the track then bears to the west following a series of cairns. Descend now towards the meadow fences ahead of you, cross the Breiðá river, pass through a gate and follow the cattle track which leads finally down to Selatrað.

What to see and do It's worth heading to the southernmost tip of the western side of the fjord, **Raktangi**, a narrow grassy promontory jutting out into the mouth of Skálafjørður, which affords superlative views across to the outskirts of Tórshavn. There's also a **monument** here in memory of all those who have lost their lives at sea.

SKIPANES, SØLDARFJØRÐUR AND LAMBI

From Skálabotnur, it's an uneventful 6km down Route 10 along the eastern shore of Skálafjørður, before the junction with Route 70 comes into view. This is the turn for all traffic heading for Norðragøta, Fuglafjørður, Leirvík and the northern islands. The small gaggle of houses at the intersection, **Skipanes**, is said to be of Viking origin; it's thought that the islands' first settlers, including Tróndur í Gøtu, once kept their ships here. **Søldarfjørður**, the altogether larger settlement that Skipanes runs into, is also one of the oldest villages on Eysturoy, although it has a tragic history. The village was originally called Sólmundarfjørður after one of two brothers, sons of the chieftain, Tróndur Tóralvsson, who first settled here. However, Sólmundur fell out with his elder brother, Skeggi (heir to the family's wealth) and unceremoniously pushed him to his death off the cliff known as Skeggjanøv; Sólmundur was later outlawed and driven from the Faroe Islands for his crime.

A couple of kilometres further on and you'll hit the junction for Route 683 which leads to the idyllically located hamlet of **Lambi**, wedged between two cliff walls overlooking the steely waters of Lambavík bay on the island's eastern shore. Down at the harbour you'll see a large rock standing all by itself in the middle of the quay; when the harbour was being constructed, nobody dared move the stone because it was believed that the Faroese elves and spirits, the *huldufólk*, lived in it. In 1707, the bay witnessed the tragic shipwreck of the *Norske Løve* which foundered on New Year's Eve, and which belonged to the Danish East India Company. The ship's bell, together with a model of the vessel, can be seen in the cathedral in Tórshavn. Although over the years there has been much talk of raising the ship – rumours have circulated for centuries that there was a large cache of gold on board – to date the vessel lies buried on the sea bed under rock and earth after a series of landslips.

GLYVRAR, SALTANGARÁ AND RUNAVÍK

Back on Route 10 and a couple of kilometres after the turn for Lambi, one of the islands' biggest conurbations begins. Although this is not Los Angeles or London, in Faroese terms a veritable mass of people live here in the half-dozen small villages that have grown together to form a 10km-long centre of population that is home to around 3,500 islanders. First off, uninspiring Glyvrar is notable only for its modern church, dating from 1927, of white walls and felt roof (though its more recent 1980s extension makes it look more like a giant folding concertina than a place of worship). Better, push on to the larger and more animated Saltangará and Runavík, virtually indistinguishable from each other, and home to a good number of services such as a hotel, bakeries, banks, restaurants, shops and the only alcohol store on Eysturoy (see *Other practicalities*, page 117).

Getting there and away Bus #440 runs every one or two hours between Runavík, Saltangará and Sóldarfjørður, where connections are available to Tórshavn; in the opposite direction it continues on to Toftir. Timetables are available at www.ssl.fo.

Where to stay and eat *Map, right.*
Hotel Runavík (*Heiðavegur 6; ☏ 66 33 33; e info@hotelrunavik.fo; www.hotelrunavik.fo; $$$$*) has 18 comfortable rooms, with private facilities; those at the front of the building look out over the harbour and should be your first choice if you stay here. Otherwise, contact the tourist office and ask if they know of any private rooms available locally. The best option for eating is the modern **MC Café & Grill** (*Heiðavegur 44; ☏ 44 44 24; ⊕ 10.00–23.00 Mon–Fri, noon–23.00 Sat & Sun; $*) with a decent chicken tikka massala (*125kr*), fish and chips (*80kr*) and burgers (*95kr*); they also serve a set lunch on weekdays for 85kr (⊕ *11.30–14.00*). Close by, **Café Cibo** (*Heiðavegur 51; ☏ 23 40 00; ⊕ 11.00–21.00 daily; $*) is a similar no-nonsense establishment rustling up a variety of snacks including chicken burgers, salmon sandwiches, fish and chips and salads for under 100kr, whilst their weekday lunch (⊕ *noon–14.00*) for 75kr.

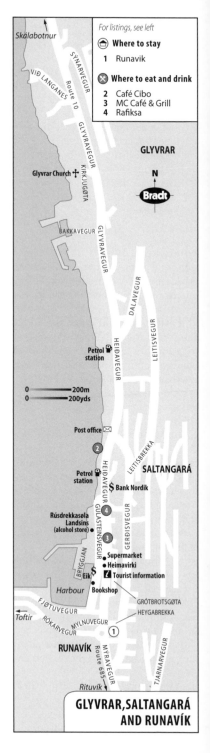

For listings, see left
🏠 **Where to stay**
1   Runavík
❌ **Where to eat and drink**
2   Café Cibo
3   MC Café & Grill
4   Rafiksa

GLYVRAR

N

Bradt

Glyvrar Church ✝

SÝNARVEGUR
VIÐ LANGANES
Route 10
GLYVRAVEGUR
KIRKJUGØTA
BAKKAVEGUR
GLYVRAVEGUR
DALAVEGUR
LEITISVEGUR
HEIÐAVEGUR

Petrol station

0   200m
0   200yds

Post office ✉
②
Petrol station
LEITISBREKKA
SALTANGARÁ
$ Bank Nordik
HEIÐAVEGUR
GULASTEINSVEGUR
GERÐISVEGUR
Rúsdrekkasøla Landsins (alcohol store) ●
④
③
BRYGGJAN
● Supermarket
● Heimavirki
ℹ Tourist information
Eik $
Harbour   Bookshop
GRÓTBROTSGØTA
HEYGABREKKA
FJØTUVEGUR
Toftir
RÓKARVEGUR
MYLNUVEGUR
①
RUNAVÍK
Route 685
MÝRARVEGUR
TJARNARVEGUR
Rituvík

GLYVRAR, SALTANGARÁ AND RUNAVÍK

Skálabotnur

The hotel restaurant, curiously decorated with old newspaper pages, is open evenings only (66 33 33; ⊕ 17.00–22.00 daily; $$) and serves a selection of fish dishes for around 200kr. Otherwise, you're looking at the altogether less appealing **Rafiksa** (44 82 37; $) at the junction of Heiðavegur and Gulasteinsvegur, serving pizzas, burgers and kebabs and a drink for around 85–100kr.

Other practicalities The Eysturoy branch of the Rúsdrekkasøla Landsins **alcohol** store (⊕ 13.00–17.30 Mon–Thu, 10.00–17.30 Fri, 10.00–13.00 Sat) is on the main road at Heiðavegur 25. There are two **banks**, Eik (⊕ 09.30–16.00 Mon–Fri) and BankNordik (⊕ 10.00–16.00 Mon–Wed & Fri, 10.00–17.00 Thu) at Heiðavegur 17 and Heiðavegur 54 respectively, both with ATMs. There is also a **post office** at Heiðavegur 57 (⊕ 10.00–16.00 Mon–Fri) and a **bookshop** at Heiðavegur 15 (⊕ 09.00–17.30 Mon–Fri, 09.00–14.00 Sat). The best **supermarket** is Bónus at Heiðavegur 40 (⊕ 09.00–22.00 Mon–Sat). The central **tourist information office** (41 70 60; e kunningarstovan@runavik.fo; www.visiteysturoy.fo; ⊕ 09.00–16.00 Mon–Thu, 09.00–15.00 Fri), one of only two on Eysturoy, is located on the main road in Runavík at Heiðavegur 26, close to the other shops and services. Inside you'll find plenty of information about local attractions and also the latest bus times if you're planning to hike around Nes or make connections back to Tórshavn.

What to see and do

Runavík Although there are no sights as such to take in here, sooner or later you're bound to end up at the **harbour** – one of the biggest and busiest in the Faroe Islands and where you can take in the goings-on of the ships and fishing boats. Otherwise, pop into the local **Heimavirki** (⊕ 14.00–17.30 Mon–Fri, 11.00–14.00 Sat) next to the tourist office at Heiðavegur 50 who stock an excellent range of handknitted woollens and other homemade items where you might just be able to pick up a bargain or two.

Toftir and Nes A mere 3km south around the headland from Runavík and you'll find yourself in **Toftir**, the last main town on Eysturoy, which stretches in an ungainly fashion from the narrow strip of land by the fjord up the hillside beyond. It's here in Toftir, at Oyrarnar 10 (opposite the junction with Høganesvegur to the stadium and above the harbour), that you'll find one of the Faroes' best-stocked woollens stores: **Navia** (⊕ 10.00–17.30 Mon–Fri, 10.00–14.00 Sat), selling all manner of sweaters, hats, gloves and coats. The Navia store here is much bigger than the outlet in Tórshavn and sometimes has sales clearance items, too. Beyond Toftir, the exposed rocky hillock at Eysturoy's southern point holds a special place in the heart of every Faroese football fan: it was here, following the quite sensational 1–0 victory of the Faroe Islands over Austria in the European Championship qualifier in 1991, that the islands' first proper **football pitch** was created. Blasting into the surrounding hillside created enough flat land to lay a pitch – with real turf – big enough to hold international matches and meeting all FIFA requirements. The **stadium** here can hold the entire population of Tórshavn, around 19,400 spectators, who flock here in their thousands, despite the ferocious winds and rain that often whip in off the surrounding fjords, to watch both qualifying matches for the national team, local inter-island games as well as athletics events. From the main road in Toftir, follow Høganesvegur up the hillside, bearing right and following signs for 'Stadion' all the way to the car park in front of a white building used as changing rooms. The international stadium is the second pitch you can see up here, located to the right of the main building. Locals proudly point out that the Toftir stadium is streets

6

ahead of its rival in Tórshavn, thanks to the superior quality of the turf here. As you leave Toftir, it's worth stopping briefly at **Fridrikskirkjan**, the modern church built between 1993 and 1994, with its steep V-shaped roof. On the opposite side of the road there's a moving **memorial** to all the local people who lost their lives at sea. The sculpture, in the form of curving metal strips, creates the form of a mother and child staring out to sea: a plaque here bears the names of those who never returned, most recently in 1994.

The handful of houses down the hill from Fridrikskirkjan make up **Nes**, a tiny hamlet which amazingly boasts its own much more beautiful **timber church**, dating from 1843 and one of the last to be built in the islands. With black-tarred walls and a slate roof, the interior of the church follows the same pattern as the other 19th-century churches in the Faroes, with unscrubbed pine walls and a carved choral screen. Indeed, the church here has played an important role in Eysturoy's religious life: the minister for the whole of the island once lived here, a role fulfilled, most prominently, by V U Hammershaimb (1867–78) who was instrumental in achieving official status for the Faroese language. Close by, just up the hill from the timber church overlooking the fjord, it's also worth having a look at the **cannon** that was erected here in 1990 to mark the 50th anniversary of the end of World War II. The gun, together with the surrounding bunkers and embattlements, was used by the occupying British forces during the war to defend the entrance to Skálafjørður. From this vantage point, there are unsurpassed views not only of the outskirts of Tórshavn, on the other side of the fjord, but also of the northern tip of Nólsoy.

From Nes, there are a number of pleasant **walks**, including a **hike** of around 3 hours that takes you up to the wind turbines that dominate the hillside above Nes and on to Toftavatn lake, noted for its rich birdlife, before returning back to Nes via Runavík. The path begins close to the junction of the main road, Route 682 (which swings around Toftavatn), and heads to the lake's southeastern corner. As you walk you may notice a wind generator high on the moors off to your right; this is used to test wind speed for possible power generation. However, it seems that the wind in the Faroes is simply too strong for these turbines to operate. Once at the lake, the track turns into a small lane, which then heads north to join Route 685 back into Runavík, roughly 1.5km to the west.

Alternatively, a **second path** leads from the village of Nes southeast across Fossdalur valley, site of the wind generator, passing the hill, Vørðan (169m) on its western side, heading for the tiny settlement of **Æðuvík**, a distance of around 2–3km. This, the most southerly place on Eysturoy, is a hamlet of no more than a dozen or so houses perched right on the shore and alarmingly exposed to the ferocious Atlantic storms. Near the rubbish dump at the north of the settlement, the old Viking parliament site, Tinghella, can still be made out.

If you time your hike right, it's possible to hike one way from Nes to Æðuvík and then take bus #442 back to Runavík, a journey of around 10 minutes (⏲ *16.05 Mon–Fri*).

UPDATES WEBSITE

You can post your comments and recommendations, and read the latest feedback and updates from other readers online at www.bradtupdates.com/ faroes.

7

The Northern Islands

The six northern islands that form the northeastern extremity of the Faroes are arguably the country's best-kept secret. These remote enigmatic islands, known as *norðoyar* in Faroese, receive little attention, even within the Faroe Islands themselves, and outside the main town of Klaksvík see relatively few visitors. Yet they are astonishingly beautiful islands, their geography of sheer sea cliffs and layer-cake mountains of scree and deep green valleys making them not only the most photogenic of all 18 islands but also the most alluring; although it takes time to get out here, it's well worth making the effort. Indeed, it also takes time to get to know the inhabitants of these remote outposts in the North Atlantic since any Faroe Islander will readily tell you they are known for their taciturn nature which is often, mistakenly, interpreted by outsiders as rudeness. Take the trouble, though, to chat to the people who scratch a living in the northern islands from sheep farming or crofting and you'll discover a genuine warmth of character and a shy curiosity about just what brings you out to these forgotten isles.

Of the six northern islands, an inner core of three are connected to each other. **Borðoy**, easily the most significant island thanks primarily to the settlement of Klaksvík, the Faroes' second town, at its southern tip, is linked to neighbouring **Kunoy** and **Viðoy** by road-carrying causeways built atop the dams that stretch across the narrow Haraldssund and Hvannasund sounds respectively. Sandwiched between Eysturoy and Kunoy, the endearing skinny length of **Kalsoy** is the most westerly of the northern islands and one of the group's most appealing destinations due to its deep valleys and towering hillsides. However, it's the last two islands that really steal the show: **Svínoy** and its tiny neighbour **Fugloy** are undoubtedly the Faroes at their most remote, elemental and enchanting. Life here is totally dominated by the whims of the mighty Atlantic, the diminutive settlements clinging to the sheer rock faces of these barren islands in the face of adversity – and some truly appalling weather.

WHERE TO GO

The best place to base yourself in the northern islands is **Klaksvík** since it's here that you'll find the greatest (albeit still limited when compared with Tórshavn) choice of restaurants, shops and accommodation. Here, you'll also find one of the most spectacular churches in the Faroes as well as a museum – and a swimming pool for those rainy afternoons. In addition, buses and ferries emanate from here so you'll generally be able to find a connection that suits. Klaksvík is also the entry point into the northern islands when arriving from the south thanks to the sub-sea tunnel from Leirvík. Striking out north from Klaksvík, Route 70 soon divides, heading west the short distance across the sound to **Kunoy**, an uneventful little

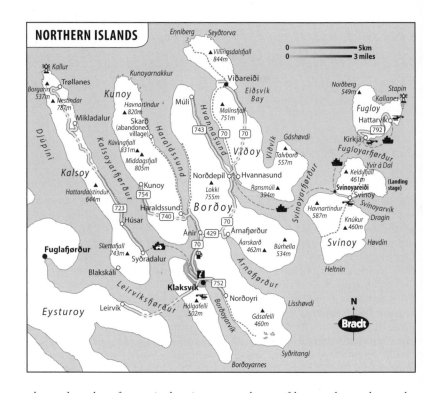

place, whose best feature is the picturesque cluster of houses that make up the eponymous village overlooking the steely waters of **Kalsoyarfjørður**, perfect for photographs and barely 12km from the centre of Klaksvík. Alternatively, heading east, the road enters a series of tunnels before emerging high above the poetically named **Hvannasund** off Borðoy's eastern shore. Before driving over the dam and road-causeway to **Viðoy**, consider a quick detour north to the now-abandoned village of **Múli**, just 6km from the junction with the causeway: a forlorn and neglected hamlet which stands as proof of the adversities of Faroese life. Across the causeway, the small harbour and jetty immediately to the east is the hamlet of Hvannasund; this is the departure point for one of the Faroes' most unforgettable boat trips aboard *Ritan* which chugs its way out to **Svínoy** and, weather permitting, to **Fugloy**, bobbing on the massive swells like a cork. From Hvannasund, Route 70 heads north via a new tunnel to **Viðareiði**, the most northerly village in the Faroes, and site of a truly remarkable collection of silverware presented to the villagers by the British government in thanks for their rescue of British sailors in 1847 as well as being the location of one of the highest perpendicular sea cliffs anywhere in the world, **Enniberg**.

If you're after a boat trip that doesn't first involve taking a bus out to Viðoy, look no further than **Kalsoy** which is linked directly to Klaksvík by regular boat; it's also the place to fully appreciate the Faroese obsession with blasting tunnels through their steep hillsides – this remote island is home to no fewer than five of them, making it an easy journey to Kalsoy's most northerly point and location for one of the best hikes in the entire northern islands and the best views anywhere in the country. Kalsoy is also home to the inordinately popular statue of the seal woman, down by the sea in Mikladalur.

Although the northern islands are not all linked to one another by road, getting around from one to another rarely poses a problem. The only things to bear in mind when travelling in this remote part of the country are that bus and ferry services are not as frequent as further south and that the weather can, and often does, lead to helicopter cancellations. The ferries, though, generally run with little disruption in all but the most appalling of conditions.

The key **bus** services are #500 which operates from Klaksvík via Hvannasund to Viðareiði, #504 from Klaksvík to Kunoy and #506 which operates on Kalsoy between Syðradalur and Trøllanes in connection with ferry arrivals from Klaksvík. The bus to Hvannasund connects with ferry sailings to Svínoy and Fugloy.

Two **ferry** services operate in the northern islands: *Sam* runs regularly out to Kalsoy from Klaksvík and *Ritan* sails out to Svínoy and Fugloy from Hvannasund either two or three times daily; see the timetable at www.ssl.fo for precise details, and note that, due to sea conditions, arrival times at Svínoy and Fugloy are only approximate and not guaranteed.

Weather permitting, the Atlantic Airways **helicopter** links Klaksvík with Svínoy and Fugloy on Sunday, Wednesday and Friday (June–August also Monday), and can provide a handy way of getting between the two islands if you're trying to see both in one day: boat from Hvannasund to Svínoy, helicopter from Svínoy across to Fugloy, allowing you to return to Hvannasund by boat from Fugloy. Remember though that bad weather elsewhere in the islands can prevent the helicopter from taking off – during one of my recent visits to Svínoy the helicopter was grounded at the airport on Vágar, unable to fly to Svínoy and pick me up, although the conditions in the northern islands were quite reasonable. If you can work it into your schedule, it's really worth trying to take a helicopter trip out here since the views of the northern islands from the air as you skim over their craggy forms are spectacular and a highlight of any trip to the Faroes.

BORÐOY

KLAKSVÍK Sitting snugly around a tight U-shaped inlet crammed with state-of-the-art ocean-going fishing trawlers, Klaksvík, with a population of around 5,000, is the second-largest settlement in the Faroes and the economic and administrative centre for the northern islands. It's here that the entire population of the six surrounding islands comes to shop and go about their everyday chores, be it going to the bank, popping into the library or sorting things out at the district council. Klaksvík owes its pre-eminence to its superbly sheltered harbour, which, ever since the town was granted municipal status in 1908, has continued to grow steadily and today is the site of one of the Faroes' largest and most successful fish-processing plants, served by the town's sizeable fishing fleet. Remarkably there's also a brewery in Klaksvík: **Föroya Bjór** [122 B4] was originally established by a local farmer and has since grown into the country's biggest and best beer producer, brewing classic European-style lager from imported hops from southern Denmark; the use of the *ö* in the spelling of the word *föroya* is an older version of today's Danicised *føroyar*.

Although Klaksvík can trace its history back to Viking times when a *ting* was held here to pronounce upon all things administrative, today's town effectively grew out of the four farms which were well established by the time a trading station was established here in 1838 during the Danish Trade Monopoly. It wasn't until the

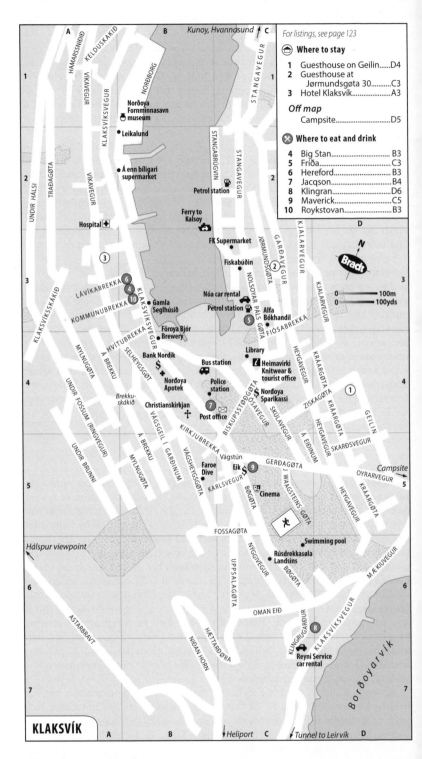

For listings, see page 123

Where to stay
1 Guesthouse on Geilin......D4
2 Guesthouse at
  Jørmundsgøta 30..........C3
3 Hotel Klaksvík.....................A3

Off map
  Campsite............................D5

Where to eat and drink
4 Big Stan...............................B3
5 Fríða....................................C3
6 Hereford.............................B3
7 Jacqson...............................B4
8 Klingran..............................D6
9 Maverick..............................C5
10 Roykstovan........................B3

KLAKSVÍK

end of the 19th century that Klaksvík made the transition from farming to fishing and acquired the modern harbour that today provides the town with its window on the world: one-fifth of the the Faroes' fish exports originate here.

Getting there and away With the advent of the tunnel to and from Leirvík, all traffic now approaches Klaksvík from the southwest along the Eysturoyarvegur. For details of public transportation to and from Klaksvík, see *Getting around*, page 121.

Where to stay Klaksvík has a handful of options. Most visitors opt for the pleasant and friendly **Hotel Klaksvík** [122 A3] (*Víkavegur 38;* 45 53 33; e *hotelklaksvik@ hotelklaksvik.fo; www.hotelklaksvik.fo;* **$$$**), which enjoys superb views out over the harbour; rooms here are a little on the plain side but comfortable and spacious. Otherwise, there's a couple of unnamed B&B options, of which the best are the comfortable **guesthouses** (**$$**) up at Jørmundsgøta 30 [122 C3] and at Geilin 29 [122 D4].

Between May and mid-September, it's possible to camp (**$**) at the town's beautifully located **campsite** [122 D5], a couple of kilometres southeast of the town centre at Úti í Grøv; the service building here contains a kitchen, washing machine and showers. Bookings for the guesthouses and campsite can be made through the tourist office (see *Other practicalities*, page 124).

Where to eat and drink Although Klaksvík is not famed for its eateries, there is at least a choice of restaurants, putting it ahead all the other towns in the northern islands.

✖ **Hereford** [122 B3] Klaksvíksvegur 45; 45 64 34; ⊕ 18.00–23.00 Thu–Sat. The best restaurant in town, serving steaks (*215kr*), tournedos (*255kr*), châteaubriand (*265kr*) & roast lamb (*250kr*). Sadly, the homely atmosphere that greets you as you enter from the street downstairs, conjured up by period furniture & high-backed chairs, is not replicated in the restaurant upstairs, where diners are slotted into wooden booths more akin to a cheap pizzeria. **$$$**

✖ **Fríða** [122 C3] Nólsoyar Pálsgøta 7; 33 33 44; www.frida.fo; ⊕ 09.00–19.00 Mon–Thu, 09.00–22.00 Fri & Sat, 14.00–20.00 Sun. Undoubtedly the best place for coffee & cakes in Klaksvík, though this homely little café, complete with outdoor terrace to the rear, also serves a filling b/fast (until 11.30) for 99kr, chicken salad (*89kr*), burgers (*129kr*) as well as wines & beers. **$$**

✖ **Big Stan** [122 B3] Klaksvíksvegur 45; 44 55 44; www.big-stan.net; ⊕ 16.30–midnight Sun–Thu, 16.30–05.00 Fri & Sat. Come here for your takeaway pizzas, shawarma & burgers – a

12-inch pizza goes for around 95kr, whilst shawarma & fries is 65kr, & burgers cost 55kr. It's also possible to eat in should you choose. **$**

✖ **Jacqson** [122 B4] Klaksvíksvegur 4; 45 88 88; ⊕ 11.00–22.00 Mon–Thu, 11.00–04.00 Fri & Sat. A welcome addition to the dining scene in Klaksvík, this new bar-bistro serves up burgers, salads, nachos & smoothies, & also has live Faroese music on Fri & Sat nights. **$**

✖ **Klingran** [122 D6] Klingrugarður 6; 45 53 14; ⊕ 07.00–21.00 daily. This bakery-cum-café is a good place for filling lunches (*78kr*) & delicious Danish pastries; on Fridays it serves a lunch buffet for 99kr while by evening there are pizzas for 80–98kr as well as fish & chips or chicken & chips for 78kr. **$**

🍺 **Roykstovan** [122 B3] Klaksvíksvegur 41; 45 61 25; ⊕ 11.00–23.00 Mon–Thu, 11.00–04.00 Fri & Sat, 14.00–23.00 Sun. Next door but one to Hereford, this enjoyable drinking den attracts an older crowd, including some seasoned sea dogs. It's a good place for a beer or two & is handy for striking up conversation with the locals.

Entertainment and nightlife Undoubtedly the best nights to be in Klaksvík are Friday and Saturday, when seemingly the entire town can be found crammed into **Maverick** [122 C5] (*Gerðagøta 6;* \ *45 45 70;* ⊕ *18.00–midnight Sun–Thu, 18.00–04.00 Fri & Sat*), a bar-cum-club, which also serves food on Saturday nights (⊕ *18.00–23.00*), attracting the town's trendy young things; come in here as a tourist at the weekend and it won't be long before someone strikes up a conversation with you wanting to know what you think about Klaksvík. Although it's not so busy on other nights of the week, if you're looking to have a beer this is definitely the best place to make for.

Klaksvík's **cinema**, Atlantis [122 C5] (*Bøgøta 5;* \ *45 69 00; www.atlantis.fo*), sits close to the head of the bay, though bear in mind that it may not be open every night of the week. The excellent **swimming pool** and **sauna**, Svimjihøllin [122 C6] (\ *45 60 37; www.svim.fo;* ⊕ *06.45–08.45 Mon–Fri, 14.00–20.00 Tue, Thu & Fri, 14.00–17.00 Wed, 10.00–17.00 Sat, 08.00–10.00 & 14.00–16.00 Sun*), are located off Gerðagøta on Jógvan Waagsteins gøta; despite what other bathers may do, you should follow the hygiene rules that apply to all swimming pools in the Faroes (as indeed a notice posted in the changing room dictates), namely, to shower naked, without a swimming costume, before entering the pool.

Other practicalities

Alcohol store [122 C6] Rúsdrekkasøla Landsins, Bøgøta 38; ⊕ 13.00–17.30 Mon–Thu, 10.00–17.30 Fri, 10.00–13.00 Sat

Banks Eik [122 C5] Bøgøta 12; ⊕ 09.30–16.00 Mon–Fri. BankNordik [122 B4] Klaksvíksvegur 7; ⊕ 10.00–16.00 Mon–Thu, 10.00–17.00 Fri. Norðoya Sparikassi [122 C4] Ósavegur 1; ⊕ 09.30–16.00 Mon–Wed & Fri, Thu 09.30–18.00. All have ATMs.

Bike rental Available at the tourist office [122 C4]; see opposite (*100kr/24hrs*).

Bookshops Alfa Bókhandil [122 C3] Nólsoyar Páls gøta 2; ⊕ 10.00–17.30 Mon–Thu, 10.00–18.00 Fri, 10.00–12.30 Sat. Leikalund [122 B2], Klaksvíksvegur 86; ⊕ 11.00–16.00 Mon–Fri, 11.00–14.00 Sat.

Car rental Nóa [122 C3], Nólsoyar Páls gøta 13; \ 75 75 75; www.noa.fo. Reyni Service [122 C7] Klingrugarður 3; \ 47 30 40; www.reyniservice.fo

Doctor Klaksvíkar sjúkrahús hospital [122 A2] Sníðgøta; \ 45 54 63

Food stores FK [122 C3] Nólsoyar Pálsgøta; ⊕ 08.00–22.00 Mon–Sat. Fiskabúðin [122 C3] Nólsoyar Pálsgøta 13; ⊕ 13.00–18.00 Mon–Thu, 10.00–18.00 Fri, 10.00–14.00 Sat (sells freshly frozen fish). Á enn bíligari [122 B2] Klaksvíksvegur 80; ⊕ 08.00–22.00 Mon–Sat

Knitwear Norðoya Heimavirki [122 C4] Tingstøðin (behind the tourist office); \ 45 68 99; ⊕ 13.00–17.30 Mon–Fri, 10.00–13.00 Sat

Library [122 C4] Tingstøðin; ⊕ 13.00–18.00 Mon–Fri, 10.00–13.00 Sat, Jun–Aug closed Sat

Pharmacy Norðoya Apotek [122 B4] Klaksvíksvegur 5; \ 47 25 00; ⊕ 09.00–17.30 Mon–Fri, 09.00–13.00 Sat

Post office [122 C4] Klaksvíksvegur 2; \ 45 50 08; ⊕ 09.00–15.00 Mon–Fri

Taxi K-Taxa \ 25 10 00. Kvikktaxa \ 59 55 55. Norðtaxa \ 27 27 70

Tourist information [122 C4] Tingstøðin 1, Norðoya Kunningarstova; \ 45 69 39; e info@klaksvik.fo; www.visitnordoy.fo; ⊕ May–Aug 09.00–17.00 Mon–Fri, 10.00–14.00 Sat; rest of the year 09.00–16.00 Mon–Fri. The friendly staff have maps & information about the town as well as the latest weather forecasts for the northern islands (a west–southwest wind generally brings clear sunny conditions to the northern Faroes). This is also the place to enquire & make bookings for cottages on some of the remoter islands. They can also help with bus & ferry timetables, essential if you're planning a trip to Svínoy & Fugloy.

What to see and do Although, in Faroese terms, Klaksvík is a steaming urban metropolis, it's still pretty hard to get lost here since the town consists essentially of just one main road (Nólsoyar Páls gøta, later becoming Klaksvíksvegur) which winds its way from the harbour entrance around the head of the inlet and back towards the open sea on the other side of the bay. Indeed, it's a pleasant place to stroll, taking in the shops and the busy goings-on in the harbour, perhaps worth a day or so's exploration before heading on to the remoter islands that lie beyond.

From the ferry berth, Nólsoyar Páls gøta leads towards the **town centre** passing a couple of clothes stores and a bookshop along the way. Just beyond here, on the right-hand side, you'll come across one of the best places in the islands to buy homemade Faroese sweaters: **Norðoya Heimavirki** [122 C4] located in a small square known as Tingstøðin beside the town library. Inside, there's not only a good selection of knitwear from some of the main manufacturers but there's also an array of jumpers hand-knitted by the women of Klaksvík. From here, Nólsoyar Páls gøta mutates into Biskupsstøðgøta as it curves around the head of the harbour, passing the Norðoya Sparikassi bank at the corner of Ósavegur and the bus station opposite. Up behind the bank, occupying part of the narrow neck of land dividing the main harbour from Borðoyarvík bay to the east, is the **swimming pool** [122 C6] and **sports ground** [122 C5]. It's from the roundabout behind the swimming pool that Eysturoyarvegur leads to the tunnel for Leirvík. At the corner of Biskupsstøð gøta and Klaksvíksvegur, which now runs the entire length of the western side of the harbour, you'll find the post office, the police station and the **brewery** with a small store (⏱ *10.00–17.00 Mon–Thu, 10.00–17.30 Fri*) selling bottles of beer and promotional goodies such as glasses emblazoned with the brewery's logo and T-shirts.

Christianskirkjan church [122 B4] (⏱ *mid-May– mid-Sep 10.00–16.00 Mon–Sat*) Opposite Föroya Bjór stands one of the Faroes' most imposing churches and Klaksvík's main sight, named after King Christian X of Denmark and consecrated in 1963. Although designed by Danish architect Peter Koch, from the outside it's easy to make out the Faroese shapes that have given this modern re-creation of a traditional church its unusual form: the tall gable walls, made of natural stone, at either end of the church are based on those at Kirkjubøur, whereas the vast floor-to-ceiling windows which punctuate the lengths of the building are representations of the gable ends of Faroese boat sheds. The extravagant interior holds a whopping **altar fresco** of *The Parable of the Last Banquet* from St Luke's Gospel, which, although originally painted by Joakim Skovgaard in 1901 to adorn the church in Viborg in Denmark, was removed from the church barely a decade later to protect it from damp. After a spell hanging in Denmark's National Art Museum, the fresco was offered to Koch who immediately donated it to Klaksvík when he was commissioned to build Christianskirkjan. The traditional **wooden eight-oared boat** hanging from the ceiling was once the largest such vessel in the islands. Built in 1890, the boat has quite a history, being used not only by the local minister who sailed out in it from his home in Viðareiði to the remoter islands to give his sermons but also by the people of Fugloy as a fishing and whaling boat. At Christmas 1913, this boat and three others were caught in a ferocious storm while out fishing; as the others went down, this boat limped home carrying the only survivors: two boys aged nine and 11 and an old man in his 70s. Coming just a fortnight after another maritime disaster off nearby Svínoy, 13 widows with over 40 children under the age of 15 were left without husbands and fathers. The other item of note inside the church is the font, which is thought to be up to 4,000 years old and was once in use in a heathen temple. Originally made during the Stone Age in Denmark and discovered in a ruined church in north Zealand in Denmark, this granite bowl was donated to Christianskirkjan by the Danish National Museum in Copenhagen.

Gamla Seglhúsið [122 B3] (*Klaksvíksvegur 48;* ☎ *21 70 55; www.gamlaseglhusid. fo;* ⏱ *14.00–17.00 Mon–Fri & Sun; admission free*) Located in an atmospheric old stone building from 1914, which once produced and repaired sails for the town's sailing ships, Gamla Seglhúsið now functions as a gallery showcasing local Faroese art over two floors. Exhibitions change on a monthly basis and all the artwork on show can also be purchased.

Norðoya Fornminnasavn (Klaksvík museum) [122 B1] (Klaksvíksvegur 86; ⊕ Jun–mid-Sep 13.00–16.00 daily; admission 20kr) Continuing past the church, the Seaman's Home and the hospital, you'll soon reach the other main sight in town: the Norðoya Fornminnasavn museum, occupying the black-tarred building of the Danish Trade Monopoly which dates from 1838. To be honest, though, the potpourri of exhibits inside is rather pedestrian and is perhaps only worth a look on a rainy day. Divided into two rooms, the museum's contents are split between the pharmacy on the first floor, which operated until 1961 and is today still stuffed with its original lotions and potions and curious bottles and tools, and a couple of other exhibition rooms which contain, predictably, all the usual suspects: fishing nets, grindstones, hooks and other equally dull bits and bobs from a previous age.

Diving trips from Klaksvík Founded in 2002 and based in Klaksvík, **Faroe Dive** [122 B5] (Vágsheygsgøta 38; m 21 89 29; e faroedive@faroedive.fo; www.faroedive.fo) have a surprisingly large number of year-round diving courses and guided diving tours at various locations around the Faroes. Previous experience is not always necessary and beginners' courses are often held in the harbour in Klaksvík. There are full details on the website.

Klaksvík Summer Festival During a long weekend in early August (exact dates can be found on www.summarfestivalur.com), Klaksvík gives itself over to the dubious musical delights of the summarfestivalur. Begun in 2004, this orgy of 80s and 90s music has grown into the Faroes' biggest music festival, attracting 12,000 people annually. In previous years adoring fans have poured into town to see the likes of Roxette, Ronan Keating, The Scorpions, Shakin Stevens and even hearthrob Kim Wilde do their thing. Tragically, in 2007 Ms Wilde was robbed of her once-in-a-lifetime opportunity to croon in Klaksvík when the weather turned truly foul and the concert had to be abandoned. Unperturbed by the vagaries of the Faroese weather, the festival goes from strength to strength and a surprisingly international cast always seems to top the bill. The latest details about the festival line-up and tickets can be seen on the website.

Hikes from Klaksvík To fully appreciate Klaksvík's highly unusual geographical location, wedged between two inlets on a narrow strip of land no more than a kilometre wide, it's worth climbing up the hills on the western edge of the town for a better perspective. The easiest viewpoint is at **Hálsur**, a mountain pass at 245m immediately behind the Sjómansheim and the hospital. To get here follow Uppsalagøta south out of town heading for the heliport (look for the windsock to guide you), then turn into **Niðan Horn** and look out for an unmade road branching off to the right and leading back in the direction of the town along the slopes of **Hálgafelli mountain** (502m) past a couple of water tanks. Follow this track and you'll come to the pass between Hálgafelli and the mountain **Klakkur** (413m), in front of you. From this vantage point there are superb views not only of Klaksvík and its two bays, Vágur and Borðoyarvík, but west through the pass across to Eysturoy. From the pass there's easy access to the two mountains, Hálgafelli and Klakkur, but sadly, in all but the best weather, their peaks are often shrouded in mist.

NORTHERN BORÐOY: NORÐDEPIL The main road out of Klaksvík leads past the tourist office and the ferry berth north along Borðoy's western shoreline, affording grand views out towards Kunoy. Barely 3km from the town centre, Route 70 splits: left drops down to sea level to cross to Kunoy, whereas Route 429, to the right, enters the single-lane 1.7km-long Árnafjarðartunnilin tunnel (the second to be built in the Faroes, in 1965) to access the island's east coast. However, after emerging blinking into the bright daylight (there's no lighting in Faroese tunnels), you're immediately plunged into Borðoy's second tunnel, Hvannasundstunnilin, dating from 1967 and just over 2km in length. Should you wish to break your journey and stretch your legs, there's a hiking path up to **Áarskarð** (the mountain above the first tunnel; 429m) and on to Klaksvík (4km; allow 2 hours one-way) which begins beside the first mountain stream on the short stretch of road between the two tunnels. Although the path is well marked with posts and cairns, the climb is quite steep at times and, indeed, until the opening of the tunnel, provided the only access between Klaksvík and the small villages to the north. The views from the top of this mountain, however, are stupendous: on a clear day you can see most of the northern islands from up here, their peaks stretching far into the distance. Incidentally, it was also in this area that a German bomber crashed into a mountainside after bombing Klaksvík harbour during World War II. Before setting off, reassure yourself of the route by having a look at the information board about the route in the lay-by between the two tunnels.

After the second tunnel, Route 70 descends past the precipitous slopes of another of Borðoy's high mountains, **Lokki** (755m), towards a cluster of houses either side of Hvannasund sound, which separates the island from neighbouring Viðoy. These twin villages, **Norðdepil** on Borðoy and **Hvannasund** on Viðoy, have together formed a single town since the construction of the causeway between them in 1972. Although the main road races past Norðdepil towards the causeway, it's worth turning off and heading into the village, home to around 200 people, to see the pretty collection of old wood-panelled houses reflected in the still waters of the sound. Economic life here is totally dependent on the impressive fish factory, one of the biggest in the Faroes, which has helped to prevent depopulation. In sharp contrast to Hvannasund across the water, Norðdepil, which consists of no more than a couple of narrow streets, dates only from the reforms of 1866 when land was made available for settlement and cultivation. Life here on the northern side of the sound has always been tougher than on the sunnier southern side around Hvannasund, where land has been cultivated since the Reformation. The harbour has always been Norðdepil's lifeblood, whereas more climatically favoured Hvannasund has been able to exploit the flat land around the sound for agriculture; the results are clear to see, for, bar a couple of wooden houses, modern concrete structures with small gardens dominate in Norðdepil.

MÚLI Just 6km north of Norðdepil along Route 743 (also known as Múlaleið), the now-abandoned hamlet of Múli, comprising three weather-beaten wooden houses built tightly together as protection against the wind and rain, bears silent witness to man's final surrender to the unforgiving forces of nature.

Just one generation ago, this was a thriving community of 30 people, working the crofts that lined the shoreline here, and fishing. However, with their menfolk often away at sea for days or weeks at a time, it soon became evident that life here was unsustainable and one by one the families of Múli drifted away for the bright lights and security of Klaksvík – at the time, Múli wasn't even reachable by road, only by boat from Klaksvík (*Másin*, which now operates from Hvannasund to Svínoy and Fugloy, was originally built to work in the northern islands and operated a circuitous route linking Klaksvík with Haraldssund on Kunoy, Múli, Viðareiði, Norðdepil, Svínoy, Fugloy and Árnafjørður). Ironically, once the road was built out here the last people moved away and the hamlet was finally abandoned in 1998. The last inhabitants were two elderly couples in their 80s and 90s, who simply were unable to exist in such a remote location. Indeed, this finger of land is one of the best places in the Faroes to experience nature in the raw: turn off your car engine, stand outside and listen to the eerie silence, disturbed only by the cries of seabirds, the crashing of the waves on this exposed shoreline, and the howl of the wind off the Atlantic.

Where to stay Without doubt, Múli is remote, but its location is also hauntingly beautiful, and should you wish to stay here, it's possible to rent one of the **houses** (**$$**) through the tourist office in Klaksvík (see page 124). There is no public transport to Múli – **bus** #500 operates only as far as Norðdepil from where you would have to walk the 6km to the hamlet if you didn't hire a car.

VIÐOY

The most northerly of all the 18 Faroe Islands, Viðoy, although not large at just 41km², is certainly one of the most impressive. Although the western coastline (location for the island's one and only road) is relatively flat and even, barely a couple of metres inland from the sea the terrain starts to rise steeply, most spectacularly around the pyramid-shaped Malinsfjall mountain (751m) which faces Múli across the northern end of Borðoy. Craggy mountaintops and soaring vertical sea cliffs can be found across the island, yet they are at their most magnificent close to Viðoy's northern tip: the third-highest mountain in the Faroes, Villingadalsfjall (844m), rears up just north of the main settlement, **Viðareiði**, conjuring up true geological splendour. From here it's possible to walk along a ridge to the Faroes' most northerly point, the **Enniberg** sea cliff, which plummets vertically to the sea over a dizzying height of 754m; naturally it's a favourite nesting spot for thousands upon thousands of seabirds which create, during the short breeding season, a truly cacophonous din from the ledges at the top of the cliff. The island's other main geographical feature is the long and desolate north-facing bay, **Viðvík**, which is a veritable trap for driftwood (the Faroese word for timber is *viður*). In a country where trees simply don't grow without man's help, driftwood was highly prized as both building material and a source of fuel. Such unforgiving terrain has naturally rendered large parts of Viðoy inaccessible; indeed, there is only around 8km of road on the entire island. Access to the island is across the causeway from Borðoy whence Route 70 passes through the modest settlement of **Hvannasund**, one of only two on the entire island, and notable as the departure point for *Ritan* which sails from here out to Svínoy and Fugloy; the jetty is located immediately to the right of the causeway when crossing from Borðoy and the ferry leaves from its right-hand side. If you're around when the boat is in the harbour, be sure to watch the deft loading operation which sees milk churns, bags of cattle feed and other essentials for island life being winched from the quay onto the boat. While you're in Hvannasund, wander along the main road which runs parallel to the sound and admire the neat allotment-style gardens adjoining many of the houses in the town (the southern aspect particularly favours the growing of potatoes, vegetables and flowers) and the painstaking work that has evidently gone into restoring some of the older wooden dwellings to their former glory.

VIÐAREIÐI From Hvannasund, Route 70 presses on north for a short distance before plunging into a new tunnel which leads through to Viðoy's east coast. The desolate stretch of road up the west coast between Hvannasund and Viðareiði, punctuated only by the former landing stage at Leiti, roughly two-thirds of the way between the two villages, began to subside and was deemed unsafe. Depending on the sea conditions it was sometimes impossible to land at Viðareiði and so an alternative landing was needed. Indeed, the landing stage at Leiti was not only used by the ferry which once ran from here around the northern islands back to Klaksvík, but also the villagers from Múli who would row across the sound on Sundays to attend church in Viðareiði. On exiting the tunnel, the new road now approaches Viðareiði from the east, finally entering the green and pleasant isthmus of land, barely 1.5km wide, which is home to the Faroes' most northerly settlement.

The views from Viðareiði are truly wonderful – across the isthmus to the east you can clearly see Fugloy, whereas, in the opposite direction, beyond the church, framed by the sea and the hills of Borðoy, there's now-abandoned Múli. Indeed, it's no surprise that Viðareiði is located here since this is the only place on the entire island flat enough to allow modern agriculture including the rearing of cattle. The main sight in the village, other than the natural surroundings, is the church and adjoining turf-roofed **vicarage**.

Getting there and away Bus #500 runs between Klaksvík and Viðareiði (*5 daily Mon–Fri, 3 daily Sat & Sun*). Timetables are available at www.ssl.fo.

Where to eat and drink Unusually for such a remote location, Viðareiði has somewhere to eat: **Matstova hjá Elisabeth** (✆ *45 12 75 or 22 24 50;* e *jenny@kallnet.fo;* ◷ *mid-May–Aug noon–21.00; rest of the year groups only by reservation*), located at the junction of Nýggivegur and Eggjarvegur in the village centre; there's also a **small shop** here selling a few minor food supplies such as coffee, tea and biscuits.

What to see and do Without a doubt, the hike up Villingsdalsfjall mountain (844m) and on towards the spine-tinglingly vertical **Enniberg sea cliff** (754m), the second-highest sea cliff in Europe, ranks as one of the highlights of any trip to the Faroe Islands. The steep hike up the mountain and the ridge walk leading out to Enniberg certainly requires stamina, plenty of time (ideally 6 or 7 hours to make the return trip) and – most importantly – good weather. The precipitous drops that dominate the northern end of Viðoy can naturally be dangerous in poor visibility.

VIÐAREIÐI'S SILVER

Inside the village church, which dates from 1892, is a breathtaking collection of altar silverware including a baptismal font donated to the congregation of the village by the British government in acknowledgement of the charity and hospitality they showed the crew of the British brig, *Marwood*, wrecked in the Faroes in January 1847. Look out too for the impressive silver crucifix hanging on the wall, donated by the Hamburg merchant Thomas Köppen in 1551. Although the silver is kept in a safe in the church, if you find the keeper of the church key (in the adjacent house) or ask at the vicarage, there's every chance you'll be shown Viðareiði's pride and joy.

Begin by following the small road that leads northwest from the former hotel and finally peters out after crossing two rivers, the second one being the Bólsá. Now follow the clear line of cairns which leads up the southern ridge of Villingadalsfjall – it's steep going all the way to the top but the summit does flatten out eventually. Once up here you'll have a bird's-eye view on a clear day of all the northern islands and will immediately appreciate the unforgiving geology of these remote outposts. From the summit, the trail leads westwards and then swings to the north and heads around a cleft in the rock. From here head north again towards Enniberg and take extreme care when approaching the cliff edge. In theory, it's possible to return to Viðareiði by descending from Enniberg down through Ormadalur valley (the valley you saw to your left when you walked around the cleft in the rock) and then along a path along the coast close to sea level; however, it's probably wise to check the viability of this route in the village before setting out. If in doubt, return via the same way you came.

However, once you've made it all the way up to the top of Enniberg, the chances are you will never see anything quite so breathtaking anywhere else in Europe – standing at the summit of Enniberg, high above the agitated waves of the North Atlantic, with a sheer drop of over 750m immediately below your feet, is a totally exhilarating experience.

KUNOY

Much more than any of the other Faroe Islands, Kunoy consists entirely of a single ridge of mountains which runs down the spine of the island at a height of 700–830m; from the top of Kunoyarnakkur, which forms the island's northernmost point, it's a sheer drop of 819m to the sea below, making this not only the Faroes' tallest sea cliff, but also one of the highest anywhere in the world. This unforgiving terrain has made human habitation here all but impossible since there are few spots with enough flat land to make both house building and farming viable; the entire island barely measures 35km². Although the east coast is characterised by a number of *botnar* or rounded valleys studded with rivers, it's not been possible to live here either, because the mountainsides are simply too steep and prone to avalanches. Indeed, there are only **two settlements** on Kunoy, one on either coast, both linked by a 3km tunnel which opened in 1988 and, together with the causeway across to Borðoy which opened the year before, effectively prevented total depopulation, which had been threatening the island until then. A third hamlet, **Skarð**, bravely located between two rounded valleys at the foot of Teigafjall (825m), was abandoned in 1919 and today makes a wonderful destination for an easy hike up the east coast (see page 131).

Kunoy is approached from neighbouring Borðoy along the causeway, which takes Route 754 across Haraldssund sound separating the two islands. Immediately over the sound, you arrive in the diminutive settlement of **Haraldssund**, notable as the probable location of an earlier Dutch settlement. A couple of kilometres south of today's hamlet there are indeed ruins of houses, known as *Hálendabúðir*, where it's thought earlier settlers may have once lived. There's no real reason to linger here and it's better to push on into the tunnel and emerge on Kunoy's west coast, opposite Kalsoy, where one of the country's most picturesque villages is more demanding of your attention.

GETTING THERE AND AWAY It's relatively easy to visit the island as a day trip from Klaksvík thanks to **bus** service #504 which runs here three times daily (*Mon–Fri only*). Indeed, an area of new housing at the entrance to the village is proof of the popularity of Kunoy as a place to live, with many people choosing the commute to Klaksvík to work, some by bus. There is no accommodation on Kunoy.

WHAT TO SEE AND DO The main settlement of the island, **Kunoy village**, enjoys a fantastic location at the foot of a rounded valley framed by layer-cake crenellations of the sheer rock walls of Lítlafjall (374m) high above the village. Originally formed of three farms, today's village has faithfully kept to these earlier boundaries and can be neatly divided into thirds. The main **centre** of the village is undoubtedly the most attractive area of Kunoy: a couple of narrow winding streets, encircling the **wooden church** dating from 1867, tightly lined with wooden houses whose gardens are seemingly overflowing in summer with sweet-smelling flowers and gnarled trees forced into ever more curious shapes by the wind. Alongside, the crystal-clear stream, which tumbles down from the mountains above, adds to the perfect tranquillity.

In theory it is possible to hike from Kunoy up over the mountain ridge and down to the abandoned village of **Skarð** on the east coast. However, on looking up at the rock walls and almost perpendicular mountainsides that bear down on Kunoy, you'd be forgiven for thinking that such a feat was ever possible. Be that as it may, the villagers of Skarð would indeed make this daunting trip every Sunday to attend church in Kunoy, returning the same way they had come. Should you be tempted to follow in their footsteps, the path first climbs the long hillside behind Norður í húsi, the third and most northerly cluster of houses that make up Kunoy village, before reaching the summit of **Middagsfjall** (805m). The rest of the path down to Skarð is incredibly steep, almost vertical in parts, and is only recommended for the most determined and experienced; before setting out you should be sure to ask the advice of the villagers as to the best way to tackle the descent and bear in mind that the course of the path is now no longer shown on maps of the area: this was always one of the Faroes' most difficult paths to negotiate. An altogether easier approach to Skarð begins north of Haraldssund, from where a track follows the eastern shoreline, passing no fewer than seven cascading rivers falling from the

---

TRAGEDY IN SKARÐ

An area of flat grassland dotted with a few ruined walls is today all that remains of Skarð after it was abandoned in tragic circumstances a century ago. On Christmas Eve 1913, all the men of the village were out fishing when they were caught in a ferocious storm with three other boats; they never returned, reducing the number of males in the hamlet to just two boys aged nine and 11 and a man in his 70s. The inhabitants of Skarð struggled on but finally gave up their battle six years later and moved away; as far as land use was concerned, Skarð had always been a marginal settlement and fishing was always required to maintain an existence here. Following the deaths of the men of the village it was sadly only a matter of time until the hamlet also died – a tragedy repeated across the Faroes in past decades.

mountain ridges above; be prepared to negotiate the water with suitable footwear and allow around three hours for the return hike.

KALSOY

The most westerly of all the northern islands, Kalsoy, weighing in at just 31km², is not only one of the easiest in the group to reach but it is also one of the most beguiling. This long slender finger of an island has the benefit of regular ferry connections to Klaksvík and some great hiking, making it a popular day-trip destination. Like its easterly neighbour, Kunoy, this island is also composed of a single ridge of mountains, which run north to south down its centre. The peaks plummet, often perpendicularly, to the sea along the west coast, rendering it entirely inaccessible, whereas the gentler east coast, where Kalsoy's four settlements are to be found, is characterised by a number of *botnar*, whose deep rounded nature has allowed some agricultural activity to take place.

GETTING THERE AND AWAY Bus #506 runs the length of the island from Syðradalur to Trøllanes several times daily in connection with ferry arrivals and departures.

WHERE TO STAY AND EAT There are a couple of houses for rent on the island, though the best is 'Pakkhúsið', overlooking the seal woman statue from its clifftop location in the hamlet of **Mikladalur** (*bookings through the tourist office in Klaksvík; see page 124 for details;* **$$$**). Located in a two-storey house in Húsar, just to the left of the children's playground, **Café Roðin** (m *22 20 60;* ⏰ *14.00–22.00 daily*) sells light snacks and coffee and also serves full meals if you phone ahead.

WHAT TO SEE AND DO
Around the island Kalsoy was once regarded as the best place in the Faroes to grow corn; look at a map today and it's quite inconceivable to think that the now-abandoned hamlet of Blakskáli, clinging to the steep slopes off the island's southwestern tip, enjoyed this privilege. An avalanche in 1809 soon persuaded the four families living there that they were better off moving to the opposite coast, and they founded the village of **Syðradalur** which today serves as the new ferry harbour for Klaksvík. Until the completion of the new jetty, the ferry arrived at Kalsoy's second settlement, **Húsar**, a couple of kilometres to the north. Indeed, arrival at either of these two villages by boat offers a spectacular view of the steep mountainsides of the rounded valleys, which bear down on three sides over the houses huddled together for protection at sea level.

From Húsar, Route 723 runs north for 11km heading for the island's main village, **Mikladalur**, and the main destination for visitors to Kalsoy. Since 2014, people have been flocking here to see the striking **statue of the seal woman** by renowned sculptor Hans Pauli Olsen. Crafted from bronze and stainless steel, the statue portrays a naked woman emerging from the body of a seal by shedding her former skin. The statue, 2.5 metres tall, is bolted onto one of the rocks by the shore below the village and has been designed to withstand waves of up to 13m. Crashing waves do indeed often break onto and over the statue, adding to the dramatic interpretation of this highly evocative piece of art. To reach the statue from the small car park in Mikladalur, walk down Bakkavegur towards the sea, then descend the 146 steps down to the shore which begin beside Pakkhúsið (the cottage for rent; see above).

During the early 80s, tunnel mania gripped Kalsoy and no fewer than five tunnels were bored through the length of it to facilitate communication between the settlements; accordingly, the island is now known to the Faroese, endearingly, as the 'recorder', due to the large number of holes that have been drilled through its length, whereas neighbouring Kunoy, which has been bored through from east to west, is known as the 'flute'. Don't think of these tunnels as wide, well-illuminated, tarmacked underpasses that can be whizzed through at top speed; they are instead pot-holed, one-lane, unlit passageways, which should be negotiated with care. There is always priority in one direction only; vehicles coming in the opposite direction should pull over into the meeting places provided, allowing those with priority to pass. Judging the distance in the pitch black between meeting places is a skill which even many Faroese drivers have yet to master.

Mikladalur enjoys an imposing location at the foot of a wide and fertile rounded valley looking out over the sea. Around 70 people live here in a couple of dozen brightly painted houses gathered around the village's stone church, which dates from 1856. Indeed, religion is alive and well in the village, as too is the abstinence movement, and any consumption of alcohol is frowned upon; the Good Templars association has been active here since 1883. Although farming the flat lands of the valley floor has been the main occupation here for centuries, things became considerably easier in 1985 with the construction of yet another tunnel into Djúpadalur valley, directly north of Mikladalur, to allow local sheep farmers to graze their animals on the valley's rich pastures; shortly after this extravagance, the money for such ventures finally dried up and the Faroes lurched towards financial bankruptcy. Until the construction of the island's fifth tunnel connecting up Kalsoy's most northerly settlement, **Trøllanes**, with the rest of the island, the only way north out of Mikladalur was to scramble up the sheer mountain path to a height of 480m before carefully negotiating the vertical slope of the rear wall of Djupadalur's rounded valley and the eastern slopes of Hádegisfjall mountain (576m) and then descending, exhausted and greatly relieved, into Trøllanes; naturally, during the long winter months, deep snow made this route impassable. Today, just three families live in this agricultural hamlet, and surprisingly for such an isolated location, it's not threatened with depopulation. It's a cheerful place with the farmers' children playing in the lanes and fields that wind between the dozen or so barns and tool sheds, giving the hamlet the appearance of one big farm. Exposed to the swells of the Atlantic, landing a boat has always been difficult here, so the arrival of the road in 1986 was a cause for great celebration. Indeed, the descent into

THE LEGEND OF THE SEAL WOMAN

One of the best known folktales in the Faroes, the Seal Woman (Kópakonan) plays out in Mikladalur on Kalsoy. A young man heads down to the shore on Twelfth Night, when, as legend has it, seals come ashore to shed their skins and dance and make merry in the moonlight, returning to the sea before sunrise. However, the man steals the skin of one of the seal women, preventing her from going back to the sea. He forces her to marry him and has several children with her. However, one day while the man is out, the woman finds the key to the chest where her skin has been hidden over many years. She steps back inside it and is transformed back into the seal she always was, returning to join her real seal husband and two pups in the chilly waters of the North Atlantic.

Trøllanes is particularly picturesque as the road winds round a couple of hairpin bends as it passes the boundary of the outfields, giving superb vistas not only of the village, but also of Kunoyarnakkur mountain (819m) across on Kunoy, and in good weather, even all the way to Enniberg (754m), three islands away on Viðoy.

Hiking to Kallur lighthouse One of the most pleasurable things to do on Kalsoy, and certainly the best way to experience the wild nature of the island, is to hike. From Trøllanes, an easy walking path (unmarked) leads out to the northernmost promontory of Kalsoy where the lighthouse, **Kallur**, enjoys what is without a shadow of a doubt the most awe-inspiring view anywhere in the country. The walk (around 30–40mins one-way) starts from a red gate, between the cattle grid and the first hairpin bend on the road down into Trøllanes; there's a small lay-by here with enough room for a couple of cars to park. From the gate, head diagonally across and up the hillside. As you walk towards the sea, you're actually rounding the flank of **Borgarin peak** (537m). Continue heading around the base of the peak, and after around a quarter of an hour or so the land begins to flatten out and you should veer slightly to the left as you finally start to leave the peak behind, at which point the lighthouse will eventually come into view. Although there is no path as such to follow and the ground in parts is rather soggy, there are plenty of narrow sheep tracks – it's simply a matter of finding one which is wide enough to walk comfortably on along the sloping hillside (not always easy). Along the way across the tussocky grass of the promontory you're likely to come across large numbers of snipe. Once at the lighthouse you'll be rewarded with a truly amazing view of no fewer than five islands: to the west you'll see the village of Gjógv, the Risin and Kellingin stacks off Eysturoy, as well as the Tjørnuvíksstakkur in the far distance off Streymoy, whereas in the opposite direction you have Kunoyarnakkur (819m) at the tip of Kunoy, followed by the Múli headland of Borðoy and finally, far in the distance, the village of Viðareiði and the Enniberg sea cliff of Viðoy. However, from this vantage point, it's not just the northern capes of the islands that impress; it is the backbone of mountains that runs down virtually every island in the northern chain that is equally demanding of your attention. Peak after peak, lined up in perfect silhouette, is clearly visible. Enjoy the spectacle; there are few places in the world that offer such stunning views.

NORTHERN OUTPOSTS: SVÍNOY AND FUGLOY

The journey that everyone who comes to the Faroe Islands wants to make is the combination of bus and ferry that leads to the country's two most remote islands: Svínoy and Fugloy. Indeed, much of the attraction of these two last places far out in the North Atlantic lies in the getting there. The weather in this exposed northeastern corner of the country often plays havoc with timetables and arriving here at all is a major achievement. A journey out here is not something to be undertaken on a whim; it requires careful planning, perseverance and not least a large amount of luck. It's certainly not a journey that is recommended to anyone who suffers from seasickness. Not only are the rolls and swells in this part of the Atlantic particularly unsettling, there is also no proper harbour on either island, which means that passengers must take their life in their hands and leap ashore from the ferry at just the right moment as the boat rises and falls up to 3m on the swell and ricochets off the quay only to be catapulted back towards the jetty as it strains on its moorings. If all this sounds alarming, and indeed it is all the more so in a northeasterly gale, rest assured that there is always someone on land to give you a hand as you fly through the air onto dry land – an experience that is likely to stay with you for quite a while. Naturally, the style of your arrival will depend on the tide and the weather, but it's as well to bear this in mind before you head off. In a strong tide, the roughest parts of the journey will be when the boat turns out of the sheltered Hvannasund sound to pass through the narrow stretch of water, Svínoyarsund, between Bergið on southern Viðoy and Tangarnir on Svínoy, as well as the final stretch across the open water of Fugloyarfjørður between Svínoy and Fugloy when the boat, quite literally, bobs like a cork.

GETTING THERE AND AWAY Sailing from Hvannasund, *Ritan* heads first to Svínoy, putting in at **Svínoyareiði** (occasionally sea conditions force it to sail around the island to land in Svínoy village instead) and then continues on to **Kirkja** and, if required, **Hattarvík**, on Fugloy. On most sailings the boat then returns from Fugloy via Svínoy, though this is by no means certain. Depending on tide conditions journey times are as follows: Hvannasund to Svínoy, 30 minutes to one hour; Svínoy to Kirkja (Fugloy) 15 minutes, with another ten minutes to reach Hattarvík. Bus connections to Hvannasund are available in Klaksvík, and, if coming directly from Tórshavn, you can always make the 08.45 sailing from Hvannasund by taking the 06.10 bus to Klaksvík (*Mon–Fri*) and then connecting on to Hvannasund.

WHERE TO STAY AND EAT Through the tourist office in Klaksvík it's possible to rent two of the houses on **Svínoy** (**$$$**; *see page 124 for details*); they sleep six to eight people each. Remember to bring all provisions with you whether you plan to stay here or not, since there are no facilities. Other than the tiny hut adjacent to the helipad, which you might be able to shelter in should it start to rain (ask around to find the keyholder), there is nowhere else to shelter from inclement weather on Svínoy.

There is now a **guesthouse** in Kirkja on **Fugloy**, the welcoming Fuglurin (m *22 63 52*; **$$**) located at Í Garðinum 7; it's also possible to get full meals here. The tourist office in Klaksvík rents out a house in Hattarvík (**$$$**); sleeping six to eight people, it must be booked well in advance. You should bring everything you need with you from Klaksvík when visiting either island as there are no shops. It's also worth bearing in mind that there is nowhere in Kirkja or Hattarvík to shelter from the rain or wind; when the wind blows in from the sea here it can be surprisingly cold, so it's worth bringing extra woollies with you in case you are left out in the cold waiting for a delayed helicopter or boat departure.

WHAT TO SEE AND DO
Svínoy From the landing stage on the island's western coast at Svínoyareiði, Svínoy's **main village** is nowhere to be seen. Don't let this put you off, since it's a straightforward walk of around ten minutes or so across the isthmus that sits between two of the island's main peaks, Keldufjall (461m) to the north and Knúkur (460m) to the south, to the main settlement, the appropriately named Svínoy. The constrained yet unusually fertile neck of land barely 33m above sea level you're traversing can often be inundated by Atlantic storms; there is no land between here and the west coast of Norway to bear the brunt of the full force of the waves. Arriving in the village, you'll be struck by the lush **pasturelands** all around. True, like most places in the Faroes, the mountains are not very far away, but what makes this village different is the wide open expanses of green so suited to agricultural use. Indeed this is the largest area of flat land available for farming anywhere in the northern islands. In addition to the couple of dairy and sheep

farms, the island also supports a **salmon-breeding plant**; you'll see the large green circular containers for this purpose to the south of the harbour. Curiously, for an island named after pigs (Svínoy means literally 'swine island') there are no pigs to be seen anywhere. Instead, the name refers to an ancient legend, according to which Svínoy was once a floating island that drifted around in the sea. An old woman tied a bunch of keys to her sow's tail so that when it next swam over to Svínoy to mate with the boar that once lived here, the island could be locked and finally anchored down.

Although there are no sights as such on Svínoy, sooner or later you'll turn up at the **church** dating from 1878. It's worth looking inside for the **gravestone of Svínoyar-Bjarni**, renowned in Viking times as the uncle of the hero of *Færeyinga Saga*, Tróndur í Gøtu. When the previous church was torn down in 1828, a gravestone bearing a cross, though no other inscription, was discovered under the floor. Its existence was well known to the islanders who have always referred to it as *Bjarnasteinur* or Bjarni's stone. Once you've wandered around the village, the best thing to do on Svínoy is to take a hike out to the island's northeastern coast from where there are good views of Kirkja over on Fugloy. From the church take the path which gently climbs the hillside on the northern side of the bay, **Svínoyarvík**. Along the way you'll pass a number of disused sheep huts before the land gradually falls towards the shoreline; the climb to the highest part of the path is only 137m. The path now descends through a wide low valley, **Yvir á dál**, which was once used for peat cutting. In fact, the promontory to the left of the valley, opposite Kirkja on Fugloy, is known as **Kallanes** or 'calling point' since it was from here that the people of Fugloy, who used to come over to Svínoy to cut peat, would call back to their village for boats to come to collect them.

Fugloy

The last Faroe Island, lost far out in the gyrating mists and fogs of the North Atlantic, Fugloy is a favourite with many visitors. Barely 11km² in size, this squat lump of basalt easily repays the effort in reaching it and has a charm all of its own. Approaching from the sea, the 30 or so weather-beaten houses that constitute the main village, **Kirkja**, home to just ten people, make a perfect picture postcard as they climb steeply up the hillside behind. The faded yellows, blues and blacks of the wooden walls merge with the greens of turf roofs and the whites of the clouds to conjure up a resonant image. Named after the church that once stood here in medieval times, Kirkja is still dominated by its **church** (the guesthouse has the key), though today's structure only dates from 1933; inside there's an **altar painting** by the Faroese artist Sámal Joensen-Mikines of Christ walking on water. Although a new road now links Fugloy's two villages, it's much more enjoyable to follow the old clifftop footpath, marked by cairns, to reach the island's other settlement, **Hattarvík** (allow about an hour one way). Although this path is not difficult, there is a story of one old woman in Kirkja who was well into her 70s before she ventured along the path; it was her wish before she died to at least see the neighbouring village of Hattarvík. From the eastern end of Kirkja, close to the tiny power-generating plant, follow the overhead power cables steeply up through the homefield to reach the beginning of the track which then loyally follows the coastline eastwards in line with the power cables and even meets up with the road at one point. Although the path is quite indistinct at times, the cairns always serve as a guideline. From up here, high on the cliffs of Fugloy, there are superlative views out over the churning waves of **Fugloyarfjørður** across to Svínoy, and if you time things right, it's an amazing sight to watch the tiny *Ritan* rolling and pitching as the boat battles its way through the swell.

After roughly 30 to 40 minutes, the hamlet of Hattarvík will come into view, superbly sheltered on three sides by the steep terraces of a rounded valley and frighteningly exposed to the Atlantic on the fourth. Less picturesque than Kirkja, the 15 or so houses here, all sitting on foundations of basalt as protection from the damp ground, are unimaginatively painted in drab browns and greys. Home to just six people, many of the houses here are now used solely as holiday homes and as a result the village appears forlorn and unkempt. Even the **stone church**, dating from 1899, with its white-and-blue-painted interior, is overtly spartan in appearance. To be frank, there's not much to detain you in Hattarvík once you've had a quick look around and it's perhaps a better idea to press on and take in some more of Fugloy's wonderful scenery. This is not a big island and with determination you can see most parts of it on a day trip. Although there are no marked paths, it's an easy walk from Hattarvík north to the Eiðsvík bay: simply follow the road out of the village, past the heliport and up to the edge of the homefield; from here it's a straightforward walk down to the bay ahead of you. Alternatively you could head northeast from this point for **Eystfelli peak** (449m) and its **lighthouse**, from where there are arresting views of the Faroes' most easterly point, the rock stack, **Stapin** (47m), where there is another lighthouse. A third option, albeit from Kirkja, is to climb to the top of **Klubbin mountain** (621m), which lies directly north of the village; the ascent through Vatnsdalur valley is steep and rocky in parts though not difficult. From the plateau, steep cliffs known as **Norðberg** (549m), making up a large part of the island's west coast, plummet to the sea and are home to thousands of seabirds that come here to nest.

7

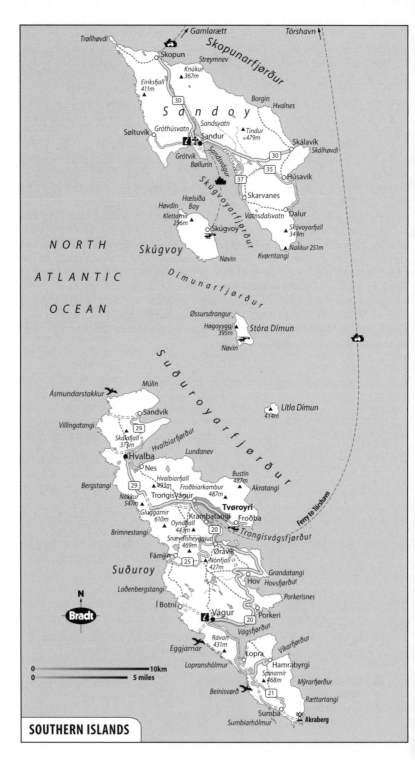

SOUTHERN ISLANDS

The Southern Islands

The five southern islands of the Faroe chain exist in a world of their own. Separated from the central group around Streymoy and, indeed, from each other, by some of the most turbulent seas you'll encounter anywhere in the North Atlantic, life here has changed little over the past decades and retains an enviably sedate quality. Immediately south of Streymoy's southern point, **Sandoy** is the first of the five, and at 112km² is the fifth-biggest of all the Faroe Islands. As its name suggests, Sandoy is known for its sweeping sandy beaches and, accordingly, this is one of the gentlest of all the islands. Here the countryside is characterised by rich undulating pasturelands and low rounded hilltops; a more striking contrast to the vertical cliffs and layer-cake mountains of the northern islands is hard to imagine. Indeed, Sandoy's highest peak, **Tindur** (479m), is barely half the size of mountains further to the north.

Marooned in the sea off the island's southern coast, **Skúgvoy**, an egg-shaped lump of rock measuring a mere 10km², is about as remote as you can get in the southern islands. Although its western shoreline consists of 400m-high cliffs that rise like a wall out of the sea, the eastern side of the island, location for the one and only village, is altogether less severe and the relatively flat lands around the Áldarsá river, which drains the island's peaks, have been successfully cultivated. However, Skúgvoy is best known for its rich birdlife, in particular its colonies of auks and guillemots.

To the southeast lie the two smallest of the Faroe Islands: **Stóra Dímun** and **Lítla Dímun**. Quite incredibly, the larger of the pair, Stóra Dímun, an imposing tooth-shaped island, whose scenic cliffs plummet precipitously to the ocean making sea landings all but impossible, is inhabited. A single family farms the flat land on the mountaintop – their link with the outside world is provided by the Atlantic Airways helicopter which calls in here three times a week, bringing much-needed supplies. Of all 18 Faroes, only Lítla Dímun is uninhabited; consisting of angular cliffs that rise together to form a craggy peak, human occupation here is simply not possible. Consequently, there is no public transport to the island, though there are arresting views of this barren rocky outcrop from the ferry which sails from Tórshavn to **Suðuroy**, the most southerly of all the Faroe Islands. It's claimed that the weather here is a little warmer and more stable than elsewhere in the country, and although this may well be true, you're unlikely to notice any appreciable difference in the climate. Characterised by four deep fjords that have gnawed their way into the heart of the island, the rugged and dramatic coastal scenery here is truly spectacular: soaring peaks, bleak moorland studded by mountain tarns which glitter a brilliant blue, and majestic sea cliffs teeming with birdlife. Indeed, if the wind is blowing hard on Suðuroy, the seascape is memorably dramatic.

WHERE TO GO

The first place to head for on Sandoy is the main village, **Sandur**, a short drive of around 8km from the ferry port, **Skopun**, on the north coast. The unusual wooden church here, dating from 1839, is the main draw; archaeologists have now established that no fewer than six churches have stood on this spot since the 1000s. Thanks to Sandoy's gentle terrain, the island is perfectly suited to hiking: an easy coastal path leads from Sandur south to the hamlet of **Skarvanes** before striking off across the island's southern reaches towards the picturesque village of Dalur. From here it's possible to continue on to **Húsavík**, where remains of a medieval manor house stand beside a beach of black-basalt sand. Another hike leads west to the untrammelled delights of **Søltuvík**, a remote windswept bay of jagged shores which offers some of the best coastal scenery anywhere in the Faroes whereas **Skálavík**, on the east coast, is the place to head for Sandoy's best accommodation option. There's more superlative hiking to be had on neighbouring **Skúgvoy** – an ideal destination for a day trip, particularly popular with birdwatchers, from Sandur on board the regular ferry across Skúvoyarfjørður. Since Stóra Dímun can only be visited with permission from the farmer who works the land here, it's probably best to move on in favour of Suðuroy where both **Tvøroyri**, a busy harbour village, and **Vágur**, a pleasant little place with an excellent art museum, make agreeable places to base yourself. Nearby in **Fámjin** on the west coast you'll find the original Faroese flag which is proudly displayed in the village church, whilst **Porkeri** boasts a traditional wooden church. Arguably best of all, though, is the daunting expanse of the Atlantic which reaches out before you as you stand at the Faroes' southernmost point, **Akraberg**, perfectly marked by two towering radio transmitters and a red-domed lighthouse.

GETTING AROUND

All **ferry** routes to the southern islands begin from Streymoy. Skopun on **Sandoy** is connected to Gamlarætt on Streymoy by *Teistin*, which sails between the two islands roughly nine times a day; journey time is 30 minutes. From Sandur, tiny *Sildberin* makes the 35-minute journey over to Skúgvoy three times daily with additional sailings on certain days of the week (see the timetable for this route for precise details). If you're planning to visit the island as a day trip from Streymoy, you will need to be on the first boat out of Gamlarætt bound for Skopun (currently 07.30) in order to reach Sandur for the 08.30 sailing to Skúgvoy. For details of the bus service on Sandoy, see below.

Getting to Suðuroy is a much more drawn-out affair since sailing time from Tórshavn aboard *Smyril* is 2 hours. Generally there are two or three sailings daily to Krambatangi, the harbour for Tvøroyri. The sea conditions down to Suðuroy can be rather sporty – taking a seasickness pill before setting off is no bad idea. There is no ferry link between Sandoy and Suðuroy – the only way to sail between the two is to backtrack to Tórshavn. However, it is possible to fly between Skúgvoy and Suðuroy on Wednesday and Friday (June–August also Monday) on board the Atlantic Airways helicopter. The helicopter also flies between Tórshavn and Skúgvoy on Sunday, Wednesday and Friday (June–August also Monday) before continuing on to Stóra Dímun. Suðuroy is only connected to Tórshavn by helicopter on Wednesday and Friday (June–August also Monday).

Bus services in the southern islands are generally good. On Sandoy, bus #600 runs several times daily (connecting with ferry sailings) Skopun–Sandur–Skálavík, complementing the #601, which operates Sandur–Húsavík–Dalur. On Suðuroy, the services are: #700 Sumba–Vágur–Tvøroyri and #702 Fámjin–Tvøroyri–Sandvík.

SANDOY

SKOPUN Roughly 1,400 people live on the island of Sandoy, predominantly in two main villages: Skopun and Sandur. It's the modern settlement of Skopun that handles all ferry traffic to and from Streymoy. Indeed, as the ferry swings into the harbour here, good views of the couple of streets that serve as the village **centre** slowly unfold, banking up the hillside beyond in tight, neat rows. Barely 150 years old, Skopun's fortunes are closely linked with the hulking fish factory dominating the quayside, processing the fish landed by the village's modest fleet of trawlers. The only thing to do in Skopun is to head up the hill to see what was once the biggest **postbox** in the world: from the café, continue up the hill to the supermarket, where you turn left and then immediately right. As tall as a house, the blue mailbox looms large on the hillside and is even used by fishermen as a landmark; it seems a couple of local men were determined to get Skopun into the *Guinness Book of Records*. Otherwise there's little reason to linger in Skopun and it's a better use of time to have a look at **Trøllhøvði**, a tiny island off Sandoy's northernmost point. Once part of the farm of Kirkjubøur, incredibly there's grazing for around 50 or so sheep on the island's steeply sloping hillsides that peak at a height of 106m. However, it's certainly no easy task bundling the sheep into boats in the autumn when it's time for the annual round-up – the only way down from the grazing areas is via a ladder, which is anchored into the rockface. You can hike out to **Høvdasund**, the sound which separates the island from Sandoy, in around an hour from Skopun; take the road which leads up past the **church** (and later turns into a walking path) leading up towards **Gleðin mountain** (269m) which you can see in front of you. You climb to the plateau at a height of 200m, and before the land falls away steeply to the sea, you'll have a wonderful view of Trøllhøvði. According to legend, the island is actually the head of a troll who was trying to fasten Sandoy and Nólsoy together by pulling on a rope. However, after putting the rope around his neck, he tugged a little too hard and his head fell off.

SANDUR From Skopun, Route 30 climbs up away from the sea to approach the pass which leads into Traðadalur, the lush broad V-shaped valley which runs the length of this western part of Sandoy, one of the most fertile areas in the whole country. Incidentally, the switchback route through the valley was the first road to be completed in the Faroes, in 1917. At its southern end, the valley is punctuated by two small lakes, **Gróthúsvatn** to the west of the road and the larger **Sandsvatn** to the east, a favourite spot for autumn anglers when spawning sea trout struggle up the short stream that connects the lake to the sea. Beyond the lakes, Sandur strings out in an ungainly way across the narrow promontory that separates the two bays, **Grótvík** and **Sandsvágur**. Named after the dunes of black-basalt sand – the only ones in the Faroes and the only place in the country where marram grass (*Ammophila arenaria*) grows – at the head of Sandsvágur, Sandur is not an immediately appealing place, though it is the only village on the island to have any services to speak of.

Where to stay

Sandoy is one of the few islands to offer accommodation out in the wilds; the wilderness stay at **Norðasti Hagi** (**$$** *pp*), formerly accommodation for sheep farmers whilst out tending their flocks in the outfield, is a perfect opportunity to get back to basics. There's no electricity or flush toilet in this simple wooden hut with three rooms northeast of Sandur, but what it lacks in mod cons, it more than makes up for in terms of location. Perched on the Borgin hills on Sandoy's totally uninhabited northeastern shore, this is the place to come to commune with nature. Access is only on foot; reckon on two to three hours hiking from either Sandur or Skálavík; the tourist office can make group bookings (see *Other practicalities*, below). Should you wish for something a little more comfortable, the tourist office also rents out entire **houses** across Sandoy for 400–850kr per night. The office can also help with planning a trip across to Skúgvoy, including accommodation, and has further information about some of the hiking routes listed on page 145.

Other practicalities

There are no cafés or restaurants in Sandur, but there is a small **supermarket** (⊕ *09.00–17.30 Mon–Thu, 09.00–19.00 Fri, 10.00–17.00 Sat*) at Heimasandsvegur 52 selling all the everyday essentials and a **bakery** (*07.30–18.00 Mon–Fri, 07.30–15.00 Sat*), opposite the church, at Heimasandsvegur 33. There's a branch of Eik (⊕ *09.30–16.00 Mon–Fri*) at Heimasandsvegur 60 with an **ATM**. Next door, at number 58, there's a **post office** (⊕ *14.00–15.30 Mon–Fri*) and a branch of the **alcohol store**, Rúsan (⊕ *14.00–17.30 Mon–Thu, 14.00–19.00 Fri, 10.00–14.00 Sat*). The helpful **tourist information office** at Mørkin Mikla 3 (✆ *36 18 36*; e *info@ visitsandoy.fo; www.visitsandoy.fo*; ⊕ *Apr–Aug 09.00–noon & 13.00–16.00 Mon–Fri, rest of year 10.30–13.30 Mon–Fri*) is in the centre of the village, just off the main road close to the bank, and beyond the junction for the road to Skálavík.

What to see and do

Located by the side of the main road at the entrance to the village, opposite the junction with Koytugøta, is the **Bygdarsavn homestead museum** (⊕ *Jun–Aug 14.00–16.00 daily; admission 30kr*), housed in a traditional turf-roofed dwelling with coarsely hewn floorboards and low ceiling (ideal for keeping in the heat). Dating from 1812 and once the home of a local fisherman and farmer, it is Sandur's main attraction. The house was occupied until 1938 and today provides a snapshot of what life was like in the Faroes in the early 20th century. Both rooms in the house have been kept exactly as they were when the occupant died: everything from pots and pans, woodworking tools to an elegant old grandfather clock dating from 1860 are on display. Close by at Uttan Á 11, **Listasavnið á Sandi art museum** (⊕ *open by appointment on tel 21 19 24 or 36 16 17; admission 50kr*) contains a respectable collection of contemporary Faroese art spanning a century or so, including several works by Sámal Joensen-Mikines, whose *Illveður, Velbastaður* from 1964 perfectly conjures up the stormy mood of the Faroese sky. Local fisherman Sofus Olsen collected the works during his lifetime and bequeathed his collection to the town on his death. The museum can be hard to find – you'll find it just beyond the church and the bakery, opposite number 28 on the main road, Heimasandsvegur. Overlooking the still waters of Sandsvágur bay, the village

church is the other building of note. Though this fine example of wooden church architecture with black-tarred walls, turf roof and white-painted belfry dates only from 1838, the site has been occupied by no fewer than five earlier churches; the first church was built according to traditional Norwegian stave design during the Viking period of AD1000–1100. Whilst here, take a wander behind the church (walk towards the cliffs keeping the church behind you) and look for the **grave** unearthed during an archaeological dig in 1989. Inside, experts discovered the remains of a skeleton, thought to be that of a woman, dating from the Viking period. Indeed, excavation work is now continuing in the cliff face and the churchyard, beyond the grave, where erosion has revealed remains of an extensive settlement.

WEST TO SØLTUVÍK Just 3km west of Sandur along an unnumbered single-track lane that begins just before the village museum, the remote and wild bay of Søltuvík is one of the most beautiful spots in the whole of the Faroes and is a must for any visitor to Sandoy. The perfectly formed arched bay, backed by a sandy beach littered with boulders and curiously shaped rocks and tiers of low green hills, is truly idyllic. The wide and open nature of the landscapes around the bay is quite unusual for the Faroe Islands, noted more for their jagged and rocky mountains. From the end of the lane, a wooden gate gives access onto the beach where, if you're lucky, you may be able to spot seals in the shallow water. There can be few more tranquil places in the islands from which to watch the sun go down over the Atlantic on a warm summer's evening or the waves crash with tremendous force onto the shore here. However charming the bay may look on a warm sunny day, this stretch of coastline is noted for a series of shipwrecks, which have claimed many lives over the centuries. Perhaps the most tragic occurred in November 1895 when the steamer *Principia* foundered on rocks during an atrocious storm. It had been on fire and drifting for three days before running aground in Søltuvík, where the single survivor managed to cling to a plank of wood and float across to Kirkjubøur on Streymoy, where he was finally rescued. The table that stands in the *roykstova* in the farmhouse at Kirkjubøur is made from this piece of wood. From beyond the solitary house, which enjoys views out over the bay, a hiking path leads north following the coast to Tröllhøvdi (see page 141) and ultimately back to Skopun.

SOUTH TO SKARVANES Eight kilometres south of Sandur along Routes 30 and 37, the picturesque hamlet of Skarvanes boasts one of the best views in the Faroes. From this exposed hillside location on the western shore of Sandoy, you can see four different islands stretched out in the distance: Skúgvoy, followed by both Stóra and Lítla Dímun, and finally, Suðuroy. The hamlet itself is equally appealing: a cluster of just seven brightly painted wooden houses, huddled beside a waterfall cascading down from Gjófelli mountain up above the settlement, makes a perfect picture-postcard scene. Sadly though, Skarvanes (whose name probably originates from the shags that once gathered on the promontory here) today belongs to one of the ever-increasing number of dying Faroese villages. During the early 1800s, the place was known as the home of the bird painter, Diðrikur á Skarvanesi, who no doubt painted the shags for which his village was known.

SKÁLAVÍK Back on Route 30, just 2km after the junction with Route 37 to Skarvanes, there's a choice of directions: southeast leads to Húsavík and ultimately to Dalur, whereas northeast heads to Skálavík, a fishing village that is now home to the only accommodation on Sandoy: the tastefully appointed **Hotel Skálavík** (✆ 34 59 00; e booking@hotelskalavik.fo; www.hotelskalavik.fo; $$)

at Eiler Jacobsens gøta 1. Rooms here offer superb value for money; they are modern, bright and fresh and decked out with harmonious Scandinavian designs and colours. The hotel was originally built by the Immanuel Foundation which was established by local man, Eiler Jacobsen, who died in 2010, though it is now owned by Smyril Line. Eiler was a self-made businessman who worked his way up from his early days as fisherman and wanted to give something back to the place where he lived. The hotel also boasts a children's play area, outdoor jacuzzi, massage room and **restaurant** (⊕ *noon–14.00 & 18.00–21.00 daily*) which serves lunch for 95kr as well as more substantial evening meals such as pork tenderloin in mushroom sauce or steamed salmon with potatoes and peas, both for 175kr, as well as burgers (*55kr*) and pizzas (*85kr*). The hotel rents bikes for 99kr (*3hrs*) as well as its jacuzzis (*199kr per hour*). In addition, behind the hotel there are three wooden cabins which you can rent for a barbecue evening (*3hrs; 799kr inc food*). Sadly, although Skálavík has little to offer the visitor in itself, it is one of the access points to the **Norðasti Hagi wilderness stay** at Borgin on Sandoy's northeast coast (see page 142 for details). From the village, take the lane running to the northwest through the outfield, which eventually peters out and becomes a walking path. Stout waterproof shoes are required to tackle this route since it crosses a number of rivers as it climbs up the mountain of Tvøfelli from where you can see the cliffs at Borgin.

HÚSAVÍK At the Skálavík road junction, Route 35 heads southeast to the endearing little village of Húsavík, an altogether more attractive place than Skálavík, which occupies a commanding position at the head of a sandy beach. Although the village itself, home to around 90 people, is pretty enough, consisting of both modern and traditional turf-roofed houses, it's the remains of a **medieval farm** that have really put this little place on the map. Before the beach, at the entrance to the village, you'll come to a narrow footbridge that leads over a small stream to the remains of Heimi á Garði, reputed to have been the home of the legendary **Guðrun Sjúrðardóttir** of Bergen, once the richest woman in the Faroe Islands. Over the centuries various folk tales about her have been handed down from generation to generation and naturally it's impossible to know exactly where the truth lies. However, according to one version of events, she had two of her servants buried alive for committing a minor offence. Another story claims that she was nothing more than a poor peasant girl from Skúgvoy who had the good fortune to find a golden horn belonging to local chieftain, **Sigmundur Brestisson**. Guðrun then dutifully sent her newly found treasure to the king who rewarded her with so much money that she could afford to buy not only all the land in Húsavík but also a good slice of Shetland, too. You have to hunt around a little in Húsavík to find the remains: cross the bridge by the blue postbox and you'll see the ruins which consist of a stone floor and surrounding low walls. Close by, the tiny house built of basalt, known as **á Breyt**, is a typical example of an early 20th-century Faroese family dwelling.

While the doors remain closed, take the liberty to peek through the window to see the extremely simple interior: a kitchen with an earthen floor and a wood-panelled sitting room with a couple of stoves for heating. Walking past the church towards the beach, you'll find a collection of 200-year-old *gróthús* or **stone storage huts** once used to keep fish and meat. Standing side by side on the grassy foreshore, these huts with their unruly turf roofs make a great photograph when viewed against the surf. It's possible to **camp** in Húsavík (⟍ *36 17 71; 50kr/tent*) at the site next to the beach, opposite the building marked 'Sólarris'.

DALUR From Húsavík it's a hair-raising 5km journey around the towering headland, Kinnartangi, on a single-track lane with blind corners that hugs the side of the mountain high above sheer cliffs before finally dropping down into **Dalur**, one of the most picturesque places in the southern islands, sheltered in a perfectly formed bowl-shaped valley. This delightful cluster of multi-coloured houses sits contentedly at the foot of a river, which empties into the sea by the harbour on the eastern edge of the village. The main reason to come here is to walk out to the cliffs at Sandoy's southern tip, **Skorin**, from where there are great views towards Skúgvoy and the two Dímuns. The trail out here begins where the river enters the village, close to the point where the main road swings east to enter the village proper. The minor road out to Skorin was built during World War II to help defend the islands from German attack, passing to the west of **Skúgvoyarfjall mountain** (349m) before leading all the way out to the cliffs (the highest point, known as **Nakkur**, is 251m) which are a good place to watch birds. Unusually for a place so off the beaten track, Dalur has summer accommodation: **Eiriksgarður** (✆ *36 14 02;* $ *pp, min 10*) offers accommodation in double rooms (bring your own sleeping bag) with a kitchen. There's also a **campsite** here (*50kr*) with a shower and toilet block.

HIKING IN SOUTHERN SANDOY: DALUR TO HÚSAVIK/SANDUR

Thanks to its relatively flat terrain, Sandoy makes for some great hiking. The best trail on the island leads from Dalur back over Gjófelli mountain to **Skarvanes** before following the coast north through Djúpidalur valley and leading back into Sandur. Alternatively, after leaving Skarvanes it's possible to head off to the northwest and hike over to **Húsavík** instead.

From **Dalur** the path begins at the western end of the village at the point where the lane down to Skorin branches off south; go straight on heading west. Here the path starts to climb as you ascend the hill in front of you; at the summit (300m) you'll see a lake to your left, **Vatnsdalsvatn**, surrounded by boggy marshland. The climb is now over and you make a steep descent down the southern slopes of Gjófelli into Skarvanes. If you opt to walk east back over to Húsavík, you'll find the path right in the village climbing immediately up the hillside behind the houses here. As you climb, hope for good weather because the ascent offers superlative views – in clear conditions you can see out past Grótvík bay on Sandoy all the way to Mykines far in the distance. Continue past the small tarn, **Dúnjavatn**; the path then skirts the western slopes of Dúnjaheyggjur hill before coming to **Klovastein**, two large rocks which appear to be a single large stone cut clean in two. According to local superstition, anyone who walks between them will die before the year is out. Pass the sheepfold that lies ahead of you and you'll reach Route 35 which runs between Sandur and Húsavík. Bus #601 runs from here to both destinations.

Alternatively, from Skarvanes it's possible to continue north heading straight for **Sandur**. Take the main road, Route 37, out of the village to the point where it begins to swing inland a little; if you reach **Stóravatn** lake in front of you, you have gone too far. At this point you'll come to a footpath that hugs the coast and weaves around the western edge of the lake through Djúpidalur valley. Pass the rocks you can see immediately offshore and you'll soon come to the main road, Route 30, into Sandur; when you reach the road it's around 2km further into the village.

SKÚGVOY

Settled during the early Viking period, the 10km² island of Skúgvoy (also spelt Skúvoy) may not be one of the larger of the Faroes, but it's certainly made its mark on the country's history. It was here that one of the main characters of *Færeyinga Saga*, **Sigmundur Brestisson**, lived and farmed. Indeed, he is accredited with the building of the first church in the islands in line with the Christianisation of the country around AD1000; sadly, nothing remains of this first church, and the unremarkable church on the island today dates from the last century only. According to the *Saga*, however, Sigmundur's farm was raided and set on fire by his arch-rival, the heathen **Tróndur í Gøtu**, whose men then harried Sigmundur, leaving him no option but to throw himself into the sea from the northern end of the island, **Høvðin**, to escape imminent death. Bizarrely, with the coast of Sandoy within sight, he washed up instead down in Sandvík in northern Suðuroy, no doubt the unfortunate victim of the unpredictable Faroese tides. Exhausted and suffering from hypothermia, he set foot ashore only to be cut to the ground by local farmer, **Tórgrímur the Evil**, who then stole Sigmundur's gold ring. His body was brought back to Skúgvoy and his grave can still be seen in the walled graveyard, Ólansgarður, a little south of the present church, where Sigmundur built his original church; you can reach the churchyard by walking for around five minutes past the church and the heliport and over the cattle grid. A triangular stone in the graveyard etched with a cross, known to the islanders for centuries as Sigmundarsteinur (Sigmund's stone), is considered to mark his final resting place.

GETTING THERE AND AWAY The **ferry** *Sildberin* sails from Sandur to Skúgvoy roughly three times daily (*35mins*). Most sailings have to be booked in advance (✆ *29 31 17*). There is a **helicopter** service to and from Skúgvoy on Sunday, Wednesday and Friday (June–August also Monday).

WHERE TO STAY AND EAT The tourist office in Sandur has one **house** for rent (**$$$**) on Skúgvoy (see page 142 for details). There is also a small **food shop** in the village as well as a post office at Fløttavegur 7 (⊕ *15.00–16.00 Mon, Wed & Fri*).

WHAT TO SEE AND DO Today, Skúgvoy, home to around 20 people, is an altogether less bloodthirsty sort of place and is better known for its rich **birdlife**; the island's Faroese name is 'island of the skuas'. Although many of these birds no longer frequent the island, there are still other large colonies of seabirds on the island's western cliffs waiting to be discovered. The people of Skúgvoy once made a living from bird hunting, and, although many species are now protected by law, there are calls for a complete ban on bird hunting on the island. However, the gathering of birds and eggs by hunters suspended on long ropes dangling down the vertical cliffs is still practised today. Although it's not fully known why, the vast numbers of guillemots that once bred on the island have been greatly reduced – it's thought they're victims of dwindling fish stocks rather than hunting. One of the best places to watch birds is around the northern end of the island; from the main village, take the farm track that leads up through the homefield to its end, then head off west up the hill, **Klettarnir** (256m), with **Hælsiða bay** to your right. Here, there are large numbers of puffin burrows. Descending from the hilltop towards an area of flat land on the northwest coast, you'll see the sea cliffs that form the headland, **Høvdin** (134m), to your right where there are still good numbers of guillemots to be seen. Look out also for cormorants, fulmars and razorbills, which can all be seen here. You're likely at this point to come under attack from frighteningly large numbers of arctic tern, the pluckiest of all the island's birds, intent on delivering a sharp blow to the top of your head with their pointed beaks. Protect yourself by carrying a stick above your head, or by raising your arm in the air; the birds will then strike this, as the highest point, instead of screeching towards your tender scalp. From this point, it's possible to continue south along the **bird cliffs** of Skúgvoy's west coast, which fall away vertically into the sea from a height of around 400m, towards a hill at the southern end of the island, **Heyggjurin mikli** (300m). A farm track begins by the lake here and leads back towards the southern end of the village.

STÓRA DÍMUN

The Faroes don't get any more remote – or indeed breathtakingly dramatic – than Stóra Dímun. A diamond-shaped island fortress halfway between Sandoy and Suðuroy, this enigmatic island measuring barely 2.5km² has fascinated sailors for centuries. The entire length of the west coast is one vertical sea cliff, reaching a dizzying 395m at its highest point, the wonderfully understated **Høgoyyggj** (high island). The rest of the island is no less forbidding; in fact at no point are the perpendicular cliffs lower than 100m, which makes landing a boat here a highly hazardous business. This is the most difficult landing in the entire country, and, until the helicopter began flying here in the 1980s, the islanders often didn't set eyes on the supply boat which bravely attempted to put in at Stóra Dímun for months at a time. The island's southern landing stage can only be used in calm conditions or in a northerly wind that shelters it from the ferocious swell (the only other suitable place is the exposed headland, Breiðanes, on the eastern coast, although this is not commonly used). From the landing stage, a set of steps, chiselled into the 100m vertical rockface, leads steeply up to the farmhouse which is surrounded by 2m-thick stone walls, anchored down with steel ropes against the brute force of the wind. In winter, when the weather is at its worst, walking outside the protective enclosure requires stamina.

WHAT TO SEE Stóra Dímun really is one of the world's last places. Since you cannot stay overnight here and you cannot book a day return on the helicopter, visiting is not possible. You can, however, see the island from the Smyril ferry as she sails between Tórshavn and Suðuroy. In fact, the only human habitation is found on the island's southern slope, where, in addition to the **farmhouse** and a few other farm buildings such as a slaughterhouse, there's a **lighthouse** and a helipad – and, err, that's it. Quite incredibly, the farm here has been occupied since the days of the Settlement, although the current farmer's family only managed to live here year-round once the regular helicopter service was established. From behind the farmhouse a steep slope streaks upwards towards the island's flat top where the lush high pastures are considered to be some of the best in the entire Faroe Islands. In its heyday, the farm here supported up to 50 cattle, over 600 sheep and 36 people, who survived on collecting eggs and birds from the cliffs as well as farming the land. Life was never easy here, and many people fell to their deaths from the clifftops or died at sea; it's even claimed that since Viking times barely a handful of inhabitants of Stóra Dímun have died of natural causes in their beds. Indeed, in 1874 the minister of Sandoy, who was duty-bound to visit the island twice a year to hold a service in the island's church, fell whilst climbing the steps from the landing stage and was killed instantly. Ruins of the last church to stand on the island, dating from 1873, can still be seen close to the farmhouse; it was torn down in 1923 to make room for a new structure which never saw the light of day because the farmer himself was killed.

LÍTLA DÍMUN

The baby of the Faroese family, Lítla Dímun, with a total area of just 1km², is the only Faroe island never to have been inhabited, though it is owned by around

40 people from Hvalba and Sandvík on Suðuroy. With little wonder, as resembling a volcano rising out of the sea to a height of 414m, this round cone-shaped lump of rock is an island too far – even for the Faroese. Its precipitous cliffs and lack of farming land make it only suitable for sheep grazing – indeed, since Norse times sheep have been brought out here in boats to graze during the summer months. In fact, the island once supported an unusual breed of brown sheep (brought by the Irish hermits who first settled the Faroes) known for their short coarse wool, until they were all slaughtered in 1844 to make room for another variety. Although there has never been any permanent human habitation on Lítla Dímun, the Faroese have long been drawn here in search of birds and eggs and there are plenty of stories of those who came but became stranded by bad weather, forced to kill birds and sheep to survive until they could next put to sea to escape. Undoubtedly the most infamous of the island's visitors was Viking chieftain **Sigmundur Brestisson**, who also grazed his sheep here. In the summer of 1004, whilst he was on the island to round up his animals, he came under attack from Tróndur í Gøtu. Cunningly, Sigmundur managed to give Tróndur the slip and escape in his boat, leaving his arch-rival marooned and forced to light a fire to signal for help and, ultimately, rescue. The southwestern point of the island is still known as **Sigmundarberg** (Sigmund's mountain).

Once a year (usually once in either June or July), **boat trips** operate from Hvalba on Suðuroy to Lítla Dímun; the June tour usually gives visitors the chance to spend the night on the island in tent accommodation, whereas the second tour allows around eight hours on the island, though at 1,500kr per person it's an expensive pleasure. The trip is not recommended to anyone who suffers from vertigo since the ascent to reach the top of the island and the only area of flat land is steep to say the least; details are available on www.ldimun.com or by calling 23 75 75 (Faroese only). Since there is no other public transport to Lítla Dímun, the best way to appreciate this uninhabited island is to see it from the sea; as it journeys between Tórshavn and Suðuroy, *Smyril* sails along its eastern cliffs, allowing unsurpassed views of the towering rock walls which, like those of its big brother, Stóra Dímun, rise sheer out of the water for around 100m, before tapering towards the island's peak. Incidentally, the root of the name Dímun is of Celtic origin (*stóra* and *lítla* are Faroese for 'big' and 'little'), composed of two elements: *di* meaning 'two' and *muin* signifying a 'ridge' or a 'mountaintop'. The name occurs elsewhere in the Nordic region, and also in Shetland, to describe this readily identifiable geographic feature.

SUÐUROY

The biggest and best of the southern islands, Suðuroy, is the fourth-largest Faroe Island and the chain's most southerly. A good two-hour journey by boat south from Tórshavn, this island is a world apart – the 5,000 islanders are claimed not only to be the most friendly of all the people in the Faroes, but also the most emotional, a quintessentially un-Faroese trait, taking readily to flailing their arms and hands around, in true Mediterranean fashion, when in discussion. As a visitor you'll be warmly welcomed across the island, not least because Suðuroy sees so few tourists, but also because the islanders are at pains to point out how different their lives are from those of the 'city-slickers' in Tórshavn. Bemoaning their fate as the Faroes' most southerly (read: forgotten) island is also a well-rehearsed sport. The well-appointed new ferry sailing between Suðuroy and Tórshavn, the fifth in the long line of *Smyrils*, is the latest sop from the government to keep the southerners smiling.

At 30km in length, but barely ever more than 5km in width, this is an up-and-down sort of a place; there's only one road, which runs across the island from coast to coast. Virtually the entire west coast consists of steep bird cliffs which rise to a height of 472m in the northwest, where Prestfjall mountain sits precariously right on the cliff edge. In contrast, the tamer east coast is altogether more accessible and it's here that most of Suðuroy's villages and agricultural land are found. The highly indented eastern shoreline is likely to be where you'll spend most of your time, namely between the main settlements, **Tvøroyri** and its satellite villages in the north, and **Vágur** in the south from where some of the southern islands' best hiking trails radiate. All sailings are to the newly constructed ferry jetty at **Krambatangi**, on the western shore of Trongisvágsfjørður, immediately opposite the main town, Tvøroyri, which is the best place to start your wanderings.

TVØROYRI AND AROUND Another textbook example of a linear settlement, Tvøroyri is home to around 850 people and stretches over 2.5km or so from the head of the superbly sheltered Trongisvágsfjørður fjord to its mouth at Høvðatangi point. Its streets run in parallel lines, banking steeply up the green hillsides behind, which reach a height of around 300m. All activity takes place on the one long main road and down on the harbourside; the busy goings-on and the sheer number of small craft moored on the jetties here are good indicators of the town's prosperity. Whereas the eastern shore of Trongisvágsfjørður is relatively densely settled, the western coast of the inlet is all but devoid of habitation. Other than the ferry quay at **Krambatangi**, the only place of note is **Øravík**. Barely more than a handful of houses, it's a wonderfully wild location to visit with views out over the sea in one direction, back towards some of Suðuroy's craggy peaks in the other.

Getting there and away Access to Tvøroyri and indeed the rest of Suðuroy is most easily done by the **ferry** *Smyril* which sails direct from Tórshavn, taking around 2 hours. **Buses** run in connection with ferry arrivals and departures, linking the terminal Tvøroyri and destinations to Sumba; timetables are at www.ssl.fo. The distance from the ferry landing into Tvøroyri is around 3km and could be walked, if necessary, in 30–40mins. However, it is also possible to fly by **helicopter** to Froðba, just east of Tvøroyri, three times a week.

Where to stay *Map, page 150.*
For accommodation, you need to decide whether you want to be in the town or outside. The best place in Tvøroyri is the excellent **Gistingarhúsið undir Heygnum** (\ 37 20 46; e guesthouse@kallnet.fo; www.guest-house.dk; **$$**), located below the church and enjoying superb views out over the fjord. Clean, airy and spacious, the rooms here all share facilities but have stripped pine floors and there's a well-appointed kitchen, lounge area and private garden to boot which makes this guesthouse a real home from home and a sound choice. There's also a rowing boat which guests can use free of charge. Alternatively, the new **Gistingarhúsið í Miðbrekkuni** (*Miðbrekkan 12;* \ 25 97 97; e gista@gista.fo; www.gista.fo; **$**) has a handful of unadorned rooms sharing facilities in the town centre, where there's also a kitchen for self-catering. Just down the hill, the functional **Hotel Tvøroyri** (*Miðbrekkan 5;* \ 37 11 71; **$$$** inc b/fast) is also right at the heart of things, just a stone's throw from the shops, overlooking the harbour, though with rather compact and uninspiring rooms. Otherwise, back at Krambatangi, there's the option of sleeping onboard *Smyril* (\ 29 30 45; e smyril.catering@ssl.fo; **$$$**) while she is docked here every night (except Friday night, when she is in Tórshavn).

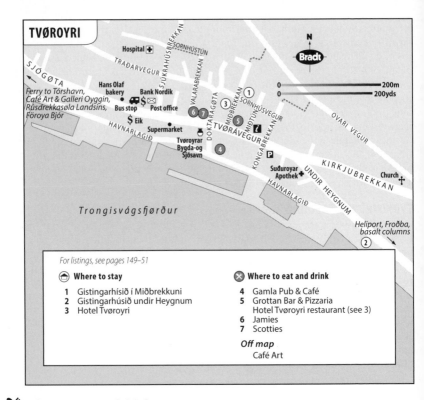

TVØROYRI

For listings, see pages 149–51

Where to stay
1 Gistingarhísið í Miðbrekkuni
2 Gistingarhúsið undir Heygnum
3 Hotel Tvøroyri

Where to eat and drink
4 Gamla Pub & Café
5 Grottan Bar & Pizzaria
   Hotel Tvøroyri restaurant (see 3)
6 Jamies
7 Scotties

Off map
   Café Art

✕ Where to eat and drink   *Map, above.*

Eating in Tvøroyri is, unfortunately, limited. By far the most agreeable option in the evening is **Jamies** (*Valarabrekkan 2;* m *37 21 72;* ⊕ *11.00–13.00 & 17.00–23.00 & 02.00–06.00 Fri, 17.00–23.00 & 02.00–06.00 Sat, 17.00–23.00 Sun; $*) in the centre of town, which serves up excellent fish and chips (*85kr*), succulent Scottish beef (*220kr*) and 12-inch pizzas (*75–100kr*). At lunchtime, your best bet is the atmospheric **Gamla Pub & Café** (⊕ *09.00–23.00 Mon–Thu, 09.00–03.45 Fri & Sat, 15.00–21.00 Sun; $*), down at the harbour, by the end of Doktaragøta, which serves a set meal for either 70kr or 90kr. This creaking, old timber building once served as the town's main store and warehouse and even boasts the original shop counter, complete with an ancient cash till; cakes, sandwiches and coffee are also available here during the day. By evening this places mutates into a pub busy with fishermen and workers from the fish factory next door. Otherwise, **Hotel Tvøroyri** serves lunch between noon and 13.30 weekdays (*150kr*) and pizzas on Saturday and Sunday evenings (⊕ *18.00–23.00*); there's also a pub in the basement (⊕ *11.00–late Mon–Fri, 16.00–late Sat & Sun*). **Café Art** (❧ *37 16 69;* ⊕ *14.00–18.00 Tue–Sun*), a little out of town at Sjógøta 184, rustles up coffee and cakes and shrimps or salmon if you order in advance; the café is licensed and also serves wine. For an evening drink at the weekend, try **Scottys**, next door to Jamies, at Tvørávegur 25 (❧ *37 21 72;* ⊕ *17.00–04.00 Fri & Sat*) or the new Grottan Bar & Pizzaria (❧ *37 01 71;* ⊕ *17.00–23.00 Fri–Sun*), which, as the name suggests, also serves pizzas (from 65kr). Alternatively, **Rúsdrekkasøla Landsins** (⊕ *14.00–17.30 Mon–Thu, 12.00–17.30 Fri, 10.00–13.00 Sat*) is beside the main road, opposite the ferry port, Krambatangi, where there's also an outlet of **Föroya Bjór** (⊕ *10.00–17.30 Mon–Fri*), selling beer and a few other items such T-shirts bearing the brewery's sheep logo. The main **supermarket** is Bónus (⏲ *09.00–22.00 Mon–Sat*) on the main street above the harbour. At Sjógøta 14 you'll find the Hans Olaf **bakery** (⏲ *07.00–17.30 Mon–Fri, 07.00–noon Sat*) selling fresh bread and cakes.

Other practicalities The tourist information office, **Kunningarstovan á Tvøroyri** (✆ *61 10 80*; ✉ *info@tvoroyri.fo; www.visitsuduroy.fo*; ⏲ *08.00–noon & 13.00–16.00 Mon–Thu, 08.00–noon & 13.00–15.00 Fri*), can be found on the main road between the museum and the church at Tvørávegur 37. Though there's a limited amount of printed matter available here, the staff are very friendly and know the island like the back of their hands. Tvøroyri has two **banks**: BankNordik at Sjógøta 4 (⏲ *10.00–16.00 Mon–Wed & Fri, 10.00–17.00 Thu*) and Eik, Sjógøta 15 (⏲ *09.30–16.00 Mon–Fri*), both with ATMs. The **post office** (⏲ *noon–15.00 Mon–Fri*) is next to BankNordik at Sjógøta 4, while the **pharmacy** Suðuroyar Apotek (✆ *36 03 00*; ⏲ *09.00–17.30 Mon–Fri, 09.00–noon Sat*) can be found at Undir Heygnum 4.

What to see and do

In the town It was Tvøroyri's protected location on a deep fjord that gave rise to the establishment in the mid-19th century of a branch of the Danish Trade Monopoly – an event that in effect created the town of today, the fourth largest in the Faroes. Following the dismantling of the monopoly in 1856, the town received a couple of fishing sloops, bought secondhand from England, which took a leading role in creating the Faroese industrial revolution. A **fish factory**, still in existence today, was soon required to process the tonnes of fish being landed in Tvøroyri, which, together with today's modern ocean-going trawlers stationed here, have helped create the basis for the town's economic advance.

The best place to get to grips with the town's history is at the **Tvøroyrar Bygda-og Sjósavn museum** (⏲ *Jun–Aug 14.30–17.30 Sun; admission 30kr; check at the tourist office if closed*) in the town centre, close to the harbour. Located in a former doctor's residence and surgery that dates from 1852, the museum canters through the most significant periods of the town's development. Inside, the evocative black-and-white photographs depicting local women washing the fish their husbands had landed, before it was salted and sent for export, are certainly an instant reminder of the past. It's worth glancing too at a few of the museum's other curiosities: a pair of old leather football boots from 1932 (the first Faroese football club was founded in 1892); the whopping 35cm-long shoes, size 53, once worn by a former Suðuroy policeman, Martin Christiansen; and the first typewriter ever used on the island (from 1910), which involved the user typing with one finger and moving a pointer to the desired key on the keyboard before striking the character – such was the demand for the new-fangled machine that it had to be shared between the local post office and town hall who each received it for one or two days at a time.

Located around a 10-minute walk west out of town towards the head of the fjord at Sjógøta 184, **Galleri Oyggin** (✆ *37 16 69*; ⏲ *14.00–18.00 Tue–Sun*) showcases the work of local artist Palle Julsgart: pottery, sculptures, paintings, lithography – the list goes on and most things are for sale. Palle's vivid use of colour in his Faroese landscape paintings is particularly pleasing. Upstairs from the gallery you'll find Café Art (see page 150).

The other sight in Tvøroyri lies a further 5 minutes' walk east along the main road: the village **church** (get the tourist office to arrange the key for you; see above for details). Unusually, the current structure, dating from 1908, was built in Lillestrøm in southern Norway before being shipped in sections to the Faroes. Its Norwegian influence is clear to see and its form is quite unlike any other in the islands. This monumental structure, with room inside for 600 worshippers, was donated to the town by a local family of merchants, and became an arresting sign of their wealth – they owned a fishing fleet of 30 or so ships and ran stores in several villages up and down the island.

Around Tvøroyri Continuing a further couple of kilometres past the church towards the mouth of the fjord will bring you to the original Viking settlement of **Froðba**, now essentially an overspill village. The hamlet is named after one of the area's earliest settlers, the Danish king, Froði, who actually never had any intention of coming to the Faroes. He was en route for Ireland when he ran into fog and, drifting helplessly, arrived in the mouth of Trongisvágsfjørður, where he settled, naming his new home, in true egotistical Viking fashion, after himself and his farmstead, or *bø*. Marking the eastern end of Froðba, the helipad is the place to start looking for one of Suðuroy's most unusual geological features: an entire row of **vertical basalt columns** formed in the rock that look like stone tree-trunks growing out of the sea. You'll find them by the roadside, just after the helipad and before a sharp left-hand bend which takes the road further up the hillside.

From Froðba a narrow road built by the British for defence purposes during World War II leads up the hill behind the settlement to a viewpoint known as Nakkur (325m), from where there are stirring views out over the Atlantic north towards Lítla and Stóra Dímun, Sandoy and also Skúgvoy; reckon on about an hour on foot to reach Nakkur. However, for those wishing to continue, a footpath leads off to the northwest, scaling the heights of **Froðbiarkambur** mountain (487m), the tallest peak on the entire east coast.

Hikes from Tvøroyri The two most popular hikes from Tvøroyri both begin from Trongisvágur, the tiny cluster of houses that nestles around the head of the fjord. One leads northwest to **Hvalba**, the other southwest to **Fámjin**. Bus connections on the #701 are available in both destinations to bring you back to Tvøroyri. The path to Hvalba (6.5km climbing to a height of 350m; reckon on 2 hours one way) begins a couple of kilometres outside Trongisvágur along Route 29 to Hvalba. Look out for two solitary huts either side of the road just after you have passed a river flowing down from the hills on your right. From the right-hand hut, take the path up through the ravine here, **Mannagjógv**, between the two peaks, **Tempilsklettur** (493m) to the left and **Eggin** (389m) on the right; the worst of the climb is now over. From here the track becomes less steep and is quite level as it goes over **Hvalbiarfjall**. Arriving at the highest cairn, there's a small rise in the terrain, which allows tremendous views east to the two Dímuns, Skúgvoy, Sandoy and the lake, Vatnsdalur, which attracts many birds during the summer months and is a good place for watching ducks and waders; to the west you can clearly see Hvalba. In the distance you should be able to make out the three large rocks known as **Sigmundarsteinar** after the Viking chieftain, Sigmundur Brestisson, of *Færeyinga Saga*. According to the *Saga*, he carried them up here and local folklore has it that anyone who walks between them will either become suddenly old or, if that wasn't bad enough, die before the end of the year. Should the weather turn whilst you're up here, be sure to follow the cairns. In the winter of 1917 one man became stranded up here when the fog came down and it began to snow. To pass his time while waiting to be rescued, he dismantled and then rebuilt one of the cairns time after time. Beyond the rocks, the path descends down **Káragjógv ravine** and it is quite steep in parts. It finally meets up with Route 293 near the hamlet of **Nes** in Hvalbiarfjørður east of Hvalba, from where it's a walk west of around a kilometre or so into the village itself.

The trail to Fámjin begins on the southern side of Trongisvágur just north of the couple of houses that are **Líðin**. This hike is roughly 2 hours in duration one way and covers similar terrain as that to Hvalba. Begin by climbing the gentle slopes of **Oyrnafjall mountain** (443m). Don't go all the way to the top; instead you follow the path as it skirts the western side of the peak, squeezing through the **Valdaskarð pass** which you can see in the distance. The fabulous rounded valley you have to your right up here, **Hvammabotnur**, has sides reaching a magnificent 569m, making them the highest point on the island. Once through the pass you're into another rounded valley dominated by the blue waters of **Kirkjuvatn** at its foot. The path now leads down the eastern side of the lake into the village of Fámjin.

NORTH TO HVALBA AND SANDVÍK From Trongisvágur, Route 29 heads northwest through a particularly lush valley, where there's even a plantation of trees to spot on your left as you leave the town behind. Soon the road enters Hvalbiartunnilin, the very first road tunnel (around 1.5km long) to be built in the Faroes, in 1963, which connects the harbour of Tvøroyri with the more rural agricultural lands to the north of Suðuroy. As the road emerges from the tunnel, the narrow lane to the right leads to the islands' only still-functioning coal mine, which produces modest amounts of the black stuff to this day. Begun as early as 1780, the seam covers an area of around 20km² between Trongisvágur and Hvalba where over the years a number of mines were sunk to extract the coal. During World War II the Faroese exported it to England to help with the war effort. The coal is, however, of poor quality and is today used only for the home market. As you drive the last couple of kilometres between the tunnel exit and Hvalba you will see remnants of three former mines that, tragically, all collapsed.

BARBARY PIRATES AND THE RAID ON HVALBA

Barbary pirates, also known as Ottoman corsairs or Barbary corsairs, were seaborne raiders who operated out of ports along the North African coast, predominantly Algiers, Tunis and Tripoli, from the 16th century onwards. At this time, the Barbary Coast, as it was known, was administered by the **Ottoman Empire**, which explains why, in the Faroes at least, the pirates were known as **Turks**. The threat posed by the pirates was only finally eradicated in 1830 by the French conquest of Algiers. Though they primarily attacked ships and settlements in and around the western Mediterranean, the pirates also engaged in raids as far afield as the Faroes and Iceland. In 1629, the pirates launched an attack on Hvalba in Suðuroy, although there are conflicting reports of whether two or three ships were involved. Tradition has it that many of the villagers were killed in the raid and that 30 local women and children were captured to be sold as slaves in North Africa. However, as the ships were leaving after the attack, one or two of them (again, reports vary) were dashed on the rocks and sank with all hands on deck; 300 bodies were washed ashore by the tide. The locals set about buring the bodies on the shoreline, and indeed the grave mounds can still be seen to this day (see page 154). It is possible that some of those bodies were those of captured villagers from Hvalba. Ballast composed of stones not present in the Faroes, yet common around the Mediterranean, has been discovered at the site, which has been greatly eroded over the ensuing centuries.

Hvalba spreads right across Suðuroy at a narrow isthmus, a fertile, hospitable shelf of land whose rocky, sea-battered old landing place, among the cliffs on the western side, is well worth a look. It was here at Hvalba in 1629 that Barbary pirates made a surprise attack, looted the village and took many of the inhabitants to be sold as slaves. The Faroese were too poor to raise the ransom money and the unfortunates were never seen again. However, the pirates' ships foundered on the rocks and the bodies of 300 of those on board were washed ashore in the village. They were buried at a spot along the beach known as **Turkagravir**, which can still be seen today; just before arriving in Hvalba, take the road to Nes and look for the sign 'Turkagravirnar' beside a grassy mound on the left-hand side of the road when approaching Nes.

From Hvalba, it's a further 5km to end-of-the-road **Sandvík**, the most northerly settlement on Suðuroy, enjoying superb views out to Lítla Dímun, which is today still owned by local farmers who graze some of their sheep there. According to the *Færeyinga Saga*, Sigmundur Brestisson, who had brought Christianity to the islands, was surprised by his pagan enemies on his farm in Skúgvoy. To save his life, Sigmundur had to jump into the sea and swim for it (albeit with two of his men on his back). He managed the shore at Sandvík some 15km away and collapsed on the sandy beach here. But, just to prove there's no justice in the world, the first person to find him, a local farmer aptly named Tórgrímur the Evil, immediately cut off his head. In fact, the land around Sandvík, so named after its sandy beach, was once the pasturelands of the Hvalba farmers until 1810, when the first settlement was founded here. The picturesque **wooden church**, dating from 1840, which today stands at the centre of this tiny hamlet beside a traditional **farmer's cottage** (closed to the public but perhaps worth a peek through the window into the large kitchen which takes up the lion's share of the building) is really the only reason to tarry.

Sandvík is one of the best places on Suðuroy to see **puffins**: take the narrow road up out of the village to the west where it peters out at the foot of Glyvraberg mountain (366m). From here a footpath leads out to the coast, where, off to the right, you'll see the rock stack, **Ásmundarstakkur** (109m). Its flat grassy top is a favourite nesting place for hundreds of these comical birds.

WEST TO FÁMJIN

One of the nicest spots on Suðuroy, Fámjin is a beautiful small village, ringed on its eastern side by a series of low-stepped hills that gradually merge up into the mountains at the centre of the island. It's not solely the picturesque quality of the harbour and the houses here that makes Fámjin so special to the Faroese. Instead, it's the presence of that potent symbol of nationhood, the flag, that brings carloads of misty-eyed home-grown tourists here. Ask around in the village for someone to open the church (dating from 1875) for you, and you'll see what all the fuss is about. In a glass cabinet hung on the rear wall is the original Merkið or **Faroese flag**. A red cross fringed with blue on a white background, this flag was the brainchild of local student **Jens Oliver Lisberg** (1896–1920) and two of his friends, who were studying at Copenhagen University when they hit upon the radical idea of creating a flag for their country to further their own dreams of independence for the Faroes. Although it was first flown following a church service in Fámjin in June 1919, it took several more decades until the flag was officially recognised. During World War II, the occupying British forces forbade all Faroese shipping to fly the red-and-white flag of occupied Denmark, instead encouraging the islanders to fly their own flag instead. The Faroese skipper **Hans Mikkelsen**, sailing to Aberdeen from the Faroes during the war under a British escort, became the first man to raise the flag at sea. Ignoring protests from the Danish authorities, a British government announcement made on the BBC on 25 April 1940 effectively made the move official, to much jubilation in the Faroe Islands. Ever since, this day has been celebrated as 'Flag Day'; with the advent of Home Rule in 1948, the Merkið had finally come of age and was adopted as the national flag of the Faroe Islands. Just outside the church entrance, Jens's grave can be seen; his gravestone was erected by the Faroese Students' Association to mark his death in 1920 at the age of just 24. Diagonally opposite the church in a small building beside the stream at the junction of Neystavegur and Fossavegur, you'll find a simple **café** (⊕ *Jun–Aug afternoons daily, also Sat morning*) with outdoor tables on a paved terrace at the rear overlooking the sea and serving coffee and waffles.

If the 9km drive to Fámjin from Øravík along the very windy Route 25, which climbs up through the Øraskarð pass between the two peaks, Snæválsheyggjur (469m) and Nónfjall (427m), doesn't appeal there's an excellent hike that will also take you to Fámjin, beginning at the hotel in Øravík. It leads steeply up the hillside behind the hotel towards the **Øraskarð pass** where it meets up with Route 25. Unlike the road, the path doesn't weave around hairpin bends to make the ascent: it just goes up and up until it reaches the summit of the pass. From here, the going is considerably easier and the trail leads around the southern slopes of Snæválsheyggjur before dropping gracefully into Fámjin, arriving a little south of the church. Remember that there are no facilities in Fámjin, and it's therefore a good idea to bring with you everything you think you'll need. Bus #703 runs back to Tvøroyri.

SOUTH TO HOV AND PORKERI
From Øravík, Suðuroy's main road, Route 20, plunges into a tunnel on its way south, avoiding a circuitous detour around the Høvðaberg and Grandatangi headlands, which separate Trongisvágsfjørður from Hovsfjørður fjord to the south. As you leave the tunnel, **Hov** comes into view. Today it is an innocuous small village, but during Viking times it served as a heathen place of sacrifice. According to the *Færeyinga Saga*, the powerful chieftain Havgrímur once lived here. Today, amazingly, it's still possible to make out his **burial mound**, which lies in a field above the village. You can get here by taking the old road up out of the village towards Tvøroyri and turning right at the sign marked Havgrímsgrøv, from where it's a further 100m walk. During the late 19th century, an excavation of the mound was made and remains of bone and iron fragments were discovered. The other notable feature in Hov is the wooden village church, which was moved here in 1942 from Vágur where it first stood from its inauguration in 1862. From Hov it's a straightforward drive of 5km to unusually named **Porkeri** (pronounced POR-churi), inhabited since Viking times. Although the main road passes the village by from above, it's worth the small detour into this busy fishing settlement to see the tar-walled, turf-roofed **church**, dating from 1847, and its small collection of trinkets inside donated by sailors who were rescued by local people when their ships foundered. The overgrown churchyard that surrounds the church is particularly pleasing to the eye and makes a charming photograph when viewed with the sea as a backdrop.

VÁGUR
From Porkeri, Route 20 now hugs the shoreline of Suðuroy's second great fjord, **Vágsfjørður**, passing the hamlet of **Nes** (former home of artist Ruth Smith (see pages 156–7), bound for the island's second town, Vágur (pronounced 'vaa-vur'), a thriving shipbuilding centre, fishing port and wool-spinning town that is home to around 1,300 people.

🏠 **Where to stay and eat** To be honest, other than the excellent museum (see below), there's not much to delay you in Vágur, but should you wish to stay here as an alternative base to Tvøroyri, you'll find comfortable and well-appointed accommodation at **Hotel Bakkin** (✆ *37 39 61;* e *hotelbakkin@olivant.fo; www. hotelbakkin.com;* **$$** *inc b/fast*), whose ten brightly painted rooms (two have private facilities; five have views of the fjord) at Vágsvegur 69 contain tasteful modern Scandinavian furniture. Although this place serves more as a hotel for visiting workmen and tradesmen than tourists, you'll be assured of a warm welcome. There's generally food available here: lunch (⊕ *noon–13.00; 90kr*) and dinner from 17.00 every evening, when the hotel serves up pizzas (*85kr*) and fish and chips (*75kr*).

Other practicalities Vágur's Suðuroyar Sparikassi **bank** (⊕ *09.30–16.00 Mon– Fri*) is on the main road through town at Vágsvegur 60 and has an ATM, while next door at No 62, you can find the **supermarket** (⊕ *09.00–18.00 Mon–Fri*) and the modest **Torgið shopping complex**, where there's a couple of other shops and another ATM. The **library** (⊕ *09.00–16.00 Mon–Fri*) and the **tourist office** (*both* ✆ *23 93 90;* ⊕ *09.00–16.00 Mon–Fri*) are located together, opposite the bank, at Vágsvegur 57.

Remarkably, Vágur has a new 50m **swimming pool** and fitness centre, **Páls Høll** (*Faroe Islands Aquatic Centre; www.palsholl.com;* ⊕ *06.45–08.45 & 15.00– 19.00 Mon, Wed & Fri, 15.00–19.00 Thu, 09.45–17.00 Sat, 08.45–10.45 & 14.00– 17.00 Sun*) located on the southern side of the fjord, next to the power plant, at Á Oyrunum 17. Comprising sauna, spa, gym and pool, the project was inspired by local elite swimmer Pál Joensen, who, despite not having anywhere to practise, went on to win silver in the European Swimming Championships in Istanbul in 2012 – the first swimming medal ever taken by the Faroe Islands (see *Appendix 3*, page 168).

What to see and do What activity there is in Vágur is concentrated on the one main road; you'll find a small **stone memorial** near the shipyard celebrating the launching in 1804 of *Royndin Fríða* (*The Good Endeavour*), the first sea-going ship to be built and owned by the Faroese since the early Middle Ages – a tribute to the efforts of national hero, Nólsoy Páll, who led resistance to the Danish Trade Monopoly in the 19th century (see pages 11–12). The main sight in Vágur is the rather fanciful new **Gothic stone church** built in 1927, which replaced the town's former church, now moved to Hov. While you're in town, it's worth having a quick look in Suðuroy's main knitwear store: the **Heimavirki** (⊕ *10.00–17.30 Mon–Fri, 10.00–13.00 Sat*), which specialises in hand-knitted traditional sweaters; you'll find it in the town centre at Vágsvegur 47.

Don't miss the excellent **Ruth Smith savn** at Vágsvegur 101 (m *22 12 15; www. ruthsmithsavn.com; 30kr*). The museum has no set opening times, so to gain access, call Maud on ✆ 57 30 44 or pop into the radio and TV repair shop just outside, which also holds the key. This modest little museum showcases the work of one of the Nordic countries' least known and most underrated watercolour artists, Ruth Smith (1913–58). Born in Vágur, Smith moved to Denmark at the age of 17, where she attended the Art Academy of Copenhagen before moving back to the Faroes and the village of Nes, just east of Vágur, where she painted many of her landscapes. Inspired by Cézanne, Smith managed to capture the magical light of her native islands in many of her paintings, which are considered to represent the Realist style, although much of her landscape work is strongly influenced by Impressionism. The museum holds some of her best-known works, including her self-portrait from 1941, full of captivating maroons and deep reds, which represents an unsung classic of the genre as well as some of her paintings of Nes – often a bright jumble of blues, greens and whites so representative of the Faroe Islands. Although the artist was a keen and strong swimmer, she drowned in the chilly waters of Vágsfjørður at the age of 45; it's thought she may have committed suicide.

AROUND VÁGUR

Vágseiði At the eastern end of the village, Eiðisvegur leads past the small lake, Vatnið, that you'll see at the head of Vágsfjørður, to a narrow isthmus of land known as **Vágseiði**, where the distance between the west and east coast of Suðuroy is just 1km. From the 19th to the earlier part of the 20th century, the natural harbour here, Kleivin, served as Vágur's main fishing port, extended by dynamite blasting in 1929. Take extra care if you venture down to the water's edge here as the sea can be rough at this point and waves can break onto the harbour area.

Eggjarnar cliffs For some truly superlative views of the Suðuroy coastline, head up to the Eggjarnar cliffs on the island's west coast, opposite Vágur. With your own car, take the first right, Eggjavegur, after the the filling station at the head of Vágsfjørður. This narrow road zig-zags up the hillside to Eggjarnar (in total a drive of around 10–15 minutes from the centre of Vágur); you can drive all the way to the top, although the road is narrow and in poor condition in parts. The abandoned buildings on the clifftop once formed part of a so-called LORAN navigation station for aircraft and shipping; this rather old-fashioned system has now been replaced by GPS. Take extreme care when you reach the end of the road because there is no fence here and there's a sheer drop of 200m from the clifftop to the sea below. On a clear day you can see all the way down to the dramatic **Beinisvørð cliffs** to the south.

Lopra and Sumba From Vágur, it´s now a short drive of around 6km to the tiny village of **Lopra**, where a whaling station once operated down by the harbour from 1901 to 1953. However, there's nothing to see of the former site today; instead, Lopra is known as the location of Frítíðarhúsið, a collection of four comfortable two-bedroom self-contained **apartments** (m 22 11 14; www.lopransdalur.fo; **$$**) with full kitchen for rent year-round. Lopra is about as remote as you can get in the Faroes and it's certainly a long way from Tórshavn – if you're looking for splendid isolation, the apartments here are hard to beat. Indeed, holed up here when winter storms tear down the valley, you can be forgiven for thinking that the roof could blow off at any moment. Lopra is served on request (↘ 23 95 50) by bus #700 to and from Sumba; timetables are at www.ssl.fo. Whilst you're here, be sure to have a look at **Lopranseiði**, another narrow isthmus of land where the extremely short distance between Suðuroy's east and west coasts is quite impressive. In 1742 a handsome sailing ship belonging to the Dutch East India Company, the *Westerbeek*, ran aground and sank here – the crew managed to climb ashore by shinning along the ship's mast, which came into contact with the steep cliffs as the ship began to list. Several members of the *Westerbeek*'s crew stayed in the Faroes and married local women. You'll see a sign for Lopranseiði off to the right of Route 21, just before the left turn into Lopra itself.

At Lopra you have a choice of routes: the main road enters a tunnel bound for Sumba and Akraberg, while the old road climbs up over the hills and twists and turns on its way south. The Faroes' most southerly village, **Sumba**, long one of the islands' most isolated villages and where traditions are still strong, is known for its talented group of **chain dancers** who, over the years, have brought international recognition to this peculiarly Faroese art.

Beinisvørð cliffs Just before the tunnel at Lopra, take the right turn signed for Um Hestin to reach one of the real highlights of Suðuroy: the breathtaking, 470m-high Beinisvørð cliffs, which are the Faroes' second-highest vertical sea cliffs.

On their eastern, landward side, the cliffs are denoted by an unbelievably steep grassy slope that soars skywards to the tip of the craggy triangular peak that marks the very highest point of Beinisvørð. From here, the cliffs plummet on their seaward side vertically into the North Atlantic below and can be seen for miles around, totally dominating any view from Lopra and Sumba (and can even be seen from the *Smyril* ferry as she swings in towards Tvøroyri). Risking life and limb, generations of local men from Sumba have abseiled down the sheer cliff face in search of seabirds and their eggs, which once were an important source of food – tragically, many paid the ultimate price. Over the years, the dramatic nature of Beinisvørð has even inspired several poets, who have used the cliffs as a potent symbol of independence in their work; today they proudly feature on the Faroese 50kr banknote. You can get close to the cliffs on the old Lopra–Sumba road at a spot known as Hesturin (the location of a radio mast at a sharp bend in the road), from where, with care, it's possible to walk to the cliff edge. From Beinisvørð the road then descends gradually towards the junction for Akraberg and Sumba itself. On the western side of Sumba, there are good views of the verdant slopes of Beinisvørð from just before the tunnel entrance. Alternatively, you can view the cliffs from a distance at Eggjarnar, near Vágur, as explained on page 157.

LAND'S END: AKRABERG From Sumba, it's barely another 2km along the road which climbs up out of the village to **Akraberg** and the most southerly point of the Faroe Islands. This wonderfully remote rocky promontory, which juts out proudly into the crashing waves of the North Atlantic, is a suitably enigmatic spot. At the end of the road there's a picnic table and a viewpoint. It's thought that the original inhabitants of Akraberg were heathen Frisians who never converted to Christianity – there are legends about them in Faroese folklore – and that they survived here through piracy from around 1040 to 1350, when they succumbed to the Black Death. Their settlement was down on the shoreline and has long since vanished into the sea. In more recent times, during World War II, British soldiers were regularly here, maintaining the **lighthouse** and a **radar station** that scanned the sea and skies south of the Faroes; some of the pillboxes they built as part of anti-invasion preparations are still standing.

What to see and do Beyond the end of the road, if you climb over the stile and follow the lane that leads down to the two red houses with green roofs on the cliff edge, you can reach the red-domed **lighthouse** itself: from the larger of the two houses a path leads off to the right to the light. Take extreme care because the cliffs here are vertical and there are no fences. The small shed clinging for dear life to the top of the clifftop, beyond the lighthouse, houses the foghorn. The lighthouse and the accompanying houses, which were home to the lighthouse keeper and his family, were built by the Danes in 1909. The light is fitted with guy wires to withstand the ferocious winds for which Akraberg is justifiably known across the islands. The last family to live here finally left after the hurricane of December 1988 which destroyed their car and caused severe damage to their home; when the hurricane was at its height they were so afraid that the upper part of the house would be ripped straight off that they tried to get down into the stone cellar for protection. Unfortunately access to the basement is only possible from the outside of the house and the family decided it was simply too dangerous to set foot outdoors; the lighthouse is now automatic.

In addition to the lighthouse, Akraberg is also dominated by the 141m-high guyed **radio mast**, which was built to pump out Faroese radio's 531kHz mediumwave signal to shipping off the Faroes. Erected in 1990, the mast (the one to the left of the road when looking at the lighthouse) broadcasts the signal generated by a transmitter, which is located in one of the adjacent service buildings. The current transmitter dates from 2008 when it was taken into operation to replace the original one, which had become unreliable. Today, broadcasting with a power of 100kW, the signal can be clearly heard by shipping in Faroese waters and also across much of the north of Scotland during daylight hours, and, of course, further afield during the hours of darkness. The mast, to the right of the road, was once part of a navigation station for aircraft and shipping, though it is no longer in use.

NEAREST LANDFALL TO THE FAROES Akraberg is a great place to sit and contemplate not only the breathtaking beauty of these 18 barren and windswept islands lost in the North Atlantic, but also their remoteness: from here, the nearest landfall is not the Shetland Islands, as many Faroese people mistakenly believe, but two uninhabited Scottish islands: **North Rona** (71km northeast of the Butt of Lewis in the Outer Hebrides and 75km northwest of Cape Wrath on the Scottish mainland) which lies 257km to the south; and the skerry, **Sula Sgeir**, which lies 258km from Akraberg and 18km west of North Rona.

Gain instant respect by pointing out that the nearest Shetland Island to Akraberg is **Foula**, 284km to the southeast. Fittingly, Foula was the last of all the Shetland Islands where Norn, the now-dead sister language to Faroese (see box, page 18), was still spoken as a first language in the 18th century. Still today in Faroese, the Hebrides (to which North Rona and Sula Sgeir belong) are known as the *suðuroyggjar* or 'southern isles': a clear linguistic sign that the Vikings considered the islands south of the Faroes as part of their domain. Indeed, the Hebrides and the Isle of Man, collectively known in English as the *Sudreys* (from Old Norse *suðreyar*), were under Norse rule for around 600 years.

8

Appendix 1

LANGUAGE

Faroese, a member of the family of Germanic languages, is most closely related to Danish, Icelandic, Norwegian and Swedish. Speakers of the above languages will notice many words and grammatical structures in common with Faroese. The closest language to Faroese is Icelandic; indeed, when Faroese and Icelanders speak to each other in their native tongues there is a good degree of mutual comprehension, much as there is between Spanish and Portuguese. The distance between Faroese and the continental Scandinavian languages, Danish, Norwegian and Swedish, is so great that there is no common ground for comprehension.

Although English is also related to Faroese, it's unlikely that you will be able to understand much written or spoken Faroese because, over the centuries, these languages have evolved along different lines. Whereas English lost its original case endings, inverted word order and genders, Faroese has maintained these and other grammatical features which, initially, make it difficult for English native speakers to learn even the simplest phrases. However, with perseverance, it is possible to learn some rudimentary phrases even if the complexities of the grammar remain beyond your grasp. Having said that, it's not necessary to speak Faroese to enjoy a holiday in the Faroes since most islanders speak at least some English (knowledge of English is at its most extensive in and around Tórshavn and the other main towns), and where no English is spoken, there's always the possibility of falling back on one or other Scandinavian language (notably Danish and Norwegian) if you can. However, mastering a couple of phrases in Faroese (at the very least, the bare essentials: hello, thank you, goodbye, etc) is sure to impress – manage more and you'll have Faroese jaws dropping at your every turn.

PRONUNCIATION Since Faroese was first written down only in 1846, the spelling of many words is based on their etymology rather than their current pronunciation. This naturally confuses matters for anyone trying to learn the language. Below is a guide to the pronunciation of vowels and consonants, though, naturally, the best way to perfect your pronunciation is to listen carefully to native speakers. Stress in Faroese usually falls on the first syllable of a word. Vowels followed by a double consonant are pronounced short, whereas those followed by a single consonant or none at all are long. We have excluded vowels and consonants where pronunciation is similar to that of English.

á	as in French *oi* in *moi*
av + consonant	as *ow* in exclamation *ow!*
ð	is never pronounced except when before *r* becoming *g*. Otherwise incorporated into surrounding vowels.
ðr	as *gr* in *grey*

ei	as *eye*
dj, ge, gi, gy, gey, gj and **ggj**	as *j* in *jam*
g	silent when between vowels
hj	as *y* in *yellow*
hv	as *kv* when at the beginning of a word
í and **ý**	as in French *oui*
ke, ki, ky, key, kj	as *ch* in *chat*
ll	as *dl* in *saddle*
rn	as *dn* in *hadn't*
rs	similar to *sh* in *ship* though softer
sj, sk, ske, ski, sky, skey, skj	as *sh* in *ship*
tj	as *ch* in *chat*
ó	as in the abbreviated English word *o'er (over)*
ø	as *ur* in *fur* though without the final *r*

Incidentally, the Faroese capital, Tórshavn, is pronounced *toe-ush-hown*.

GRAMMAR

Nouns Faroese **nouns** are divided into three genders: *kallkyn* (masculine), *kvennkyn* (feminine) and *hvørkikyn* (neuter). Like German, they are also declined by case: nominative, accusative, dative and genitive, depending on several factors including their role in the sentence and preceding prepositions. Endings are added to nouns to denote their case. Nouns are qualified by **articles**. The **indefinite article** (*a*) is *ein* (masculine and feminine) or *eitt* (neuter). Like nouns, articles are also declined according to case. *Ein* is conjugated as follows:

Singular	Masculine	Feminine	Neuter
Nominative	ein	ein	eitt
Accusative	ein	eina	eitt
Dative	einum	ein(ar)i	einum
Genitive	eins	einar	eins

Plural			
Nominative	einir	einar	eini
Accusative	einar	einar	eini
Dative	einum	einum	einum
Genitive	eina	eina	eina

When used with an adjective the **definite article** is masculine: *hin* stóri maðurin – the big man; feminine: *hin* raska konan – the skilful woman; neuter: *hitt* sjúka barnið – the sick child. However, when used without a preceding adjective, the definite article is attached to the end of the noun, in common with the other Scandinavian languages. For example, masculine: -*in* maðurin – the man; feminine: -*in* bygdin – the village; neuter: -*ið* barnið – the child.

Hin and *hitt* are conjugated as follows:

Singular	Masculine	Feminine	Neuter
Nominative	hin	hin	hitt
Accusative	hin	hina	hitt
Dative	hinum	hini	hinum
Genitive	hins	hinnar	hins

Plural

Nominative	hinir	hinar	hini
Accusative	hinar	hinar	hini
Dative	hinum	hinum	hinum
Genitive	hinna	hinna	hinna

Adjectives

Faroese **adjectives** precede the nouns they describe: ein *grønur* bilur – a green car; hin *grøni* bilurin – the green car, though they can also stand alone: maðurin er *stórur* – the man is big; konan er *stór* – the woman is big; barnið er *stórt* – the child is big. Adjectives are conjugated by number: ein *stórur* maður (a big man); fleiri *stórir* menn (many big men); by case: ein *stórur* maður sat har – a big man sat there; eg sá ein *stóran* mann – I saw a big man; eg møtti einum *stórum* manni – I met a big man; by gender: ein *stórur* maður – a big man; ein *stór* kona – a big woman; eitt *stórt* barn – a big child; and by comparison: stórur – størri – størstur = big – bigger – biggest (masculine).

Adjectives are **strongly conjugated** when the noun is **indefinite**: ein *sjúkur* maður – a sick man; ein *sjúk* kona – a sick woman; ein *sjúkt* barn – a sick child.

Adjectives are **weakly conjugated** when the noun is **definite**: hin *sjúki* maðurin – the sick man; hin *sjúka* konan – the sick woman; hitt *sjúka* barnið – the sick child. Otherwise the **definite** declension is used: *gamli* Andras – old Andras; Eirikur *Reyði* – Eric the Red.

Pronouns

Pronouns are generally conjugated by numbers, case and gender. The personal pronouns when used in the nominative case in Faroese are:

eg	I
tú	you (informal)
hann	he
hon	she
tað	it
vit	we
tit	you (plural)
teir/tær/tey	they (masc/fem/neuter)

Verbs

Verbs fall into two main categories: those with sound changes and those without. They are conjugated by **tense**, **number** and **person**. They also use **weak** and **strong** conjugations.

Weak conjugation

Singular	Present	Past
1st person	*eg skrivi*	*eg skrivaði*
2nd person	*tú skrivar*	*tú skrivaði*
3rd person	*hann skrivar*	*hann skrivaði*
	hon skrivar	*hon skrivaði*
	tað skrivar	*tað skrivaði*

Plural		
1st person	*vit skriva*	*vit skrivaðu*
2nd person	*tit skriva*	*tit skrivaðu*
3rd person	*tey skriva*	*tey skrivaðu*

Strong conjugation

Singular	Present	Past
1st person	*eg lesi*	*eg las*
2nd person	*tú lesur*	*tú last/tú las*
3rd person	*hann lesur*	*hann las*
	hon lesur	*hon las*
	tað lesur	*tað las*

Plural		
1st person	*vit lesa*	*vit lósu*
2nd person	*tit lesa*	*tit lósu*
3rd person	*tey lesa*	*tit lósu*

VOCABULARY
The basics

Good morning	*Góðan morgun*	Thank you	*Takk (fyri)*
Hello	*Góðan dag*	Don't mention it	*Tað var so lítið*
Good evening	*Gott kvøld*	Yes	*Ja*
Good night	*Góða nátt*	No	*Nei*
Goodbye	*Farvæl*	Excuse me	*Orsaka meg*
Bye	*Bei*		

Useful phrases

My name is …	*Eg eiti …*
How are you?	*Hvussu gongur?*
I'm fine	*Tað gongur væl*
What's your name?	*Hvussu eitur tú?*
Where are you from?	*Hvaðan ert tú?*
Where do you live?	*Hvar býrt tú?*
How old are you? (masculine/feminine)	*Hvussu gamal/gomul ert tú?*
I am … years old (masculine/feminine)	*Eg eri … ára gamal/gomul*
I (don't) understand	*Eg skilji (ikki)*
I (don't) know	*Eg veit (ikki)*
Where is …?	*Hvar er …?*
I'd like …	*Kundi eg fingið …*
Do you have any rooms free?	*Eru nøkur leys kømur?*
I'm staying for …	*Eg steðgi í …*
one day	*ein dag*
two days	*tveir dagar*
How much is it?	*Hvussu nógv kostar tað?*
Can I see it?	*Kann eg sleppa at síggja tað?*
Is breakfast included?	*Er morgunmatur uppi í?*
The bill, please	*Kann eg fáa rokningina?*
Will it be windy/rainy today/tomorrow?	*Verður tað vindur/regn í dag/í morgin?*
When does … leave?	*Nær fer … ?*
the boat/the bus	*báturin/bussurin*
The timetable will be modified on the following days	*Hesar dagar er ferðaætlan broytt*
What's included?	*Hvat hoyrir til?*

| I'm vegetarian | *Eg eri vegetarur* |
| the bill | *rokningin* |

Essential vocabulary

beach	*sandur* or *strond*	next week	*næstu viku*
bus and ferry	*farstøðin*	now	*nú*
terminal		pen	*kúlupennur*
camera film	*filmur*	pharmacy	*apotek*
coach/bus	*rutubilur*	police	*løgregla*
dentist	*tannlækni*	police station	*løgreglustøð*
doctor	*lækni*	post office	*posthús*
Faroese ferry	*Strandfaraskip*	a single ticket	*einvegis*
company	*Landsins*	taxi	*leigubilur*
guesthouse	*gistingarhús*	this evening	*í kvøld*
hospital	*sjúkrahús*	this morning	*í morgun*
hotel	*hotell*	ticket	*ferðaseðil*
library	*bókasavn*	today	*í dag*
map	*kort*	tomorrow	*í morgin*
matches	*svávulpinnar*	yesterday	*í gjár*
money	*pengar*	yesterday evening	*í gjárkvøldið*
newspaper	*dagblað*	youth hostel	*vallaraheim*

Food and drink

| breakfast | *morgundrekka* | dinner | *døgurði* |
| lunch | *morgunmatur* | | |

beef	*neytasteik*	onion	*leykur*
bread	*breyð*	orange juice	*appelsindjús*
butter	*smør*	peas	*ertrar*
carrots	*gularøtur*	plaice	*reyðsprøka*
cauliflower	*blomkál*	pork cutlet	*grísasteik*
cheese	*ostur*	potato	*epli*
chicken	*høsnarungi*	prawns	*rækjur*
coffee	*kaffi*	rice	*rís*
fish	*fiskur*	runner beans	*bønir*
garlic	*hvítleykur*	salmon	*laksur*
haddock	*hýsa*	sausage (hotdog)	*pylsa*
halibut	*kalvi*	sugar	*sukur*
herring	*sild*	toast	*ristað breyð*
jam	*súltutoy*	trout	*síl*
lamb	*lambskjøt*	whale meat and	*grind og spik*
lamb cutlet	*lambssteik*	blubber	
meat	*kjøt*	tea	*te*
milk	*mjólk*	water	*vatn*
mushrooms	*hundaland*	wine	*vín*
mustard	*sinoppur*		

Days and months

Monday	*mánadagur*	Friday	*fríggjadagur*
Tuesday	*týsdagur*	Saturday	*leygardagur*
Wednesday	*mikudagur*	Sunday	*sunnudagur*
Thursday	*hósdagur*		

January	*januar*	July	*juli*
February	*februar*	August	*august*
March	*mars*	September	*september*
April	*apríl*	October	*oktober*
May	*mai*	November	*november*
June	*juni*	December	*desember*

Numbers

Numbers Unfortunately, in Faroese, numbers one, two and three are also declined in all four cases. Numbers above three are unaffected. Examples are as follows:

1, 2, 3 (masculine)	*ein, tveir, tríggir*
1, 2, 3 (feminine)	*ein, tvær, tríggjar*
1, 2, 3 (neuter)	*eitt, tvey, trý*

4	*fýra*	20	*tjúgu*
5	*fimm*	21	*einogtjúgu*
6	*seks*	30	*tretivu*
7	*sjey*	40	*fjøruti*
8	*átta*	50	*hálvtrýss*
9	*níggju*	60	*trýss*
10	*tíggju*	70	*hálvfjerðs*
11	*ellivu*	80	*fýrs*
12	*tólv*	90	*hálvfems*
13	*trettan*	100	*hundrað*
14	*fjúrtan*	101	*hundrað og ein*
15	*fimtan*	200	*tvey hundrað*
16	*sekstan*	1,000	*túsund*
17	*seytjan*	2,000	*tvey túsund*
18	*átjan*	1,000,000	*ein miljón*
19	*nítjan*		

Appendix 2

GLOSSARY OF FAROESE GEOGRAPHICAL TERMS

Faroese	English
á	river, stream
bakki	slope
barð	promontory, headland
botnur	rounded valley, corrie, cirque
bøur	cultivated infield surrounding a village
brekka	brink, edge
byrgi	fenced-off land
dalur	valley
drangur/stakkur	sea stack
eiði	isthmus
enni	cliff face, rock wall
fjall	mountain
fjørður	fjord, sound
fossur	waterfall
gjógv	ravine, gorge, gully
hagi	uncultivated outfield
hálsur	mountain col
heiði	peat moor, heathland
heyggjur	hill
hólmur	island
høvði	promontory, headland
kambur/kjølur	mountain ridge
kinn	mountain slope
klettur	rock pinnacle
klubbi	rounded hill
knúkur	mountain summit
lið	even-sloping mountainside
múli	promontory
mýri	moorland
nakkur	sharp-edged promontory
nes	point, headland
nípa	protruding mountain ridge
oy, oyggj	island
oyri	gravel deposit
pollur	cove, anchorage
ryggur	ridge, hill line

sandur	sandy beach
skarð	narrow mountain col (pass)
stakkur	sea stack
steinur	stone, rock
sund	sound
tangi	eroded headland, tongue of land
tindur	pyramidal peak
tjørn	mountain tarn, lake
trøð	allotment
urð	scree
vágur	cove, small bay, inlet
vatn	large lake
vík	V-shaped bay or inlet
vøllur	pasture or grassland on cliff face

For a glossary of weather terms, see page 21.

Appendix 3

FURTHER INFORMATION

BOOKS English-language books on the Faroe Islands are remarkably scant. The books listed below are the pick of a meagre crop. Some of the titles are more readily accessible in the Faroes than elsewhere and are marked accordingly.

General

Day, David *Faroes UK: Faroese People at Home in the UK* Guillemot Publishing, 1998. An unusual account of Faroese life outside the Faroes, predominantly in Scotland where seemingly no Faroese household is complete without a stuffed puffin as a reminder of home.

Gilmour, Rod *The Pal Effect: A Faroe Islander's Quest for Swimming Glory* Chequered Flag Publishing, 2015. A lyrical account of how one man beat the odds to become a world and European swimming champion, galvanising a nation in the process.

Jackson, J *The Faroes: Faraway Islands* Robert Hale, 1991. An excellent contemporary account of Faroese life written within the past decade which attempts to finally put the Faroes on the map and explain what makes these remote islands so unusual yet so appealing.

Kjørsvik Schei, Liv and Moberg, Gunnie *The Faroe Islands* Birlinn Ltd, 2003. Although certainly the established authority on all things Faroese, this tome makes dry and stodgy reading. If you're looking for offbeat facts about the islands, the chances are you'll find them here. Illustrations are by the Faroese artist, Tróndur Patursson.

Miller, James *The North Atlantic Front: The Northern Isles at War* Birlinn Ltd, 2005. During the two world wars, the Faroes, along with Orkney, Shetland and Iceland, linking Europe to North America, acquired great significance. This work tells of operations along this northern front, and gives an insight into how the Faroe Islands came to be occupied by Britain whilst the rest of Denmark was under Nazi command.

Millman, Lawrence *Last Places* Houghton Mifflin, 2001. A humorous and quirky account of a visit to the Faroes as part of a North Atlantic journey. Millman seems obsessed with whale hunts and blubber – however, it's definitely one of the best contemporary reads on the Faroes, although it is now a little dated.

York-Powell, F *Færeyinga Saga: the Tale of Thrond of Gate* Ballantyne Press, 2012. A must-read for anyone interested in the flamboyant characters who lived in the Faroes during medieval times. This Icelandic saga deals essentially with the long-standing and ultimately fatal rivalry between Tróndur í Gøtu and Sigmundur Brestisson. With this book in hand you'll gain an altogether more realistic appreciation of some of the villages where history was played out to the full.

Young, G V C *From the Vikings to the Reformation: Chronicle of the Faroe Islands to 1538* Shearwater Publishing, 1979. Readily available in the bookshops in Tórshavn, this is the definitive historical account of early Faroese life from the time of the Settlement to the Reformation.

Language

Adams, Jonathan and Petersen, Hjalmar P *Faroese: A Language Course for Beginners* Stiðin, 2009. The only language course on the market and an excellent one at that. Comes in two volumes (textbook and grammar plus CDs) and will teach you all of the essentials in a lively and engaging manner as you follow the adventures of Claire and Jógvan through the islands.

Føroya Fróðskaparfelag *Faroese: An Overview and Reference Grammar* Føroya Fróðskapafelag, 2004. An authoritative and thoroughly comtemporary account of all things grammatical. If you're intent on learning Faroese, this is an invaluable resource. More readily available in the Faroes.

WEBSITES

www.faroe-island.blogspot.com The leading blog on all things Faroese, with plenty of excellent photos

www.faroepodcast.blogspot.com Join Matthew Workman as he audio guides you around the Faroes

www.visitfaroeislands.com The official Faroese tourism site

www.dmi.dk/dmi/index/faroerne/femfaro.htm Five-day weather forecast for the Faroes

www.faroeart.com Summary of the Faroese arts scene and information on the country's leading artists

www.football.fo The Faroe Islands Football Association, with details on fixtures of the national team

www.framtak.com Facts and figures about the Faroes as well as language information

www.hagstova.fo Statistics about the Faroe Islands

www.setur.fo The site of the University of the Faroe Islands, with information about the summer course in the Faroese language

www.ssl.fo Timetables and fares for Faroese public transport

www.stamps.fo Everything about Faroese stamps for the philatelist

www.tutl.com A chance to buy Faroese music online

www.kringvarp.fo The homepage of Faroese television and radio with information about frequencies as well as programming

www.whaling.fo Pro-whaling information issued by the Faroese government

www.campaign-whale.org A British-based non-profit organisation opposed to the killing of Faroese whales

Index

Page numbers in **bold** indicate major entries; those in *italics* indicate maps

accommodation 28–29
Æðuvík 118
airlines 23–24
airport, Vágar (Vága floghavn)
    42, 92–93, 94
Akraberg 158–9
alcohol *see also* Rúsdrekkasøla
    Landsins 30
Atlantic Airways 23–4, 93

banks 26
Barbary pirates 153
BBC 12, 31, 34, 155
Beinisvørð cliffs 158
birds 4–6, 100
birdwatching 5, 6, 88, 100
boat trips 60–1, 88, 135
Borðoy 119, 121–8
Bøur 95
breakfast 29
Brestisson, Sigmundur 9, 31,
    88, 144, 146, 148, 152, 154
buses 27, 42

car hire 28
chain dance 50, 66, 157
churches, timber 80
Christianskirkjan (church) 125
    see also Klaksvík
cliffs, sea
    Beinisvørð 158
    Eggjarnar 157
    Enniberg 129–30
climate 3–4, 20
consulates 23
costs 26–7
credit cards 26
culture 19
currency 2, 26
customs and duty free 33

Dalur 145
dining *see* eating

dinner 29–30, 115
diving 126
Danish language 16–18
dolphins 7–8

eating 29–30
    restaurant price codes 30
Eggjarnar cliffs 157
Eiði 104–5
    hiking 105
Elduvík 108
    hikes from 108
embassies 23
Enniberg sea cliff 129–30
entertainment 32–3
exchange rates 2
Eysturoy *102*, 103–18
    getting around 104
    northern 104–13
    southern 113–18
    where to go 103–4

Fámjin 154–5
Færeyinga Saga (story) 9, 88,
    146 *see also* Brestisson,
    Sigmundur
Faroese
    books 168–9
    geographical terms 166–7
    grammar 161–3
    language 16–18, 160–5
    websites 169
ferry 24–5, 27, 42
festivals, music 113, 126
Finsen, Niels 55
fishing 15
flag (Merkið) 12, 31, 154–5
flora 8–9
football 117, 169
Fuglafjørður 109–11, *110*
    getting there and away 109
    other practicalities 111
    varmakelda hot spring 111

Fuglafjørður *continued*
    what to see and do 111
    where to stay and eat
        110–11
Fugloy *120*, 136–7
Funningsfjørður 108
Funningur 107

G! Music Festival 113
Gásadalur 96
    hiking around 96
Gáshólmur 95, 96
gay and lesbian travellers 25–6
geography *see also* Faroese
    (geographical terms) 3
getting around the islands 27–8
getting there and away
    by air 23–4
    by sea 24–5
giving something back 35
Gjógv 105–6
    hiking around 106–7
Glyvrar 115–16, *116*
Guðrun & Guðrun *see also*
    woollens 32

Haldarsvík 82–3
Hammershaimb, Venceslaus
    Ulricus 17, 85, 91
Hattarvík 136–7
Havnar kirkja (cathedral) *see*
    also Tórshavn 52
Heinesen, William 19
health 25
helicopter 27–8
Hellur 109
Hestur 71
    getting there and away 71
highlights, Faroese 20–2
hiking, advice 26
Hirtshals 24
history 9–15
home dining 115

home rule 15
Hosvík 78
Hov 155
Hoyvíksgarður (Open-Air
  Museum) 59
Húsavík 144
Hvalba 153–4
Hvalvík 78–9
  timber church 78
Hvannasund 127

independence 14
internet 35

Jakobsen, Jakob 17, 18
Jensen, Jens-Kjeld 68–9
Joensen-Mikines, Sámal 19, 57
Joensen, Ove 68

Kaldbak see also timber
  churches 73
Kallanes 73
Kalsoy 120, 132–4
  getting there and away 132
  seal woman 132, 133
  what to see and do 132–4
  where to stay and eat 132
Kamban, Grímur 9, 107
Killing, The (TV show) 32
Kirkja 136
Kirkjubøstólarnir 58
Kirkjubøur 64–7
  getting there and away 64
  hiking 66
  other practicalities 64
  what to see and do 64–7
Klaksvík 121–6, 122
  brewery, Föroya Bjór 125
  church 125
  entertainment and nightlife
    123–4
  getting there and away 123
  hikes from 126
  museum (Norðoya
    Fornminnasavn) 126
  other practicalities 124
  summer festival 126
  tourist information 124
  what to see and do 124–6
  where to eat 123
  where to stay 123
knitwear, Faroese see woollens
Kollafjørður 77–8
Koltur 71–2
getting there and away 72
Kunoy 120, 130–2
  getting there and away 131

Kunoy continued
  what to see and do 131–2
Kvívík 84–5

Lambi 115
language 16–8, 160–5
Leirvík 112
Leitisvatn 92
library 51,111, 124
Listasavn Føroya (National Art
  Gallery) 56–7
Lítla Dímun 138, 147–8
Lopra 157
Lopranseiði 157
lunch 29

Magnus Cathedral 64–5
maps 22
Merkið see flag
Miðvágur 89–91
mobile telephones 34
money 26–7 see also exchange
  rates
Múli 127–8
music festivals 32, 113, 126
Mykines 74, 97–101
Mykineshólmur 100–1

National Art Gallery (Listasavn
  Føroya) 56–7
National Museum (Føroya
  Fornminnissavn) 58–9
natural history 59
Nes 118 (Eysturoy), 155, 157
  (Suðuroy)
Nólsoy 62, 67–70
Norðdepil 127
Nordic House see
  Norðurlandahúsið
Norðlýsið (schooner) 60
Norðragøta 112–13
  G! Music Festival 113
Norðurlandahúsið (Nordic
  House) 57–8
Norn 16, 18, 159
Norröna (ferry) 24–5
North Rona 2, 159
northern islands 119–137, 120
  getting around 121
  where to go 119–20

Ólavskirkjan (church) 66–7
Ólavsøka 30–1
Outer Hebrides 159
Oyndarfjørður 109
Oyrarbakki 104

Páll, Nólsoy 69
pirates, Barbary 153
population 2, 16
Porkeri 155
post office 34, 51, 124
price codes
  accommodation 29
  restaurant 30
public holidays 2, 31
puffins 4, 5, 100

radio 33–4, 159
religion 2, 19
rental, car see car hire
rock stacks see sea stacks
Roykstovan farmhouse 65–6 see
  also Kirkjubøur
Runavík 115–17, 116
Rúsdrekkasøla Landsins
  (alcohol store) 30
Ruth Smith Museum 156–7

safety 25
SagaMuseum 88
Saksun 79–82
Saltangará 115–17, 116
Sandavágur 91–2
Sandoy 138, 141–5
  hiking on 145
  where to stay 143–4
Sandur
  other practicalities 142
  what to see and do 142–3
seabirds 4–6
sea stacks
  Búgvin 107
  Flatidrangur 101
  Píkarsdrangur 101
  Risin and Kellingin 104
seal woman 132, 133
Selatrað 114
self-catering 29, 49
settlement 9
Seyðisfjørður 24
Sheep Letter 10
Shetland Islands 18, 159
shopping 31–2, 33, 56
Skálafjørður 113
Skálavík 143–4
Skáli 114
Skarð 131
Skarvanes 143
Skipanes 115
Skopun 141
Skúgvoy 138, 145–7
Slættaratindur 105, 106
SMS shopping centre 55

Smyril Line *see also* ferry 24–5
Søldarfjørður 115
Søltuvik 143
Sornfelli 84
Sørvágsvatn 92
Sørvágur 94–5, *95*
southern islands *138*, 139–59
    getting around 140–1
    where to go 140
stamps 32
Stóra Dímun *138*, 147
storm petrels 5, 6, 69
Strendur 114
Streymoy *74*, 75–88
    getting around 77
    where to go 76–7
Suðuroy *138*, 148–59
Sumba 157–8
Svínoy *120*, 134–6
Syðrugøta 112–13 *see also* G!
    Music Festival

tax-free 33
telephone codes 34
television 34
timber churches 80
time 2, 35
Tindhólmur 95, 96
tipping 27, 43
Tjóðsavn (National Museum)
    58–9
Tjørnuvík 83–4
Toftir 117–18
Tórshavn 39–61, *40–41* (main),
    44–5 (centre)
    accommodation *see* where
        to stay
    aquarium, Føroya Sjósavn 60
    around *62*, 63–73
    boat trips 60

Tórshavn *continued*
    buses, city 42
    campsite 47
    cathedral (Havnar kirkja) 52
    entertainment and nightlife
        49–50
    getting around 43
    getting there and away 42
    graveyard 61
    harbour 53
    library 51
    Løgting (parliament) 55
    National Art Gallery
        (Listasavn Føroya) 56–7
    National Museum (Føroya
        Fornminnissavn) 58–9
    Niels Finsens gøta 54
    Nordic House
        (Norðurlandahúsið)
        57–8
    old town 51–2
    other practicalities 51
    pubs 50
    shopping centre, SMS 55
    Skansin fort 53–4
    Tinganes 52–3
    tourist and weather
        information 43
    welcome card 43
    what to see and do 50–61
    where to eat 47–9 *see also*
        self–catering
    where to stay 43–7
tour operators 22–3
trade monopoly 11–12
travelcard 27
Tróndur í Gøtu 31, 88, 112
tunnels, new 15
    Streymoy–Eysturoy 73
    Streymoy–Sandoy 141

Tvøroyri 149–152, *150*
    other practicalities 151
    what to see and do 151–2
    where to eat and drink
        150–1
    where to stay 149

Vágar *74*, 88–97
    airport 92–3
Vágseiði 157
Vágur 155–7
    around 157
Vestaravág harbour *see*
    Tórshavn
Vestmanna 85–88, *86*
    bird cliffs 88
    SagaMuseum 88
Vesturkirkja (church) 59–60
við Áir 78
Viðareiði 129
Viðarlundin Park 56
Viðoy *120*, 128–30
Vikings 9, 59, 64, 85, 88, 146
    sundial 53

weather 22
    terms, glossary of 21
websites 169
western islands *74*, 88–101
    Vágar 88–97
    Mykines 97–101
whales 6–7
whaling 8, 15–16 *see also* við
    Áir
what to take 26
women travellers 25
woollens 32, 56, 117, 124

youth hostels 29, 47, 89

INDEX OF ADVERTISERS

62°N Incoming	2nd colour section	Regent Holidays	inside front cover
Gjáargarður Guesthouse	2nd colour section	VisitFaroeIslands	inside back cover
Hotel Streym	2nd colour section	Wanderlust	167